# GERMAN AND AUSTRO-HUNGARIAN

# AIRCRAFT MANUFACTURERS

# 1908-1918

# GERMAN AND AUSTRO-HUNGARIAN AIRCRAFT MANUFACTURERS 1908-1918

TERRY C. TREADWELL

AMBERLEY

*For my wife, Wendy, and my grandson, Rex.*

First published 2010

Amberley Publishing
Cirencester Road, Chalford,
Stroud, Gloucestershire, GL6 8PE

www.amberley-books.com

British Library Cataloguing in Publication Data.
A catalogue record for this book is available from the British Library.

ISBN 978 1 4456 0102 1

Typeset in 10pt on 12pt Sabon.
Typesetting and Origination by Amberley Publishing.
Printed in the UK.

# Contents

# Introduction

Military aviation in Germany can be traced back to 1884, when the Prussian Army began experimenting with balloons for reconnaissance purposes. So successful were these experiments that small balloon units started to spring up within the regiments. It was around this time that Count Ferdinand von Zeppelin created the first of his airships. The military hierarchy soon realised the potential of such a vehicle for reconnaissance purposes and in 1906 commissioned von Zeppelin to produce one specifically for the Army. The specifications laid down were for a semi-rigid model that could easily be deflated and inflated for transportation over land.

With the relative success of this airship came the idea of using a heavier-than-air craft, the aeroplane. The Army continued with the airships, but purchased a number of aircraft from various foreign manufacturers for testing. The whole of the aviation industry was on a learning curve, as no one really knew anything about the design and manufacture of aircraft, let alone the theory of aerodynamics and weight ratios. The men who built the aircraft, usually in sheds or basements, invariably flew the aircraft themselves and suffered a number of crashes. The cost of all this usually meant either a loss of life, or bankruptcy, so unless they were independently wealthy, or had strong financial backing, they relied heavily on luck.

Investing in the future of aviation was down to those individuals and institutions, such as the Deutsche Bank and the Dresden Bank, who had the foresight and the gambling instinct to recognise the possibilities of the aeroplane. The major stumbling block was that all investment at this level was governed by the need for profit, and this in turn depended on the needs of the domestic and foreign markets. The domestic market was unlikely to develop as there were very few people who could afford to purchase an aircraft for between 15,000 and 30,000 marks, and the foreign market was already being invaded by superior French and American companies, who were even selling their aircraft in Germany. This left one other avenue in Germany untapped – the military.

The initial problem for the Army, ostensibly the Prussian Army, as they were the cornerstone of the German military machine, was that when they purchased any aircraft, there were no military test pilots to test the aircraft. So they had to rely heavily on the honesty of the men who built the aircraft, or the test reports from the company test pilots, who themselves were still on a continuing learning curve and had a vested interest in selling the aircraft. There was also the problem of persuading the Prussian Army's hierarchy to keep up with modernisation; like many other senior Army officers of their time they were resistant to change, having been brought up to fight battles with sword and lance.

The first opportunity when the Prussian Army had to make a conscious decision regarding the use of aircraft came in 1906, when the Wright Brothers offered to sell one of their aircraft to the Prussian War Ministry. After discussions with the Inspectorate of Transport Troops, the engineers department of the War Ministry and members of the General Staff in September 1908, it was decided to reject the offer and stay with the airship. This was because in the main they had invested heavily in the Research Unit and Airship Battalion and its development from the 1890s. However, the rapid development of the aeroplane by the French soon persuaded the Germans that they were rapidly being left behind in the field of aviation.

In 1907, the Prussian Army had created the Research Unit and Airship Battalion to look into the development of military aviation. Initially the unit concentrated on the Airship Battalion, but as time progressed it became clear that although the airship had a role to play, the aircraft was to have an even greater role. Among the many requirements drawn up by the Airship Battalion was:

> The flying machine must always be able to carry two people, only one (pilot) of whom is required to operate the apparatus (aircraft). The second (observer) is entrusted solely with undertaking a military task. This latter person must be accommodated in the apparatus in such a way that he can carry out his information-gathering actively, efficiently and in safety.

The unit's authority on aircraft was Kapitän Wolfram de la Roi, and he saw aircraft not only as a reconnaissance and communications tool, but as a tool to be used to attack airships by either dropping small incendiary bombs or acid on them. He recommended to the War Ministry that they incorporate a flying school into the Research Unit, enabling the unit to examine a variety of aircraft while training pilots. He also recommended that the only aircraft used were from private manufacturers, and that potential military pilots first obtained a civilian licence from the German Aviators Association. This of course would reduce the expense of the training facilities at the school. In order to gain a foothold, if the project was taken up, Dr Walter Huth placed two French Latham aircraft and Simon Brunnhuber, his top engineer, at the disposal of the Research Unit.

A national fund was set up in 1908 called the Zeppelin Fund, which raised money for the building of Zeppelin airships, and was instrumental in persuading the War Ministry to purchase a number of these craft. Such was the support for the fund that some observers realised that some influential industrialists could affect the course of military-industrial relations widely. It was also realised that the continuing unrest in the Western world was causing a number of nations to look to their military forces in an effort to convince their neighbours that they were a force to be reckoned with. Germany was no exception, and its use of large airships showed the world that they were looking to the future, and the potential use of such craft placed them in the forefront of military might.

In one German magazine, the *Kladderadatsch*, a cartoon showed a uniformed Gallic cockerel standing on top of a dung heap, staring up at a winged Germany flying above it. In an effort to increase the German public's interest, postcards, photographs and public appearances by the aviators, who were rapidly becoming famous, blossomed. Slogans like 'For the People! By the People!' were coined in an attempt to generate a national pride in the new venture.

Kapitän von der Leith Thomsen was appointed head of a technical section for the General Staff and ordered to follow the progress of aviation, motorised transport and telegraphy. Captain Erich Ludendorff, who, fortunately, felt exactly the same way as Leith Thomsen, headed another section, which was created to observe the development of aviation. Between them they pushed the need for both airships and aircraft forward to the War Ministry, who controlled the budget.

However, the War Ministry was still not convinced and continued with the expansion of the Zeppelins. The small aircraft that occasionally buzzed around the massive Zeppelins that floated above were reduced to insignificance by the public conception of aviation at the time. Slowly but surely, however, the War Ministry started to realise the potential of the aeroplane after reports on the achievements by the French aviation industry.

The numerous reports and articles concerning the progress being made by the French and the Americans had awakened the German public's interest. This was demonstrated by the number of designs for flying machines that were starting to flood into the Government departments. These actions prompted Kapitän de la Roi to recommend that the Army put aside their prejudices and support an aviation programme.

The Airship Battalion reacted immediately, stating that the flights being made by the French and American aircraft could only be described as 'frivolous flights' and were not worth the time, effort and money required to emulate them. Leutnantgeneral Alfred von Lynker resolved the dispute by stating:

> The German army administration is presently of the opinion that its own work in the field of aviation technology is not yet absolutely necessary, since no type of flying machine has yet achieved the success that would demonstrate its suitability for military purposes. The solution to the problem should therefore be left to private enterprise, respectively factories, with which constant contact should be maintained.

Despite this setback, the construction of aircraft from private concerns continued and more and more civilians were starting to take flying lessons from the schools that were springing up around the country. Public interest in aviation had taken a giant step forward, one that the Government could not afford to ignore. The formation of the German Air Fleet League in the summer of 1908 attracted over 3,000 members within six months. The board members consisted of some of the most influential men from the world of politics and industry, and the War Ministry realised that they could no longer sit on the sidelines and just watch.

In 1909, the Army built its first airfield near Berlin, and in 1910 purchased a total of seven aircraft from various manufacturers, including the Albatros Company, who initially leased two of their aircraft to the school. The pilot training project was started on 8 July 1910, with Kapitän de la Roi in command. The Albatros machines were immediately put to use and four Army pilots were trained. In December 1910, the unit purchased the two Albatros aircraft for 24,108 marks each, and some officers and NCOs were sent to civilian flying schools for training. The end of 1911 saw aircraft involved in Army manoeuvres; the total number of aircraft purchased at this stage had risen to thirty-seven, with thirty pilots available to fly them.

At the beginning of 1909, a meeting of the German Air Fleet League had looked at a project presented by W. S. Hoffman for a military aircraft. The War Ministry ordered the Research Unit to look at the project after Hoffman had sent the plans and a model of the triplane to Oberstleutnant Hugo Schmiedecke, head of the War Department's transportation department. Initially, General von Lynker, head of the Inspectorate of Transport Troops, opposed the idea, but after pressure from the War Ministry he conceded, and on 18 February he accompanied Kapitän de la Roi when the project was presented to Emperor Wilhelm. The Emperor, a keen supporter of aviation, was impressed with the presentation, authorised the Research Unit to build the aircraft and ordered that the machine be ready for the forthcoming Imperial manoeuvres in September.

There were problems from the start, causing delay after delay, and it wasn't until 1 March 1910 that the aircraft was ready for its first flight – six months late. The delays were caused by the aircraft's designer, Hoffman, making constant alterations and the non-availability of a suitable engine. This immediately encouraged the Albatros Company to start manufacturing aircraft, as they realised that they had to get into the market early if they were to succeed.

It soon became obvious that these aircraft were a force that needed a separate organisation to control it. It was decided to establish thirty-four Feldflieger-Abteilung: eight for each of the Army Headquarters, and one for each of the twenty-six Army Corps. There was a great deal of initial resistance from some of the senior members of the old guard, who still thought that a good cavalry charge was all that was needed to dissuade the enemy. Fortunately for the German Army, this new type of warfare also had a large number of supporters, and on 1 August 1914 the Imperial German Air Force consisted of thirty Prussian Feldflieger-Abteilung and three Bavarian Feldflieger-Abteilung. Compared to the Allied air forces they were numerically inferior, but what they lacked in numbers they more than made up in organisation.

It was probably the unrest in Morocco and the Balkans that made the Prussians increase their aircraft orders after seeing the active part the aeroplane could play in reconnaissance.

In 1912, in an effort to raise money to help supplement the defence budget, the Prussian War Ministry created what was called the National Aviation Fund. It came under the direct control of the War Ministry, who oversaw the allocation of funds to technical development of military aircraft. It had been the brainchild of August Euler, who had taught Prince Heinrich of Prussia to fly, and the committee that controlled it was made up of some of Germany's most important and influential businessmen, retired politicians and senior military officers. However, the fund did not have a figurehead like Count Ferdinand Zeppelin, who was at the head of the Zeppelin Fund. Some of the cities that had raised various amounts of money through a network of fund committees were reluctant to release the money to what they thought was a faceless organisation. After reassurances from Kaiser Wilhelm himself that the money was to going to promote the furtherance of aviation and was in the national interest, a total of 500,000 marks were transferred into the National Aviation Fund.

With the threat of the First World War looming, a number of aircraft manufacturers started to look toward producing an aircraft that could be used for military purposes. Among these were three brothers, Alfred, Walter and Ernst Eversbusch, who established an aircraft manufacturing plant with the financial aid of the Bavarian Government. The Government decided to come to the aid of the brothers because they were concerned that unless they contributed to the manufacture of the aircraft, they would have no say in the equipment that would be used by Bavarian aircrews.

One of the major problems that Germany faced was that it was made up of a number of principalities and states, the two largest and most influential being Prussia and Bavaria. Of the two, the Prussians were more powerful, and there existed a very bitter rivalry between the two powers that carried on throughout the First World War; even today, traces of the rivalry still exist. Bavaria's autonomy stemmed from the Franco-Prussian War of 1870, when the Bavarian Army fought alongside the Prussian Army. After the conference at Versailles which ended the war, Prince Otto von Bismarck of Prussia, in order to create a German Empire, agreed that Bavaria and its ruling Wittelsbach dynasty be given a number of privileges as a reward for their support during the war. These included military autonomy, financial aid, an independent railway and postal system, and limited independent diplomatic privileges. However, it was the Prussian War Ministry that controlled the Bavarian Army budgetary allocation, and during the war it was the Prusso-German staff that directed the operations of the Bavarian Army.

The Bavarian War Ministry's excursion into the world of aviation had started back in 1910, when the Inspectorate of the Engineering Corps subsidised one of their officers, a Leutnant Wildt, to the sum of 20,000 marks in his attempt to build an aircraft of his own design. Despite four attempts to take off and a number of redesigns, the project failed. Determined to push on, General Karl von Brug, Head of the Engineers Corps, made contact with the Prussian War Ministry via the Bavarian liaison officer who was attached to the Prussian Army's Research Unit.

Initially, the Bavarian Government's intention was to approach the Albatros Company to acquire the rights to build their aircraft in Bavaria, but negotiations fell through. Then the Bavarian Flying Service stepped in, and at their instigation the Pfalz Company approached Gustav Otto, a financier who helped finance a new company, the Otto-Werke GmbH (*Gesellschaft mit beschränkter Haftung* – Limited Liability Company), and assisted in the development of the business. The company also acquired the rights to build the Otto biplane. The Pfalz Flugzeug-Werke was built at Speyer am Rhein in July 1913. The Otto-Werke GmbH was the first Bavarian aircraft firm, and was the brainchild of Gustav Otto. Otto had been coerced into working with the Army's newly acquired Bavarian Military Flying School and lent them one of his mechanics to train the Army personnel. The first aircraft to be produced there was not one of the Pfalz designs, but the Otto pusher biplane that was powered by a 100-hp Rapp engine. Later, Alfred Eversbusch managed to obtain a licence from the French Morane-Saulnier Company to manufacture the 'L' type Parasol monoplane.

Another company, Luftfahrzeug GmbH (LFG), had its roots back in 1906, when a company by the name of Motorluftschiff Studiengesellschaft had been created at the instigation of Wilhelm II, to carry out the manufacture of airships. The company changed its name a few years later to LFG Bitterfeld, from which sprang another company by the name of Flugmaschine Wright GmbH. This company went into liquidation in 1912, but was revived by a number of top financiers, including among them Alfred Krupp. So as not to be confused with the aircraft company Luft-Verkehrs Gesellschaft (LVG), the name Roland was added to the chosen name for the company of LFG, creating the company LFG Roland.

In the Austro-Hungarian Empire, things were not a lot better as far as the development of the aircraft was concerned. It wasn't that there were objections to the building of aircraft; it was who was building the aircraft that was the cause of some concern. Controversy surrounded Camillo Castiglioni, an extremely wealthy, Italian-born, naturalised Austrian with strong connections to the Austro-Hungarian monarchy, who was the financier behind the creation of the Brandenburg Werkes. Castiglioni already owned two aircraft manufacturing plants, the Motorluftfahrzeuggesellschaft (MLG) and the Hungarian Airship and Flying Machine Company in Budapest. Castiglioni had founded MLG in Vienna in 1909 with funds of 300,000 crowns from his parent company, the Austro-American Rubber Company. Most of the negotiations for the creation of these companies were carried out by directors under instructions and control of Castiglioni, so as not to make the authorities aware that the growing numbers of Austro-Hungarian aircraft manufacturers were under the control of one man. By the time the First World War was underway, Camillo Castiglioni also had a controlling interest in the Hansa-Brandenburg Company, Ungarische Flugzeugwerke Aktiengesellschaft (UFAG) in Budapest and the Phönix aircraft company in Vienna.

Problems for him arose when Oberstleutnant Emil Uzelac was appointed head of the Austro-Hungarian Army Airship section, a section of the Imperial and

Royal Aviation Troops (Kaiserliche und Königliche Luftfahrtruppen – KuK LFT). Uzelac was one of the champions of Austro-Hungarian aviation, having learned to fly at the age of forty-five. He soon realised that Camillo Castiglioni, to whom he had taken an instant dislike, was rapidly becoming a major influence in Austro-Hungarian aircraft manufacturing, and if he were to be allowed to continue unchecked, would take over complete financial control of the Austro-Hungarian aviation industry. Uzelac ensured that orders for aircraft were spread across the board and with various aircraft manufacturers, and that the standard of aircraft produced was of the highest quality possible, bearing in mind the lack of skilled workers and facilities.

When the LFT ordered twenty aircraft from MLG in 1912, four of these were modified Etrich trainers with side-by-side seating, and were to be ready by the end of July 1912. It soon became obvious that the completion date was far beyond the reach of the company if the stringent standards were adhered to, and they asked for the tardiness penalty to be dropped. These were refused, and by the end of 1912, when none of the aircraft had been delivered, the contracts were withdrawn and penalties issued.

Camillo Castiglioni was furious and attempted to use his considerable influence against Uzelac, as he saw his control of the aircraft manufacturing industry being threatened. However, it was to no avail; Uzelac too had powerful friends, not only in military and government circles, but also in the Prussian Army, and they threw their support behind him. Emil Uzelac was in close contact with Wolfram de la Roi, Head of the Prussian Research Unit, and Wilhelm Siegert of the Prussian Inspektion der Fliegertruppen (Idflieg) (Inspectorate of Flying Troops). These men were not about to throw money away on sub-standard aircraft and wanted everything to be of a consistently high standard. At the end of the day, both the Bavarian Army and the Prussian Army were part of the same German Empire, despite their differences. Castiglioni was being carefully watched and he knew it. He kept a tight grip on the companies that he owned but also kept a relatively low profile.

Although Siemens-Schuckert's first incursion into the world of aviation was in 1907, the company actually started life back in 1847, when it manufactured telegraph equipment. It was known as Siemens-Halske OH before it merged with the Schuckert Werke and became the famous Siemens-Schuckert company.

In 1914 war broke out, and the German Government requested that all companies respond to the war effort. Contrary to popular belief, the German Army Air Service was not ready for a war, as they had a very limited number of what could be called fighting aircraft. Within days of the war starting, the reconnaissance flights that the Fliegertruppen had been used for during training were put to good use as the war settled down into trench warfare on the ground.

German aircraft manufacturers, like their Allied counterparts, were in their infancy at the beginning of the First World War. There were a number of small manufacturing enclaves producing small sports-type aircraft, but nothing that could be construed as a military type.

As the war progressed, so did the standard and quality of German and Allied aircraft production. Two decades later, a Second World War would find these two protagonists using the lessons they had learned and the strides they had made in aviation, once again locked in mortal combat.

The Imperial German Navy's aviation section, on the other hand, was in an even worse condition. At the end of 1910, the Dockyard Department of the Naval Office recognised the potential of the aeroplane as a reconnaissance machine and allocated 100,000 marks to investigate and set up a working party to develop it.

The Naval Office ordered the Imperial Dockyard at Danzig to develop a seaplane; the Dockyard, in turn, assigned the task to a Leutnant Max Hering and naval engineer Karl Loew, with Leutnant Walter Langfeld as test pilot. The team had no experience at all in building an aircraft, so they turned to one of Germany's top aviation companies, Rumpler, for help. Within six months they produced the first of the floatplanes. This was quickly followed by two more, this time from the Albatros Company, and delivered in October 1911. The Navy was satisfied with the results and used the experience gained to work closely with aircraft manufacturers to produce a two-seat seaplane that met all their requirements. When manufacturers were approached initially, they were delighted with the thought of contracts, but envisaged technical difficulties when they saw the stringent requirements laid down by the Navy. This discouraged the vast majority of aircraft manufacturers, as they wanted only minimum co-operation with the military and to be given an almost free hand in the design and construction, which was something the Navy would not allow.

The Imperial German Navy and the Bavarian Army were in a unique position: they were not subject to the same amount of Prussian control as the other smaller states and principalities, and as such were autonomous to a certain degree. The only thing that affected the Navy's position was the inter-service rivalry which existed between the Army and the Navy, and still exists even today with armed forces throughout the world.

The Imperial Navy High Command's office had primarily dealt with manufacturers who had been supplying the Prussian Army, but because they were able to maintain their independence from any state or principality, they were able to send out new guidelines and specifications to all the manufacturers. The Navy had watched with interest the seaplane competition held in Monaco in March 1912, and in particular the American Glenn Curtiss seaplane. They ordered one of the aircraft via the Allgemeine Flug Gesellschaft (AFG) with the idea of taking the best ideas of the design. They then decided to sponsor competitions, and invited aircraft manufacturers to submit floatplanes and amphibians for the contests. There were a number of competitions with a large number of entrants, the vast majority of which came nowhere near matching the requirements of the Navy. Four did though; Albatros, Ago, Aviatik and Rumpler all offered to deliver aircraft to the Navy's requirements. The first seaplane to be used by the Navy, however, was the Albatros, after it had successfully taken off from the Baltic Sea during trials.

Among the manufacturers was Flugzeugbau Friedrichshafen (FF), who specialised in seaplane construction. Created in 1912 by Friedrich Kober, a close friend of Count Zeppelin, the company opened up its workshop in an old Zeppelin hangar on the shores of Lake Constance. The first aircraft produced was a modified copy of a Glen Curtiss floatplane and the first trials of the aircraft took place in October 1912. The trials were a complete success and so impressed the Navy that almost all the early contracts were given to the FF Company.

Between 1911 and 1914, the Navy purchased thirty-nine aircraft: sixteen Albatros, nine Ago, six Friedrichshafen, four Rumpler, one AEG, one Gotha, one Oertz and one MLG. The Navy was, in effect, still in the experimental stage as regards aircraft and still relied heavily on the airship.

On 1 April 1913, the Imperial German Navy established an aviation section that was followed on 3 May by a Naval Flying Unit. The unit set up a contest for the manufacturers to produce a seaplane that could operate over the open sea. The intention was for the contest to be held over the Baltic or North Seas, but the manufacturers complained that this was far too risky and so the contest was moved to Lake Constance. Initially, there were ten aircraft entered in the competition, but when the trials began only two firms, Albatros and Ago, had entered aircraft. Not satisfied, in November 1913, the Naval Office ordered the American Curtiss flying boat and the English Sopwith flying boat. Only the Curtiss aircraft was delivered, and that failed tests when subjected to high seas. One Austrian flying boat was purchased from MLG, and after tests it was accepted, but it was to the Flugzeugbau Friedrichshafen that they ultimately turned, and the company became the largest supplier of aircraft to the Navy.

Two more companies who specialised in the manufacture of floatplanes came to the fore soon afterwards: the Oertz and Hansa Brandenburgische Flugzeugwereke. The latter became the second largest manufacturer of German naval aircraft, and had been founded by Camillo Castiglioni, whose dominance, as mentioned earlier, was the cause for some concern to the Austro-Hungarian aircraft manufacturing industry.

The Oertz Company was a subsidiary of the Hamburg Yacht Company, which, like many other boat-builders, saw the opportunity to move into a different field of transport using their existing skills. Very few made the transition, as they found the technical side far too difficult, but Oertz did, albeit only briefly. Their designer/owner, Dipl.Ing. Max Oertz, produced a total of twelve flying boats from four different designs, the Oertz W.4, W.5, W.6 and W.8. All the aircraft used Maybach IV engines mounted inside the hull, which turned pusher propellers by means of a series of gears. All were biplanes, with the exception of W.6, which was a tandem-wing biplane. The beam of the hull was slightly wider than normal, which gave it extra stability. In 1916, the company was absorbed into the Hansa-Brandenburg Company, where the skills of its workforce were soon put to good use.

The Chief of the Admiralty Staff, Admiral Hugo von Pohl, had started pressurising the War Ministry for aeroplanes at the beginning of 1914. He saw them not only as defensive weapons against enemy airships and aircraft, but as both a reconnaissance and offensive weapon to be used in support of the Fleet. He, even at this early stage, recognised the importance of such a weapon and was becoming increasingly frustrated with the lack of commitment being showed by the manufacturers.

In order to encourage more interest, the Naval Office planned to hold a competition called the Baltic Sea Flight at Warnemunde, between 1 and 11 August 1914. Eleven firms, among them Aviatik, Rumpler, Hansa-Brandenburg, Friedrichshafen, Albatros and Ago, entered a total of twenty-six aircraft. Before the competition could get under way, the First World War broke out and the Navy commandeered all the aircraft entered. The motley collection of aircraft was ill-equipped for what lay before them and, indeed, some were worse than useless.

At the beginning of the war, the German Imperial Navy had a total of twenty-four aircraft at various stations, the majority of which were not seaworthy and none of which could be considered as training or combat aircraft. In fact, the Navy were building air stations without having any aircraft to put in them. A massive sum of 6,000,000 marks for aircraft and airships was allocated for German naval aviation, compared to 670,000 crowns for the Austro-Hungarian Navy. The German Navy approached a number of aircraft manufacturers, but they were only interested if they were subsidised. By the time the First World War started, the two major manufacturers supplying aircraft to the Navy were Flugzeugbau Friedrichshafen and Hansa Brandenburgische Flugzeugwerke.

One of the Navy's most supportive and influential figures in aviation at the time was Prince Heinrich of Prussia, the Kaiser's younger brother. He had learned to fly in 1910 at the age of forty-eight, and was an avid aviation enthusiast. At the beginning of the war he was appointed Grossadmiral of the naval forces in the Baltic (Oberbefehlshaber der Ostseestreitkräfte), much against the advice of the Kaiser's naval advisors. They thought that Prince Heinrich was too much of a playboy who liked to dabble in aviation, and his appointment looked like nepotism. He surprised everyone, however, with his natural leadership, dedication and ability to plan, using aviation to a larger degree than anyone else had even considered. He even persuaded Konteradmiral Ehler Behring, not renowned for his enthusiasm about aviation, to change his mind and place aircraft on the armoured cruiser SMS *Friedrich Carl*. During engagements in the Baltic, aircraft were used for aerial mine-laying and for reconnaissance.

The first German torpedo aircraft operations were carried out during this period. In April 1917, the German Navy started a campaign using torpedo-carrying seaplanes based at Zeebrugge. They would attack British ships in the English Channel, and even though they only sunk three ships for the loss of three seaplanes from anti-aircraft fire, the terror value was immense. The sinking of the ships, considering the torpedoes were only 1,000 lb in weight, was quite an achievement. Larger torpedoes could not be carried, as the British found out when they attempted to do so.

The use of the aircraft as an offensive weapon was highlighted on 11 August 1918, when German seaplanes intercepted six British motor torpedo boats on a mission in the Heligoland Bight. During the engagement the six torpedo boats were destroyed without a single loss to the Germans. The battle has gone down in history as being the greatest loss suffered by a navy from an aerial attack; it wasn't until the Battle of Bismark Sea in 1943 that anything was comparable with it.

Prince Heinrich's enthusiasm rubbed off on a number of other admirals, including Vice-Admiral Reinhard Scheer, who, in his book after the war, bemoaned the fact that there were not enough scouting seaplanes at the High Seas Fleet's disposal.

Austria-Hungary's Kaiserlich und Königlich Kreigsmarine – KuK (Imperial and Royal Navy) was fortunate to have an Admiral, Rudolph Graf Montecuccoli, who was a tremendously keen aviator and would fly at every opportunity. The KuK, as it became known, had an advantage over the German Navy, inasmuch as it had had some operational experience in Albania during peacekeeping duties there in 1913. This was proved beyond doubt in May 1917, when Italy joined in the war and the KuK, with its skilled pilots and ground staff, was ordered into the skies over the Adriatic Sea to take control. This they did comfortably, despite valiant efforts from the Italians.

It has to be said that during this period both sides only had a few aerial engagements over the sea. During 1915 the KuK lost three aircraft and three pilots, and in 1916 it lost twelve aircraft and twenty pilots. These figures, when compared to the losses being suffered over the Western Front, were very small indeed, but relatively high when compared with the number of aircraft and pilots the KuK had. Almost all the aircraft operated from land bases, although there were some unsubstantiated reports of aircraft being launched from warships.

The first recorded aerial attack on a warship in European waters was by an Austro-Hungarian flying boat on 17 October 1914, when the French armoured cruiser *Waldeck Rousseau* was bombed while it was on patrol in the Adriatic Sea. Despite coming very close, the bombs caused no damage and the rifle and machine gun fire from the cruiser caused no damage to the aircraft, but it highlighted the threat that aircraft could pose. Two years later, on 16 August 1916, seaplanes of the Austro-Hungarian KuK successfully bombed and sank the British submarine *B.10* at its moorings in Venice harbour. Then, two weeks later, the French submarine *Foucault* was bombed and sunk while submerged.

Back in Germany, the number of aircraft manufacturers was growing and the production lines were now producing increasing numbers of aircraft. Siemens-

Schuckert re-activated their aviation department under the control of Dr Walter Reichel, who was assisted by Dr Hugo Natalis and designer/pilots Franz and Bruno Steffen. The company's first effort was a single-engined monoplane that had been constructed for Prince Friedrich Sigismund of Prussia. Swedish aircraft builder Villehad Forssman based it on the design of the Nieuport 17. Two of the Siemens-Schuckert Bulldogs, as they were known, were built in 1915 and submitted to the Idflieg for testing. One of the aircraft was fitted with a 100-hp Siemens-Halske Sh I rotary engine, the other with a 100-hp Mercedes S.I. Both the aircraft were rejected on the grounds of poor performance and even worse handling qualities. This highlighted Idflieg's role, inasmuch as they would not accept sub-standard aircraft no matter how desperate the war situation had become.

The Automobil und Aviatik AG & Hannoversche Waggonfabrik AG, or Aviatik Company, as it became known, was a well-known German aircraft manufacturer before the First World War. At the beginning of the war, a number of Aviatik B.I and IIs, built before the war, were pressed into service with the Imperial German Air Service as unarmed reconnaissance aircraft. Like most of the early aircraft, the pilot flew the aircraft from the rear cockpit, while the observer sat in front.

The Rumpler aircraft manufacturing company had started building aircraft in 1908, well before the First World War started. The first of their aircraft to come from their factory at the state-owned airfield at Johannisthal was the Rumpler Eindecker, based on the Taube design. A flimsy-looking machine, as indeed most of the early aircraft were, the Eindecker was powered by a 100-hp Mercedes D.I engine and saw a great deal of service in the initial stages of the war on reconnaissance missions. Also operating from the airfield at Johannisthal was the Wright Flying Machine Company that appeared in 1909. This company had been established by the Motor Airship Study Company with a capital of 500,000 marks and the intention of producing a patented copy of the Wright Flyer.

As the need for aircraft intensified, the first of the Rumpler biplanes appeared in 1914 – the Rumpler B.I. A small number were built and supplied to the German Army for training purposes and reconnaissance duties.

Another of the manufacturers that was beginning to make its mark was the Fokker Company. The name Fokker was synonymous with aviation in the First World War, and produced some of Germany's finest military aircraft. Development of Fokker aircraft started back in 1911, when Anthony Fokker produced the first of his many aircraft, the Spider. With very little interest being expressed in Holland, Anthony Fokker moved to Germany, registering his company, Fokker Aviation Limited, in the Trade Register in Berlin on 22 February 1912.

Fokker's flying school was initially the most successful part of his company, and the authorities moved his school to Schwerin-Görries in Mecklenburg and supplied him with a large number of students. They also started to purchase his aircraft as once the war had started, German aviation, in terms of aircraft, was extremely thin on the ground.

All the aircraft manufacturers came under the control of the Flugzeugmeisterei (Air Ministry) and Idflieg (Inspektion der Fliegertruppen – Inspectorate of Aviation Troops). Desperate as the situation with aircraft had become, this Inspectorate would not be pressurised into accepting aircraft that did not measure up to their strict rules of requirement. Anthony Fokker discovered this to his cost and, because of his alien status, almost lost his liberty when it was thought that he might be deliberately producing sub-standard aircraft. It was only his high-level connections that prevented his arrest.

Not all the manufacturers started life building aircraft. The Junkers Aircraft Company began not as an aircraft manufacturer, but as a manufacturer of gas water-heaters for bathtubs. One of their aeronautical engineers, Dr Hugo Junkers, was one of the most innovative engineers of his time and, during his lifetime, was awarded more than 1,000 patents covering an extremely wide variety of fields. His involvement in aviation is legendary, and for some years he had been looking at the concept of producing an all-metal monoplane aircraft. Then, at the beginning of December 1915, the Junkers J.I, also known as the E.I. appeared. The first test flight, carried out on 12 December by Leutnant Friedrich Mallinckrodt at Döberitz, was a resounding success. The thin sheet metal covering the aircraft gave rise to the name 'Tin Donkey'.

One of the largest German aircraft manufacturers of the First World War was Luft-Verkehrs Gesellschaft (LVG), located at Johannisthal, Berlin. The use of the old Parseval airship hangar at the base gave the company all the room they needed to produce some of Germany's finest two-seater aircraft. The first aircraft produced in 1912 were of the standard Farman type. Then in 1912, a Swiss aeronautical engineer by the name of Franz Schneider joined LVG from the French Nieuport company, and started building aircraft that had been designed by LVG's own designers.

In 1907, the German General Staff approached the company with a view to building a 'military' non-rigid airship. The Type-M, as it was called, was completed but was not the success anticipated. This was followed by a much larger version that by all accounts was very successful, but for some unknown reason the project was dropped. Two years later the company was approached again, this time to build three aircraft. After two years they had produced three aircraft, which at best could only be described as of mediocre quality, and the company went back to its original business of electrical manufacture.

One of the most famous German aircraft of the First World War was the twin-engined Gotha bomber built by the Gothaer Waggonfabrik Company. The origins of the company went way back before the war, when one of the first aircraft they built was of Taube (Dove) design and given the designation LE.3. Originally built for the civilian market, a number of these aircraft saw service at the beginning of the First World War after being requisitioned by the German Army as scouts. Only a small number of these aircraft were built.

One of the things that emerged from the development of German aircraft during the First World War was the rivalry and snobbery that could have stunted the growth of aviation in these formative years. A prime example was that concerning the Austrian-designed Taube. In the early part of the war the Prussian Army used the aircraft as a front-line fighter, while the Austro-Hungarian Army regarded it as nothing more than a training aircraft. Their standards were considerably higher than that of the Prussians, so many of the aircraft manufacturers were unable to meet the required level. They suffered from the belief that they could produce their own aircraft, something they talked about at great length, but never actually did anything about.

The basic difference between the Prussian and Bavarian Armies and the Austro-Hungarian Army was that the Prussians and Bavarians were not averse to using their political and social positions to their own ends, whereas the Austro-Hungarian Army had almost no political power and very little on the social side, except in the higher ranks. This meant that the Prussians and the Bavarians had a much greater say in their military expenditure, and could use civilians with impunity, whereas the Austro-Hungarian Army basically got what they were given.

Despite this difference, the 7 million marks allocated to Germany, when compared to the 1.5 million crowns allocated to the Austro-Hungarian Army, were equal when looking at capita per head. It appears that the Austro-Hungarian Army was reluctant to involve the civilian aircraft industry, as is borne out when the small Austrian aircraft industry only produced 5,400 aircraft, while the German aircraft industry produced in excess of 48,000 aircraft. Ultimately the competition in the Austro-Hungarian aircraft manufacturing industry disappeared, which left the market open for German aircraft manufacturers to enter the market. The blame for this can be laid squarely at the feet of the Army, because of its stringent standards and their reluctance to offer sufficient contracts to encourage competition.

The Prussian and Bavarian armies, however, were much more realistic and looked toward the private sector for solutions to their aviation problems. This was not to say they, too, didn't have standards; they would not put up with sloppy, sub-standard work, as Anthony Fokker, among others, later discovered to his cost. The general staff of the German military watched other nations as they continued to progress with the development of their aircraft design and manufacture, while having to push their own various ministries into giving them more money. The Prussian and Bavarian ministries, however, wanted a more cautious approach, and required more research into aviation design and development resisting the attempts to push them headlong into giving out vast amounts of money.

As the need for more aircraft appeared so the larger manufacturers expanded, forcing the smaller firms to grow or be taken over. The number of designers and skilled engineers also grew and as demands increased, so they were 'headhunted' by the larger companies, forcing a number of the smaller manufacturers out of business. In addition to this, it has to be realised that almost all the Austro-Hungarian aircraft manufacturing companies built very little of their own designs and were predominantly used to manufacture aircraft from the major German companies under licence.

It was only the best that survived, and survive they did, leaving behind a legacy for the future of German aviation.

# List of German and Austro-Hungarian Aircraft Manufacturers of the First World War

## GERMAN FIRMS

Allgmeine Electrizitäts GmbH Hennigsdorf bei Berlin.
Ago Flugzeug-Werke GmbH Johannisthal bei Berlin.
Albatros Werke GmbH Johannisthal bei Berlin and Friedrichshafen bei Berlin.
Alter, Ludwig, Werke, Darmstadt.
Automobil und Aviatik AG, Leipzig-Heiterblick.
Bayerische Flugzeug-Werke AG München.
Bayerische Rumpler-Werke GmbH, Augsburg.
Daimler Motorengesellschaft Werke, Sindelfingen.
Deutsche Flugzeug-Werke GmbH Lindenthal bei Leipzig.
Euler-Werke, Frankfurt am Main, Neiderrad.
Fokker Flugzeug-Werke GmbH, Schwerin-Gories un Mecklenburg.
Flugzeug Friedrichshafen GmbH Manzell und Warnemünde.
Goedecker Flugzeug-Werke, Mainz Gonsenheim.
Germainia Flugzeug-Werke GmbH Leipzig-Mockau.
Gothaer Waggonfabrik AG Gotha.
Halberstädter Flugzeug-Werke GmbH Halberstadt.
Hannoversche Waggonfabrik AG, Hannover-Linden.
Hansa und Brandenburgische Flugzeug-Werke GmbH.
Priest bei Brandenburg am Havel.
Hanseatische Flugzeug-Werke (Karl Caspar AG) Hamburg Fühlsbüttel.
Jeannin Flugzeugbau GmbH Johannisthal bei Berlin.
Junkers Flugzeug-Werke AG, Dessau.
Junkers-Fokker-Werke.
Kaiserlich Marineweft Reichwerft, Danzig, Kiel, Wilhelmsavhen.
Kondor Flugzeug-Werke GmbH Essen.
Linke-Hoffman Werke AG, Breslau.
Luftfahrzeug GmbH (LFG) Berlin-Charlottenburg.
Luft Torpedo GmbH Johannisthal bei Berlin.
Luft-Verkehrs GmbH (LVG) Johannisthal bei Berlin.
Flugzeugwerft Lübeck-Travemünde GmbH Travemünde-Privall.
Märkische Flugzeug-Werke GmbH. Golm-in-der-Mark.
Mercur Flugzeugbau GmbH, Berlin.
Naglo Boots-Werft, Pichelsdorf-Spandau, Berlin.

National Flugzeug-Werke, GmbH Johannisthal bei Berlin.
Nordeutsche Flugzeug-Werke, Tetlow bei Berlin.
Oertz-Werke GmbH, Reiherstieg bei Hamburg.
Ostdeutsche Albatros Werke GmbH, Schneidemühl.
Otto-Werke GmbH, München.
Pfalz Flugzeug-Werke GmbH, Speyer am Rhein.
Flugmaschine Rex GmbH, Cologne.
Waggonfabrik Joseph Rathgeber, München-Moosach.
Albert Rinne Flugzeug-Werke, Rummelsburg bei Berlin.
Rumpler Flugzeug-Werke GmbH, Johannisthal bei Berlin.
Sablatnig Flugzeugbau GmbH, Berlin.
Flugmaschine Fabrik Franz Schneider, Seegefeld bei Spandau.
Luftfahrzeugbau Schütte-Lanz, Mannheim-Rheinau; also at Zessen bei Königswursterhausen.
Schwade Elugzeug und Motorenbau, Erfurt.
Siemens-Schuckert Werke GmbH, Berlin und Nürnberg.
Union Flugzeug-Werke, Tetlow bei Berlin.
Zeppelin Werke, Lindau GmbH, Reutin und Seemos.
Zeppelin Werke Staaken GmbH, Staaken bei Berlin.


## AUSTRO-HUNGARIAN

Oesterreichisch-Ungarische Flugzeugfabrik 'Aviatik' GmbH.
K.u.K. Fliegerarsenal Flugzeugwerke Fischamend.
Ungarische Lloyd Flugzeug und Motorenfabrik AG.
Lohnerwerke GmbH.
Oesterreichische Flugzeugfabrik AG.
Phönix Flugzeugerkw AG.
Ungarische Allgemeine Maschinefabrik AG.
Thöne & Fiala.
Ungarische Flugzeugwerke AG.
Wiener Karosserie und Flugzeugfabrik.


The manufacturers listed below are the major ones and some of the minor ones selected for the text.

Allgmeine Electrizitäts GmbH. Hennigsdorf bei Berlin.
Albatros Werke GmbH. Johannisthal bei Berlin and Friedrichshafen bei Berlin.
Automobil und Aviatik AG, Leipzig-Heiterblick.
Hansa und Brandenburgische Flugzeug-Werke GmbH.
Deutsche Flugzeug-Werke GmbH. Lindenthal bei Leipzig.
Euler-Werke GmbH, Frankfurt.
Flugzeug Friedrichshafen GmbH. Manzell und Warnemünde.
Fokker Flugzeug-Werke GmbH., Schwerin-Gories un Mecklenburg.
Gothaer Waggonfabrik AG Gotha.
Halberstädter Flugzeug-Werke GmbH Halberstadt.
Hannoversche Waggonfabrik AG, Hannover-Linden.
Junkers Flugzeug-Werke AG, Dessau.
Lohner GmbH.
Luftfahrzeug Gesellschaft GmbH (LFG) Berlin-Charlottenburg.
Luft-Verkehrs Gesellschaft GmbH Johannisthal bei Berlin.

Oesterreichische Flugzeugfabrik AG (Oeffag).
Otto Werke GmbH.
Pfalz Flugzeug-Werke GmbH, Speyer am Rhein.
Phönix Flugzeugerkw AG (Austro-Hungarian).
Rumpler Flugzeug-Werke GmbH, Johannisthal bei Berlin.
Sablatnig Flugzeugbau GmbH, Berlin.
Siemens-Schuckert Werke GmbH, Berlin und Nürnberg.
Flugzeug und Maschinenfabrik Thöne & Fiala.
Wright Flying Machine Company, Johannisthal, bei Berlin.
Zeppelin Werke, Lindau GmbH, Reutin und Seemos.
Zeppelin Werke Staaken GmbH, Staaken bei Berlin.

# Aircraft Types

A. Single-engine monoplane without armament.

B. Single-engine biplane without armament.

C. Single-engine biplane with armament.

D. Single-engine, single-seat biplane with armament.

E. Single-engine, single-seat monoplane with armament.

F. Single-engine, single-seat triplane with armament (prototype models).

G. Multi-engine biplane with armament.

R. Biplane with three to six engines (known as 'Giant' aircraft).

Dr. Single-engine, single-seat triplane with armament (production models).

CL. Light C-Type two-seater biplane with armament.

GL. Light G-Type biplane with armament.

J. Single-engine, two-seater armoured biplane for infantry cooperation.

L. Multi-engine biplane with armament.

N. Single-engine aircraft with armament for night operations.

S. Single-engine, two-seater armoured biplane with armament.

DJ. Single-engine, single-seat armoured aircraft with biplane.

# Glossary

Abteilung: Squadron.
Armee-Flug-Park (AFP): Aviation Supply Depot.

Eindecker: Monoplane.

Feldflieger-Abteilung (Ffl.Abt): Field Aviation Detachment.
Feldfliegerschule: Field Flying school.
Feldwebel: Sergeant or Sergeant Major.
Fliegerarsenal (Flars): Aviation arsenal responsible for testing and accepting all army aviation materials.
Fliegerkompagnie (Flik): Operational unit.

Generalleutnant: Lieutenant-General (Major-General in USA).
Generalmajor: Major-General (Brigadier-General USA).
Generaloberst: Colonel-General (General USA).
Geschwader: Squadron.
GmbH (Gesellschaft mit beschraenkter Haftung): Limited liability Company.

Hauptmann: Captain.

IdFlieg (Inspektion der Verkehrstruppen): Inspectorate of Flying Troops.

Jagdgeschwader (JG): Group of four fighter sections.
Jagdstaffel (Jasta): Fighter section.
Jastaschule: Fighter Training School.

Kampfgeschwaden: Combat Squadron.
Kampstaffel (Kasta) (KS): Fighting section.
Kette: Flight of three or four aircraft together.
KuK (Kaiserliche und Königliche Luftfahrtruppen): Imperial and Royal Aviation Troop.

Luftfahrtuppen (LFT): Aviation troops.
Luftschifferabteilung (LA): Responsible for the development of airships and aircraft for military purposes.

MAG: Ungarische allgemeine Maschinefabrik AG.
Major: Squadron Leader.

Oberleutnant: First Lieutenant.
Oberstleutnant: Lieutenant-Colonel/ Wing Commander.
Oberst: Colonel/ Group Captain
WKF: Wiener Karosserie und Flugzeugfabrik.

# AEG
## (Allgemeine Elektrzitäts Gesellschaft)

The Allgemeine Elektrzitäts Gesellschaft was Germany's largest electric company, and at the beginning of the flight era was probably one of the few companies in Germany that was capable of financially supporting an aviation company. It wasn't until 1914, however, that they produced their first aircraft. They had investments in a number of different companies but had yet to be persuaded that the aeroplane was a worthwhile investment. Like all major companies, profit was the underlying theme that motivated them.

In 1912, a number of new aviation companies started to appear, but the one that interested the Army the most was from AEG. One of the directors of the company, Walter Rathenau, put forward a proposal that his company would buy a French Breguet for 400,000 marks, together with a licence to build the aircraft in Germany, on the condition that the Army would buy twenty-five of the aircraft in the first year. As tempting as the offer was, General von Lyncker, who wanted AEG to enter the aviation-manufacturing field, was sceptical about purchasing aircraft from an untried and untested company.

AEG went ahead and purchased one of the French Breguet, but did not purchase the licence to build the aircraft. What they did was build an unlicensed copy of the aircraft, much to the anger of the Breguet Company, thus sparing themselves the costs of having to pay a patent fee for the aircraft. Production was started at a factory at Hennigsdorf, just outside Spandau near Berlin.

In 1914, a two-seat unarmed reconnaissance aircraft, the AEG B.I, appeared in the skies over France. It was the first military aircraft produced by AEG. The B.I was selected for reconnaissance and artillery spotting duties almost from the outset of the war. It was unusual in that it had a tricycle undercarriage and a wingspan of over 50 feet. Powered by a 100-hp Mercedes D.I engine, the B.I had a top speed of 63 mph. Like all wartime weapons, necessity became the mother of invention, and within months the B.I had been superseded by the B.II, fitted with a more powerful Mercedes engine. The tricycle undercarriage had been replaced, making the aircraft a standard 'tail dragger'.

An incursion into the development of twin-engined bombers gave AEG a new impetus, when, early in 1915, the AEG I (KI) appeared. Powered by two 100-hp Mercedes D.I engines and carrying a crew of three, the aircraft proved not to be the success hoped for and only one was built. In July 1915, a slightly larger version of the G.I. appeared – the G.II. Powered by two 150-hp Benz Bz III engines, the aircraft carried a crew of three and was armed with two machine guns and carried 200kg of bombs externally. Between fifteen and twenty of these aircraft were built and were used by the Kampfgeschwader (Combat Squadron).

The AEG B.III appeared in June 1915, fitted with a 120-hp Mercedes D.II engine and a reduced wingspan (42 ft 11½ in). Once again the aircraft was used for unarmed reconnaissance missions, with a top speed of 68-75 mph. One month later, in March 1915, the first armed AEG appeared in the shape of the AEG C.I. Fitted with a 150-hp Benz Bz III engine, the C.I was virtually a B.II fitted with a more powerful engine and carrying a Bergmann machine gun in the observer's position.

In October 1915, the AEG C.II appeared – a slightly smaller version of the C.I. The fuselage was 3 feet shorter, which reduced the weight of the aircraft by some 50 lb, and reduced the wing span by 2 feet. The aircraft was equipped with bomb-carrying equipment, enabling it to carry four 10 kg bombs. Powered by the 150-hp Benz Bz III engine, with its distinctive rhino horn exhaust, the aircraft had a top speed of 86 mph.

This was followed at the end of 1915 by the radical design of the AEG C.III, in which the pilot was seated behind the observer. Powered by a 150-hp Benz Bz III engine, the aircraft only reached the experimental stage and only one was ever made. Among a number of other things, there were serious problems with the pilot's visibility during combat and landing.

By the end of the year a third type of bomber had appeared, the AEG III. This was the first of the bombers to have balanced control surfaces, and was powered by two eight-cylinder 220-hp Mercedes D.IV engines. It carried a crew of three and was armed with two manually operated machine guns and 300 kg of bombs. It had a range of 700 km and a top speed of 98 mph.

Earlier in February 1916, manufacturers were asked to produce a new two-seat fighter/reconnaissance aircraft. AEG produced the AEG C.V. Powered by a 220-hp Mercedes D.IV engine, the C.V had a top speed of 103-12 mph and could climb to 3,280 ft in less than 5 minutes. One was built and entered for the competition, but the Albatros C.V proved to be a far better aircraft and was selected.

At the beginning of 1916 the German Army High Command started a programme called the R-plane, which was designed to replace the airship with a long-range bomber/reconnaissance aircraft. A number of aircraft manufacturers were approached, including AEG.

Some of the other aircraft companies, such as Siemens-Schuckert, Albatros and Aviatik among others, had been working on such an aircraft since the middle of 1914. AEG's staff had had some considerable experience in building bombers, but nothing on the scale of the R.I that was to eventually appear.

In charge of the project was former Deutsche Flugzeug-Werke (DFW) test pilot Oberleutnant Brückmann, with Chief Engineer Ing. Sander and his assistants, Dipl.Ing. Werner Zorn and Professor Oesterlein. The aircraft was a real *tour de force*, and consisted of a number of revolutionary designs, including an all-steel fuselage, mixed steel and duralumin wings and electrically operated tailplane trim controls. The R.I was powered by four 260-hp Mercedes D.IVa engines, the first of which was started by a single Bosch inertia starter and then the remaining three engines 'clutch started'. On the prototype model, each engine had its own radiator; these were later replaced by two large radiators that consisted of four separate units mounted on the centre-section struts. They also had four-bladed propellers, which, surprisingly, were later replaced by two-bladed ones.

The first flight took place on 14 June 1918, and a number of problems manifested themselves. The most serious was that with the engines throttled right back and with the elevator full down, the nose of the aircraft continued to rise. To enable the aircraft to make a safe landing, all available weight had to be moved forward.

Allocated the designation of R.21, the bomber carried out a number of other test flights, and it was decided that the propellers were not suitable. Returned to the propeller factory, they were fitted with additional glued sections. The propellers were returned to AEG with the warning that it would be at least ten days before the glue had set properly. Impatient to get the aircraft into the air again, Oberleutnant Brückmann had the propellers fitted within four days of their return. Dipl.Ing. Zorn warned Brückmann that it was unsafe to fly the aircraft. On 3 September 1918 the aircraft took to the air, but within one hour tragedy struck. One of the propellers flew apart, causing the cardan shaft to tear loose and shatter the centre-section structure. The result was that the AEG R.21 broke apart in the air, killing all seven members of the crew.

Test pilot Max Fiedler, who was flying a Rumpler C.I chase plane as an escort, described the accident:

I recall being slightly over the R.21 at about 6,000 feet, when Brückmann, celebrating the event, waved a cognac bottle as the R.21 swung to the left and then a right bank. There was a flutter and suddenly the wings folded back. It was a terrifying sight.

Production was immediately halted until the problems were sorted out, but the main problem had been identified almost immediately.

AEG received a contract for a second R.I, designated the R.II, but the project was never completed.

In December 1916, two models of the AEG C.VII appeared, the difference between the two being that one had straight wings, while the other had a heavily-swept upper wing and a large spinner on the airscrew. Only one of each was built.

Another single model was built in 1917, the AEG C.IV N. This was a single-engined night bomber. Based on the design of the C.IV, the C.IV N had a wingspan of 50 ft 2 in, was powered by a 150-hp Benz Bz III engine and had a flight endurance of 4 hours. It was not a great success and only one was built. This was followed by the C.VIII, an experimental two-seater with multi-spar wings and radiators situated either side on the fuselage that closely resembled ears. Powered by a 160-hp Mercedes D.III engine, the C.VIII had a top speed of 106.25 mph and could climb to 3,280 feet in 3.8 minutes.

An incursion into the field of single-seat fighters in March 1917 produced the AEG D.I. Powered by a 160-hp Mercedes D.III engine, this stocky little fighter was capable of a top speed of 137 mph. It was built in limited numbers, and was flown in combat by Leutnant Walter Höhndorf, who was killed in the aircraft on 5 September 1917.

Two further prototypes were produced, differing only in the fact that they had 'ear'-type radiators fitted either side of the fuselage. There was even a triplane version produced, the AEG Dr.I, but it proved to have no more performance value than the previous three models.

The arrival of the triplane prompted AEG to produce an experimental version, the AEG C.VIII Dr. Similar to the C.VIII in design, even down to the unusual tail surfaces, the aircraft proved to be no better than the C.VIII and development was not pursued.

Early in 1918, another experimental single-seater triplane was produced, the AEG P.E. (Panzer Einsitzer). It had an armoured fuselage, covered in aluminium sheets, and tubular wing spars. Powered by a 195-hp Benz Bz IIIb engine, the fighter was capable of a top speed of 103.75 mph. It was armed with twin Spandau forward-firing machine guns, and was capable of carrying four small bombs. Just before the Armistice, another fighter aircraft appeared from the factory – the AEG DJ.I. Derived from the AEG P.E., the DJ.I was powered by the 195-hp V.8 Benz Bz IIIb engine and, like the P.E.'s fuselage, was covered in armoured aluminium. It had a top speed of 112 mph and a climb rate of 830 feet per minute. It was designed as an armoured, single-seat ground-attack fighter whose British equivalent was the Sopwith Salamander, but before it could be put into production the war ceased and the main protagonists were at peace, albeit for just over twenty years.

## SPECIFICATIONS

### AEG B.I

| | |
|---|---|
| Wingspan: | 50 ft 10¼ in (15.5 m) |
| Length: | 34 ft 5½ in (10.5 m) |
| Height: | 11 ft (3.3 m) |
| Weight Empty: | 1,430 lb (650 kg) |
| Weight Loaded: | 2,464 lb (1,117 kg) |
| Maximum Speed: | 56 mph (95 km/h) |
| Ceiling: | Not known |
| Endurance: | 4 hours |
| Engine: | One 100-hp Mercedes D.I |

### AEG B.III

| | |
|---|---|
| Wingspan: | 50 ft 10¼ in (15.5 m) |
| Length: | 34 ft 5½ in (10.5 m) |
| Height: | 11 ft (3.3 m) |
| Weight Empty: | 1,430 lb (650 kg) |
| Weight Loaded: | 2,464 lb (1,117 kg) |
| Maximum Speed: | 69 mph (110 km/h) |
| Ceiling: | Not known |
| Endurance: | 4 hours |
| Engine: | One 120-hp Mercedes D.II |

### AEG C.I

| | |
|---|---|
| Wingspan: | 42 ft 10½ in (13.7 m) |
| Length: | 26 ft 1 in (8.0 m) |
| Height: | 11 ft (3.3 m) |
| Weight Empty: | 1,562 lb (710 kg) |
| Weight Loaded: | 2,475 lb (1,125 kg) |
| Maximum Speed: | 81 mph (130 km/h) |
| Ceiling: | 9,840 ft (3,000 m) |
| Endurance: | 4 hours |
| Engine: | One 150-hp Benz Bz.III |
| Armament: | One free-firing machine gun mounted in the observer's cockpit |

### AEG C.II

| | |
|---|---|
| Wingspan: | 38 ft 10½ in (12.0 m) |
| Length: | 23 ft 3 in (7.1 m) |
| Height: | 11 ft (3.3 m) |

| | |
|---|---|
| Weight Empty: | 1,495 lb (680 kg) |
| Weight Loaded: | 2,640 lb (1,200 kg) |
| Maximum Speed: | 86 mph (138 km/h) |
| Ceiling: | 9,840 ft (3,000 m) |
| Endurance: | 4 hours |
| Engine: | One 150-hp Benz Bz.III |
| Armament: | One free-firing machine gun mounted in the observer's cockpit |
| | Four 10 kg bombs |

## AEG C.II (Experimental)

| | |
|---|---|
| Wingspan: | 39 ft 4¼ in (12.0 m) |
| Length: | 21 ft 4 in (6.5 m) |
| Height: | 10 ft 10 in (3.3 m) |
| Weight Empty: | 1,511 lb (687 kg) |
| Weight Loaded: | 2,721 lb (1,237 kg) |
| Maximum Speed: | 99 mph (158 km/h) |
| Ceiling: | 9,840 ft (3,000 m) |
| Endurance: | Not known |
| Engine: | One 150-hp Benz Bz.III |
| Armament: | None |

## AEG C.IV

| | |
|---|---|
| Wingspan: | 44 ft 2 in (13.4 m) |
| Length: | 23 ft 5½ in (7.1 m) |
| Height: | 11 ft (3.3 m) |
| Weight Empty: | 1,760 lb (798 kg) |
| Weight Loaded: | 2,464 lb (1,117 kg) |
| Maximum Speed: | 98 mph (181 km/h) |
| Ceiling: | 16,400 ft (4,998 m) |
| Endurance: | 4 hours |
| Armament: | One forward-firing synchronised Spandau machine gun |
| | One manually operated Parabellum machine gun in observer's position |
| Engine: | One 160-hp Mercedes D.III six-cylinder, in-line, water-cooled |

## AEG C.IV.N (Only one built)

| | |
|---|---|
| Wingspan: | 50 ft 2½ in (15.2 m) |
| Length: | 23 ft 11½ in (7.3 m) |
| Height: | 10 ft 10 in (3.3 m) |
| Weight Empty: | 1,936 lb (880 kg) |
| Weight Loaded: | 3,080 lb (1,400 kg) |
| Maximum Speed: | 90 mph (143 km/h) |
| Ceiling: | 16,400 ft (4,998 m) |
| Endurance: | 4 hours |
| Armament: | One forward-firing synchronised Spandau machine gun |
| | One manually operated Parabellum machine gun in observer's position |
| Engine: | One 150-hp Benz Bz.III |

## AEG J.II

| | |
|---|---|
| Wingspan: | 44 ft 2 in (13.4 m) |
| Length: | 23 ft 7½ in (7.2 m) |
| Height: | 11 ft (3.3 m) |
| Weight Empty: | 3,201 lb (1,452 kg) |
| Weight Loaded: | 3,828 lb (1,732 kg) |
| Maximum Speed: | 93 mph (172 km/h) |
| Ceiling: | 16,400 ft (4,998 km/h) |
| Endurance: | 2½ hours |
| Armament: | One forward-firing synchronised Spandau machine gun |
| | One manually operated Parabellum machine gun in observer's position |
| Engine: | One 160-hp Mercedes D.III six-cylinder, in-line, water-cooled |

## AEG Dr.I (Triplane)

| | |
|---|---|
| Wingspan: | 30 ft 10 in (9.3 m) |
| Length: | 20 ft (6 m) |
| Height: | 7 ft 6 in (2.2 m) |
| Weight Empty: | 1,562 lb (708.5 kg) |
| Weight Loaded: | 2,134 lb (967.9 kg) |
| Maximum Speed: | 106 mph (196 km/h) |
| Ceiling: | 14,600 ft |
| Endurance: | 4-5 hours |
| Armament: | One forward-firing synchronised Spandau machine gun |
| Engine: | One 160-hp Mercedes D.III six-cylinder, in-line, water-cooled |

## AEG C.VII

| | |
|---|---|
| Wingspan: | 36 ft 5¼ in (11.1 m) |
| Length: | 20 ft 4¼ in (6.2 m) |
| Height: | 7 ft 6 in (2.2 m) |
| Weight Empty: | 1,668 lb (758 kg) |
| Weight Loaded: | 2,462 lb (1,118 kg) |
| Maximum Speed: | 103 mph (165 km/h) |
| Ceiling: | 14,000 ft (4,267 m) |
| Endurance: | 4-5 hours |
| Engine: | One 160-hp Mercedes D.III six-cylinder, in-line, water-cooled |

## AEG C.VIII (Experimental)

| | |
|---|---|
| Wingspan: | 31 ft 2 in (9.5 m) |
| Length: | 22 ft 8 in (6.9 m) |
| Height: | 7 ft 6 in (2.2 m) |
| Weight Empty: | 1,760 lb (800 kg) |
| Weight Loaded: | 2,552 lb (1,160 kg) |
| Maximum Speed: | 106 mph (170 km/h) |
| Ceiling: | 14,000 ft (4,267 m) |
| Endurance: | 4-5 hours |

| Engine: | One 160-hp Mercedes D.III six-cylinder, in-line, water-cooled |

## AEG C.VIII Dr (Triplane)

| | |
|---|---|
| Wingspan Upper: | 36 ft 9 in (11.2 m) |
| Middle: | 35 ft 5 in (10.8 m) |
| Lower: | 25 ft 1 in (7.7 m) |
| Length: | 22 ft 8 in (6.9 m) |
| Height: | 7 ft 6 in (2.2 m) |
| Weight Empty: | 1,562 lb (708.5 kg) |
| Weight Loaded: | 2,134 lb (967.9 kg) |
| Maximum Speed: | 103 mph (190 km/h) |
| Ceiling: | 14,000 ft (4,267 m) |
| Endurance: | 4-5 hours |
| Engine: | One 160-hp Mercedes D.III six-cylinder, in-line, water-cooled |

## AEG D.I

| | |
|---|---|
| Wingspan: | 27 ft 10½ in (8.5 m) |
| Length: | 20 ft 1 in (6.2 m) |
| Height: | 8 ft 8½ in (2.65 m) |
| Weight Empty: | 1,507 lb (685 kg) |
| Weight Loaded: | 2,068 lb (940 kg) |
| Maximum Speed: | 137 mph (220 km/h) |
| Ceiling: | 16,400 ft (5,000 m) |
| Endurance: | 4-5 hours |
| Engine: | One 160-hp Mercedes D.III |
| Armament: | Twin Spandau machine guns and provision for four small bombs |

## AEG D.J

| | |
|---|---|
| Wingspan: | 36 ft 9 in (11.2 m) |
| Length: | 21 ft 8 in (6.6 m) |
| Height: | 7 ft 6 in (2.2 m) |
| Weight Empty: | 2,600 lb (1,179 kg) |
| Weight Loaded: | 3,106 lb (1,408 kg) |
| Maximum Speed: | 103 mph (190 km/h) |
| Ceiling: | 13,920 ft (4,242 m) |
| Endurance: | 4-5 hours |
| Engine: | One 195-hp Benz Bz.IIIb V-8, in-line, water-cooled |
| Armament: | Twin Spandau machine-guns and provision for four small bombs |

## AEG G.I (Only one built)

| | |
|---|---|
| Wingspan: | 52 ft 6 in (16.0 m) |
| Length: | 28 ft 4½ in (8.65 m) |
| Height: | 12 ft 9½ in (3.90 m) |
| Weight Empty: | 2,552 lb (1,160 kg) |
| Weight Loaded: | 3,199 lb (1,954 kg) |

| | |
|---|---|
| Maximum Speed: | 78 mph (125 km/h) |
| Ceiling: | 14,760 ft (4,500 m) |
| Endurance: | 4-5 hours |
| Engine: | Two 100-hp Mercedes D.I |
| Armament: | None |

## AEG G.II

| | |
|---|---|
| Wingspan: | 53 ft 2 in (16.2 m) |
| Length: | 29 ft 10½ in (9.1 m) |
| Height: | 12 ft 9½ in (3.90 m) |
| Weight Empty: | 3,190 lb (1,450 kg) |
| Weight Loaded: | 5,434 lb (2,470 kg) |
| Maximum Speed: | 87 mph (140 km/h) |
| Ceiling: | 14,760 ft (4,500 m) |
| Endurance: | 4-5 hours |
| Engine: | Two 150-hp Benz Bz.III |
| Armament: | Two/three free-firing machine guns and provision for 200 kg bombs |

## AEG G.III

| | |
|---|---|
| Wingspan: | 60 ft 6 in (18.44 m) |
| Length: | 30 ft 2¼ in (9.2 m) |
| Height: | 12 ft 9½ in (3.90 m) |
| Weight Empty: | 4,268 lb (1,940 kg) |
| Weight Loaded: | 6,633 lb (3,015 kg) |
| Maximum Speed: | 99 mph (160 km/h) |
| Ceiling: | 14,760 ft (4,500 m) |
| Endurance: | 4-5 hours |
| Engine: | Two 220-hp Mercedes D.IV |
| Armament: | Two free-firing machine guns and provision for 300 kg bombs |

## AEG G.IV

| | |
|---|---|
| Wingspan: | 60 ft 4½ in (18.40 m) |
| Length: | 31 ft 10 in (9.70 m) |
| Height: | 12 ft 9½ in (3.90 m) |
| Weight Empty: | 5,280 lb (2,400 kg) |
| Weight Loaded: | 7,986 lb (3,630 kg) |
| Maximum Speed: | 103 mph (165 km/h) |
| Ceiling: | 14,760 ft (4,500 m) |
| Endurance: | 4-5 hours |
| Engine: | Two 260-hp Mercedes D.IVa, six-cylinder, in-line, water-cooled |
| Armament: | Two Parabellum free-firing machine guns and provision for four small bombs |

## AEG G.V

| | |
|---|---|
| Wingspan: | 89 ft 4½ in (27.24 m) |
| Length: | 35 ft 9½ in (10.8 m) |

| | |
|---|---|
| Height: | 14 ft 9½ in (4.5 m) |
| Weight Empty: | 5,940 lb (2,700 kg) |
| Weight Loaded: | 10,120 lb (4,600 kg) |
| Maximum Speed: | 91 mph (145 km/h) |
| Ceiling: | 14,760 ft (4,500 m) |
| Endurance: | 5-6 hours |
| Engine: | Two 260-hp Mercedes D.IVa, six-cylinder, in-line, water-cooled |
| Armament: | Two Parabellum free-firing machine guns and provision for 1,320 lb (600 kg) bombs |

## AEG R.I

| | |
|---|---|
| Wingspan: | 118 ft 1½ in (36.0 m) |
| Length: | 63 ft 11½ in (19.5 m) |
| Height: | 20 ft 10 in (6.35 m) |
| Weight Empty: | 19,845 lb (9,000 kg) |
| Weight Loaded: | 28,003 lb (12,500 kg) |
| Maximum Speed: | Not known |
| Ceiling: | Not known |
| Endurance: | 5-6 hours |
| Engine: | Four 260-hp Mercedes D.IVa |
| Armament: | Five Parabellum free-firing machine guns |

# Albatros Flugzeugwerke GmbH

The Albatros Flugzeugwerke produced their first aircraft in 1912, the Albatros L.3, a single-seat scout type. This was followed by the L.9, a single-seat scout type designed by Claude Dornier, who later was to join the Zeppelin Company as their chief designer.

The Albatros company, co-founded and owned by Dr Walter Huth, had been in existence since 1909 and was founded with a capital of 25,000 marks. It was situated, together with other aircraft manufacturers, at the airfield at Johannisthal, near Berlin. As the Prussian Army became more and more interested in aviation, the manufacturers came up with a variety of offers in an attempt to secure contracts from them. On 2 October 1909, Dr Huth approached the War Ministry and offered to buy a French Latham aircraft for the military and supply an instructor to train military pilots, if they would pay for any repairs and maintenance costs. The offer was declined as the Wright Company had offered a similar package – for free. This prompted the Chief of the General Staff, General von Moltke, to put forward a recommendation that the War Minister sanction the training of suitable officers as pilots. At the end of 1909, von Moltke had been well aware that the French were already buying numbers of aircraft in addition to building some of their own, and were training military pilots.

The General Inspectorate of Military Transportation tried to maintain an impartial stance towards the various aircraft manufacturers, or so it was thought. For some unknown reason, they seemed to favour the Albatros Company, but this came to a head in 1911 when Otto Weiner, one of the directors of Albatros, urged Colonel Messing of the Inspectorate not to deal with the Luftverkehrsgesellschaft (LVG), claiming that the company was just a sale agent for Albatros. The LVG Company was owned by Arthur Mueller, and he allegedly persuaded Otto Weiner that the Army would rather deal with him than Albatros. Albatros claimed, however, that they reserved the right to sell directly to the Army and LVG would receive 750 marks for each aircraft sold. The fact that the LVG Company had saved the Albatros Company from collapse in the spring of 1911, after it had had a request for a subsidy from the Army rejected, seems to have been forgotten by Otto Weiner. LVG had purchased four aircraft from Albatros at a cost of 100,000 marks, which enabled the company to continue production.

The War Ministry supported LVG's complaint of unfair dealing, and ensured that all transactions concerning the contracts issued for the purchase of aircraft from the various companies was done on the basis of ability to provide.

The first of the Albatros reconnaissance/trainers, the B.I, appeared in 1913. The aircraft was initially used as a trainer, but with the outbreak of war it was used both as a trainer and reconnaissance aircraft. Powered by a 100-hp Mercedes D.II engine, the B.I had a top speed of 65 mph and an endurance of 4 hours. Only a small number were built before being replaced by the B.II. The B.II, like the B.I, had an extremely strong, slab-sided fuselage made up of four spruce longerons covered with plywood. As in all the early aircraft, the pilot sat in the rear cockpit, which gave him a very limited view for take-off and landing. Used for training and reconnaissance duties, the B.II was replaced by the B.III with only minor modifications.

The arrival of Allied fighter aircraft prompted the development of a faster reconnaissance aircraft. Albatros produced the (OAW – Ostdeutsche Albatroswerke) C.I, powered by the 150-hp Benz engine, but only two were built. A second Albatros, the (OAW) C.II built in 1916, powered by a straight eight Mercedes D.IV engine was produced. This time only one was built.

Early in 1915, the company embarked on a singularly ambitious project, a four-engined bomber. Designed by Konstr. Grohmann, the Albatros G.I, as it was known, had a wingspan of 89 ft 6½ in (27 metres), a wing area of 1,485 sq ft (138 sq metres) and a fuselage length of 39 ft 4¼ in (12 metres). It was a very large aircraft. On the lower wing, four 120-hp Mercedes D.II engines in nacelles were mounted, driving four tractor propellers. The first flight took place on 31 January 1916, and was flown by a Swiss pilot, Alexander Hipleh. The G.I became the forerunner of the G.II and G.III, although the two latter aircraft were twin-engined bombers.

A completely different design early in 1916 produced the Albatros C.II. Called the Gitterschwanz (Trellis-tail), the design was of the pusher type, looking very similar to the De Havilland DH 2. Powered by a 150-hp Benz Bz III engine, the C.II did not measure up to expectations and only one was built. This was quickly followed by the Albatros C.IV, which reverted back to the original basic design. A 160-hp Mercedes D.III engine was fitted into the C.III fuselage, to which a C.II tail assembly and undercarriage were fixed. Again, only one of these aircraft was made.

A purely experimental model, the Albatros C.V Experimental, was built at the beginning of 1916. This had a wingspan of 41 ft 11½ in, supported by I-struts in an effort to test the inter-plane bracing. Powered by an eight-cylinder 220-hp Mercedes D.IV engine, the C.V Experimental supplied a great deal of information to Albatroswerke. The C.VI followed soon afterwards, and was based on the C.III airframe and powered by a 180-hp Argus As III engine, giving the aircraft a top speed of 90 mph and enabling it to carry enough fuel for a 4½-hour flight duration. In 1917, a night bomber version, the C.VIII N, evolved. Bombs were carried beneath the lower wings, but it was only powered by a 160-hp Mercedes D.III engine. Only one was constructed.

At the same time as the night bomber was being built, a two-seat fighter/reconnaissance aircraft, the Albatros C.IX, was being made. With a straight lower wing and a considerably swept upper wing it presented an unusual aircraft, but only three were built. This was followed by one version of the Albatros C.XIII, and again it was for experimental purposes. A return to the original design of the two-seater reconnaissance produced the Albatros C.XIV. There was one difference: the C.XIV had staggered wings, and again only one was built. The C.XIV was later modified into the C.XV. It was too late for the development of this aircraft in any numbers, as the end of the war came.

The air supremacy of the Imperial German Air Service during 1916 had been gradually eroded by the rapid development of the Allied fighter aircraft. In a desperate attempt to gain control again, the Albatros Werkes was approached to design and build a fighter that would do just that. Looking at the highly manoeuvrable Nieuport that was causing some of the problems, the company's top designer Robert Thelen set to work and produced a design that combined speed and firepower. If his aircraft couldn't outmanoeuvre the Nieuport, the Albatros could catch it and blast it out of the sky.

A 160-hp Mercedes engine or the 150-hp Benz, which was enclosed in a semi-monocoque plywood fuselage, powered the first of the Albatros series, the D.I. The cylinder heads and valve gear were left exposed, as this gave assisted cooling and greater ease of access for the engineers who had to work on the engine. Engine cooling was achieved by mounting two Windoff radiators, one on each side of the fuselage and between the wings, and a slim water tank mounted above and toward the rear of the engine, at an offset angle slightly to port. The extra power given to the aircraft enabled the firepower, twin, fixed Spandau machine guns, to be increased without loss of performance.

The fuselage consisted of three-eighths thick plywood formers and six spruce longerons. Screwed to this frame were plywood panels, and the engine was installed with easily removable metal panels for both protection and ease of maintenance. The wings, upper and lower, and the tail surfaces were covered with fabric. The fixed tail surfaces and upper and lower fins were made of plywood. The control surfaces were fabric covered over a welded steel-tube frame with a small triangular balance portion incorporated in the rudder and the one-piece elevator.

The undercarriage, a conventional, streamlined steel-tube V-type chassis, was fixed to the fuselage by means of sockets, and sprung through the wheels with rubber shock cord.

The Albatros was a very satisfactory aircraft to fly, but it was discovered to have a major drawback during combat. The top wing, because of its position to the fuselage, obscured the pilot's forward field of vision. The problem was solved by cutting out a semi-circular section of the top wing in front of the pilot, and by lowering the wing so that the pilot could see over the top.

The first Jasta to receive the Albatros D.I, on 17 September 1916, was Jasta 2, which was commanded by the legendary Oswald Boelcke. Three weeks later Boelcke was killed when his Albatros was in involved in a mid-air collision with his wingman Erwin Böhme as they both dived into attack the same British aircraft, a DH.2 of No. 24 Squadron RFC.

In the middle of 1916, the German Naval High Command decided that it would be a good idea to have a single-seat fighter floatplane as a defence aircraft. The Albatros D.I was used as the basis of the Albatros W.4, although the latter was considerably larger in overall dimensions. The wingspan was increased by 1 metre.

Late in 1916, the Albatros D.III appeared with subtle, but noticeable changes to previous models. However, by the summer of 1917, this too had been superseded by the Albatros D.V and D.Va, just as the S.E.5s and SPADs (Société Pour Aviation et ses Dériéves) of the Allies started to regain control of the skies. The same problem seemed to dog the Albatros throughout its lifetime: the lower wing had a tendency to break up in a prolonged dive. In one incident, Sergeant Festnter of Jasta 11 carried out a test flight in an Albatros D.III, when at 13,000 feet the port lower wing broke up, and it was only his experience and a great deal of luck that prevented the aircraft crashing into the ground. Even the legendary Manfred Freiherr von Richthofen experienced a similar incident on 24 January 1917, while testing one of the new Albatros D.IIIs that had recently arrived at Jasta 11.

Tests were carried out, and it was discovered that the single spar was positioned too far aft, causing vibration which increased as the dive continued. This eventually resulted in the structure of the wing collapsing under the erratic movement. A temporary stopgap was achieved by fitting a short strut from the V interplane to the leading edge. Instructions were then given to pilots not to carry out long dives in the Albatros, which, as one can imagine, drastically reduced the faith pilots had in the aircraft, especially when under combat conditions.

A large number of the Jagdstaffels (fighter sections) were being supplied with the Albatros III and IV, and once again superiority in the air passed to the Germans. Those pilots rapidly becoming famous as 'Aces' were flying the Albatros IIIs and IVs, among them Werner Voss and Prinz Friedrich Carl of Prussia. The latter, who commanded a Flieger-Abteilung unit, kept an Albatros IV with Jasta 2 for his personal use. The superiority of the Albatros IIIs and IVs, however, was short-lived, with the arrival of the Sopwith Triplane and the SPAD S.VII, and later the S.E.5 and Sopwith Camel. The Germans quickly realised that every time they came up with a superior design, the Allies countered it with an even better one. The Allies also had the advantage of being able to turn to a variety of aircraft manufacturers, whereas the Germans were limited in their choice.

The Albatros Werke were pressurised into improving the Albatros, with the result that the Albatros D.V was developed. The D.V had a major change to the shape of the fuselage. The D.III fuselage, with its flat sides, was replaced with an elliptical fuselage. The aileron cables were routed through the top wing instead of the lower wing, but the wing structures were the same. Fitted with a 200-hp Mercedes D.IIIa six-cylinder, in-line water-cooled engine, the increased speed of the D.V started to redress some of the balance of air power, but was not sufficient to make any substantial difference. Even the appearance of the D.Va, although it was a superior aircraft to the D.V, did nothing to improve the German air superiority.

The company was not being idle: the Albatros was being developed, and an experimental model, the D.IV, produced. With the fuselage of a D.Va and the wings of a D.II, the experimental fighter was powered by a specially geared version of the 160-hp Mercedes D.III engine, which allowed the engine to be completely enclosed in the nose. There were a number of insurmountable problems with the engine and the project was scrapped. Two months later, in August 1917, another experimental fighter appeared, the D.VII. It was powered by a V8 195-hp Benz Bz IIIb engine, which gave the aircraft a top speed of 127 mph and a climb rate of almost 1,000 feet per minute. Again only one model was built.

The appearance of the Albatros Dr.I in 1917 was to assess the possibilities of producing a triplane. After many tests, the aircraft was deemed to be no better than the D.V and was not continued. Then at the beginning of 1918 another triplane appeared, the Albatros Dr.II. The heavily staggered triple wings were braced with very wide struts, and ailerons were fitted to all the wingtips. Powered by a V8 195-hp Benz IVb engine with frontal-type radiators that were mounted in the centre section between the upper and middle wings, the speed of the aircraft was affected considerably because of the drag caused by the position of the radiators.

A two-seater reconnaissance/bomber appeared at the beginning of 1918, the Albatros J.II. Powered by a 220-hp Benz IVa engine, which gave the aircraft a top speed of 87 mph, the J.II was armed with twin fixed, downward-firing Spandau machine guns and one manually operated Parabellum machine gun in the rear cockpit. The downward-firing guns protruded through the floor of the fuselage, between the legs of the undercarriage. Four examples were built, but it arrived after the Junkers J.I, and the success of the J.I overshadowed the J.II to the extent that no more were built.

A number of prototypes made their appearance early in 1918, the first being the Albatros D.IX. It was powered by a 180-hp Mercedes D.IIIa engine, giving it a top speed of 96 mph. Only one was built. A second model appeared, the Albatros D.X, powered by a V8 195-hp Benz IIIb engine. This gave the aircraft a top speed of 106 mph. At a fighter competition at Aldershof it initially outperformed all the other competitors, but was unable to sustain the performance throughout. Again, only one model was built. The Albatros D.XI that followed was the first Albatros aircraft to use a rotary engine. Fitted with the Siemens-Halske Sh III of 160-hp, it was installed in a horseshoe-shaped cowling with extensions pointing toward the rear. These extensions assisted in the cooling by sucking air through the cowling. Two prototypes were built; one with a four-bladed propeller, the other was a twin-bladed model.

Two prototype Albatros D.XIIs followed, both fitted with different engines, but fitted with a Bohme undercarriage, which for the first time featured compressed-air shock absorbers. Neither aircraft was considered for production.

The Albatros D.V model was the most famous of all the Albatros aircraft, and was assigned to various Jastas in May 1917. In an attempt to bolster flagging morale, pilots were encouraged to emblazon their aircraft in ways that would personalise them. Baron Manfred von Richthofen had his Albatros D.V 1177/17 painted all red, as was his later version No. 4693/17, hence the name given to him by the Allies, 'The Red Baron'. Eduard Ritter von Schleich had his Albatros D.V painted all black and became known as the 'Black Knight'. By May 1918 there were 131 Albatros D.Vs and 928 D.Vas in operational service, but by now it was too late, the war was over.

One other aircraft appeared in 1917 and that was the Albatros G.I. Built by the Ostdeutsche Alabatroswerke GmbH, they had been contracted to build three bombers for the Staaken company. Otto Weiner and Dr Walter Huth had created Ostdeutsche Alabatroswerke GmbH in Schneidemühl on 23 April 1914. The latter had been one of the founders of Albatros Flugzeugwerke GmbH when it had been in Johannisthal. Although bearing the name of Albatros, the company was initially independent, that is until 1917, when it was taken over by the Albatros Flugzeugwerke GmbH.

The Albatros G.I led to the development of the G.II and G.III, and it was this that persuaded the authorities to award the three Staaken aircraft contract to the Albatros Company.

## SPECIFICATIONS

### Albatros B.I

| | |
|---|---|
| Wingspan: | 47 ft 6¼ in (14.5 m) |
| Length: | 28 ft 1½ in (8.5 m) |
| Height: | 10 ft 4 in (3.15 m) |
| Weight Empty: | 1,643 lb (747 kg) |
| Weight Loaded: | 2,376 lb (1,080 kg) |
| Maximum Speed: | 66 mph (105 km/h) |
| Ceiling: | 9,840 ft (3,000 m) |
| Endurance: | 4 hours |
| Engine: | One 100/110-hp Mercedes six-cylinder, in-line, water-cooled |
| Armament: | None |

### Albatros B.II

| | |
|---|---|
| Wingspan: | 42 ft 0 in (12.8 m) |
| Length: | 25 ft 0½ in (7.63 m) |
| Height: | 10 ft 4 in (3.15 m) |

| | |
|---|---|
| Weight Empty: | 1,591 lb (723 kg) |
| Weight Loaded: | 2,356 lb (1,071 kg) |
| Maximum Speed: | 66 mph (105 km/h) |
| Ceiling: | 9,840 ft (3,000 m) |
| Endurance: | 4 hours |
| Engine: | One 100-hp Mercedes six-cylinder, in-line, water-cooled |
| Armament: | None |

## Albatros B.III

| | |
|---|---|
| Wingspan: | 36 ft 1¼ in (11.0 m) |
| Length: | 25 ft 7½ in (7.8 m) |
| Height: | 10 ft 4 in (3.15 m) |
| Weight Empty: | 1,591 lb (723 kg) |
| Weight Loaded: | 2,356 lb (1,071 kg) |
| Maximum Speed: | 66 mph (105 km/h) |
| Ceiling: | 9,840 ft (3,000 m) |
| Endurance: | 4 hours |
| Engine: | One 100-hp Mercedes six-cylinder, in-line, water-cooled |
| Armament: | None |

## Albatros C.I

| | |
|---|---|
| Wingspan: | 42 ft 4 in (12.9 m) |
| Length: | 25 ft 9 in (7.85 m) |
| Height: | 10 ft 4 in (3.15 m) |
| Weight Empty: | 1,925 lb (875 kg) |
| Weight Loaded: | 2,618 lb (1,190 kg) |
| Maximum Speed: | 90 mph (145 km/h) |
| Ceiling: | 9,840 ft (3,000 m) |
| Endurance: | 2½ hours |
| Engine: | One 160-hp Mercedes D.III |
| Armament: | One Parabellum machine gun in observer's cockpit |

## Albatros C.III

| | |
|---|---|
| Wingspan: | 38 ft 4¼ in (11.6 m) |
| Length: | 26 ft 3 in (8.04 m) |
| Height: | 10 ft 2 in (3.1 m) |
| Weight Empty: | 1,872 lb (849 kg) |
| Weight Loaded: | 2,976 lb (1,349.9 kg) |
| Maximum Speed: | 87 mph (161 km/h) |
| Ceiling: | 11,000 ft (3,352 m) |
| Endurance: | 4 hours |
| Engine: | One 150-hp Benz Bz III six-cylinder, in-line, water-cooled |
| Armament: | One fixed forward-firing Spandau machine gun<br>One manually operated Parabellum machine gun in observer's cockpit |

## Albatros C.V

| | |
|---|---|
| Wingspan: | 41 ft 11¼ in (12.78 m) |
| Length: | 29 ft 4½ in (8.9 m) |

| | |
|---|---|
| Height: | 14 ft 9¼ in (4.5 m) |
| Weight Empty: | 2,253 lb (1,024 kg) |
| Weight Loaded: | 2,387 lb (1,585 kg) |
| Maximum Speed: | 106 mph (170 km/h) |
| Ceiling: | 16,400 ft (5,000 m) |
| Endurance: | 3 hours |
| Engine: | One 220-hp Mercedes D.IV eight-cylinder, in-line, water-cooled |
| Armament: | One fixed forward-firing Spandau machine gun |
| | One manually operated Parabellum machine gun in observer's position |

## Albatros C.VI

| | |
|---|---|
| Wingspan: | 38 ft 4½ in (11.7 m) |
| Length: | 26 ft 11¼ in (8.0 m) |
| Height: | 10 ft 6 in (3.2 m) |
| Weight Empty: | 1,826 lb (830 kg) |
| Weight Loaded: | 2,954 lb (1,343 kg) |
| Maximum Speed: | 91 mph (145 km/h) |
| Ceiling: | 11,000 ft (3,352 m) |
| Endurance: | 4 hours |
| Engine: | One 180-hp Argus As III six-cylinder, in-line, water-cooled |
| Armament: | One fixed forward-firing Spandau machine gun |
| | One manually operated Parabellum machine gun in observer's position |

## Albatros C.VII

| | |
|---|---|
| Wingspan: | 41 ft 11¼ in (12.78 m) |
| Length: | 28 ft 6½ in (8.7 m) |
| Height: | 11 ft 9¼ in (3.6 m) |
| Weight Empty: | 2,176 lb (989 kg) |
| Weight Loaded: | 3,410 lb (1,550 kg) |
| Maximum Speed: | 106 mph (170 km/h) |
| Ceiling: | 16,400 ft (5,000 m) |
| Endurance: | 3 hours |
| Engine: | One 200-hp Benz Bz.IV six-cylinder, in-line, water-cooled |
| Armament: | One fixed forward-firing Spandau machine gun |
| | One manually operated Parabellum machine gun in observer's position |

## Albatros C.VIII N

| | |
|---|---|
| Wingspan: | 54 ft 11¼ in (16.7 m) |
| Length: | 24 ft 1 in (7.3 m) |
| Height: | 11 ft 9¼ in (3.6 m) |
| Weight Empty: | 2,176 lb (989 kg) |
| Weight Loaded: | 3,410 lb (1,550 kg) |
| Maximum Speed: | 84 mph (135 km/h) |
| Ceiling: | 16,400 ft (5,000 m) |
| Endurance: | 3 hours |
| Engine: | One 160-hp Mercedes D.II six-cylinder, in-line, water-cooled |

Armament: One fixed forward-firing Spandau machine gun
One manually operated Parabellum machine gun in observer's position

## Albatros C.IX

| | |
|---|---|
| Wingspan: | 34 ft 1½ in (10.4 m) |
| Length: | 26 ft 11½ in (8.2 m) |
| Height: | 8 ft 11½ in (2.7 m) |
| Weight Empty: | 1,738 lb (790 kg) |
| Weight Loaded: | 2,530 lb (1,150 kg) |
| Maximum Speed: | 97 mph (155 km/h) |
| Ceiling: | 16,400 ft (5,000 m) |
| Endurance: | 2 hours |
| Engine: | One 160-hp Mercedes D.III six-cylinder, in-line, water-cooled |
| Armament: | One fixed forward-firing Spandau machine gun<br>One manually operated Parabellum machine gun in observer's position |

## Albatros C.X

| | |
|---|---|
| Wingspan: | 47 ft 1½ in (14.36 m) |
| Length: | 30 ft 0¼ in (9.1 m) |
| Height: | 11 ft 2 in (3.4 m) |
| Weight Empty: | 2,310 lb (1,050 kg) |
| Weight Loaded: | 3,669 lb (1,668 kg) |
| Maximum Speed: | 109 mph (175 km/h) |
| Ceiling: | 16,400 ft (5,000 m) |
| Endurance: | 3 hours |
| Engine: | One 260-hp Mercedes D.IVa six-cylinder, in-line, water-cooled |
| Armament: | One fixed forward-firing Spandau machine gun<br>One manually operated Parabellum machine gun in observer's position |

## Albatros C.XII

| | |
|---|---|
| Wingspan: | 47 ft 1½ in (14.36 m) |
| Length: | 29 ft 0¼ in (8.8 m) |
| Height: | 10 ft 8 in (3.25 m) |
| Weight Empty: | 2,246 lb (1,021 kg) |
| Weight Loaded: | 3,606 lb (1,639 kg) |
| Maximum Speed: | 109 mph (175 km/h) |
| Ceiling: | 16,400 ft (5,000 m) |
| Endurance: | 3 hours |
| Engine: | One 260-hp Mercedes D.IVa six-cylinder, in-line, water-cooled |
| Armament: | One fixed forward-firing Spandau machine gun<br>One manually operated Parabellum machine gun in observer's position |

## Albatros C.XIII

| | |
|---|---|
| Wingspan: | 32 ft 9½ in (10.0 m) |

| Length: | 25 ft 7¼ in (7.8 m) |
| Height: | 8 ft 10½ in (2.7 m) |
| Weight Empty: | 1,540 lb (700 kg) |
| Weight Loaded: | 2,332 lb (1,060 kg) |
| Maximum Speed: | 103 mph (165 km/h) |
| Ceiling: | 16,400 ft (5,000 m) |
| Endurance: | 3 hours |
| Engine: | One 160-hp Mercedes D.III six-cylinder, in-line, water-cooled |
| Armament: | One fixed forward-firing Spandau machine gun |
| | One manually operated Parabellum machine gun in observer's position |

## Albatros C.XIV

| Wingspan: | 34 ft 1½ in (10.4 m) |
| Length: | 22 ft 7½ in (6.9 m) |
| Height: | 8 ft 10½ in (2.7 m) |
| Weight Empty: | 2,090 lb (950 kg) |
| Weight Loaded: | 3,047 lb (1,385 kg) |
| Maximum Speed: | 103 mph (165 km/h) |
| Ceiling: | 16,400 ft (5,000 m) |
| Endurance: | 3 hours |
| Engine: | One 220-hp Benz IVa six-cylinder, in-line, water-cooled |
| Armament: | One fixed forward-firing Spandau machine gun |
| | One manually operated Parabellum machine gun in observer's position |

## Albatros C.XV

| Wingspan: | 38 ft 5½ in (11.8 m) |
| Length: | 24 ft 6¼ in (7.5 m) |
| Height: | 10 ft 11½ in (3.3 m) |
| Weight Empty: | 1,890 lb (859 kg) |
| Weight Loaded: | 2,904 lb (1,320 kg) |
| Maximum Speed: | 103 mph (165 km/h) |
| Ceiling: | 16,400 ft (5,000 m) |
| Endurance: | 3 hours |
| Engine: | One 220-hp Benz IVa six-cylinder, in-line, water-cooled |
| Armament: | One fixed forward-firing Spandau machine gun |
| | One manually operated Parabellum machine gun in observer's position. |

## Albatros Dr.I (Triplane)

| Wingspan: | 28 ft 7 in (8.6 m) |
| Length: | 24 ft (7.3 m) |
| Height: | 7 ft 11 in (2.4 m) |
| Weight Empty: | 2,600 lb (1,179 kg) |
| Weight Loaded: | 3,106 lb (1,408 kg) |
| Maximum Speed: | 103 mph (190 km/h) |
| Ceiling: | 13,920 ft (4,242 m) |
| Endurance: | 4-5 hours |
| Engine: | One 160-hp Mercedes D.III six-cylinder, in-line, water-cooled |

Armament:                Twin Spandau machine guns

## Albatros Dr.II (Triplane)

| | |
|---|---|
| Wingspan: | 32 ft 10 in (9.9 m) |
| Length: | 20 ft 3 in (6.1 m) |
| Height: | 11 ft (3.3 m) |
| Weight Empty: | 1,487 lb (674 kg) |
| Weight Loaded: | 2,013 lb (913 kg) |
| Maximum Speed: | 103 mph (190 km/h) |
| Ceiling: | 13,920 ft (4,242 kg) |
| Endurance: | 4-5 hours |
| Engine: | One 195-hp Benz IVb V-8, in-line, water-cooled |
| Armament: | Twin Spandau machine guns |

## Albatros D.I

| | |
|---|---|
| Wingspan Upper: | 28 ft 2½ in (8.5 m) |
| Wingspan Lower: | 26 ft 5 in (8.0 m) |
| Length: | 24 ft 0 in (7.3 m) |
| Height: | 9 ft 6 in (2.8 m) |
| Weight Empty: | 1,426 lb (646 kg) |
| Weight Loaded: | 1,980 lb (898 kg) |
| Maximum Speed: | 109 mph (201 km/h) |
| Ceiling: | 18,000 ft (5,486 m) |
| Endurance: | 2 hours |
| Engine: | One 160-hp Mercedes D.IIIa six-cylinder, in-line, water-cooled |
| Armament: | Twin Spandau machine guns |

## Albatros D.II

| | |
|---|---|
| Wingspan Upper: | 27 ft 8 in (8.4 m) |
| Wingspan Lower: | 26 ft 3 in (7.9 m) |
| Length: | 24 ft 0 in (7.3 m) |
| Height: | 8 ft 10 in (2.7 m) |
| Weight Empty: | 1,404 lb (636 kg) |
| Weight Loaded: | 1,958 lb (888 kg) |
| Maximum Speed: | 109 mph (201 km/h) |
| Ceiling: | 18,000 ft (5,486 m) |
| Endurance: | 2 hours |
| Engine: | One 160-hp Mercedes D.IIIa six-cylinder, in-line, water-cooled |
| Armament: | Twin Spandau machine guns |

## Albatros D.III

| | |
|---|---|
| Wingspan Upper: | 29 ft 6 in (8.9 m) |
| Wingspan Lower: | 28 ft 6 in (8.6 m) |
| Length: | 24 ft 0 in (7.3 m) |
| Height: | 9 ft 10 in (2.9 m) |
| Weight Empty: | 1,457 lb (660.8 kg) |
| Weight Loaded: | 1,953 lb (885 kg) |
| Maximum Speed: | 108 mph (200 km/h) |
| Ceiling: | 18,000 ft (5,486 m) |

| | |
|---|---|
| Endurance: | 2 hours |
| Engine: | One 170-hp Mercedes D.IIIa six-cylinder, in-line, water-cooled |
| Armament: | Twin Spandau machine guns |

## Albatros D.IV

| | |
|---|---|
| Wingspan: | 29 ft 8½ in (9.0 m) |
| Length: | 24 ft 0 in (7.3 m) |
| Height: | 9 ft 6 in (2.89 m) |
| Weight Empty: | 1,496 lb (678.5 kg) |
| Weight Loaded: | 2,013 lb (913 kg) |
| Maximum Speed: | 103 mph (214 km/h) |
| Ceiling: | 18,000 ft (5,486 m) |
| Endurance: | 2 hours |
| Engine: | One 160-hp Mercedes D.III six-cylinder, in-line, water-cooled |
| Armament: | None |

## Albatros D.V

| | |
|---|---|
| Wingspan Upper: | 29 ft 6 in (8.9 m) |
| Wingspan Lower: | 28 ft 6 in (8.6 m) |
| Length: | 24 ft 0 in (7.3 m) |
| Height: | 9 ft 6 in (2.89 m) |
| Weight Empty: | 1,496 lb (678.5 kg) |
| Weight Loaded: | 2,013 lb (913 kg) |
| Maximum Speed: | 116 mph (214 km/h) |
| Ceiling: | 18,000 ft (5,486 m) |
| Endurance: | 2 hours |
| Engine: | One 170-hp Mercedes D.IIIa six-cylinder, in-line, water-cooled |
| Armament: | Twin Spandau machine guns |

## Albatros D.Va

| | |
|---|---|
| Wingspan Upper: | 29 ft 6 in (8.9 m) |
| Wingspan Lower: | 28 ft 6 in (8.6 m) |
| Length: | 24 ft 0 in (7.3 m) |
| Height: | 9 ft 4½ in (2.8 m) |
| Weight Empty: | 1,515 lb (687 kg) |
| Weight Loaded: | 2,066 lb (937 kg) |
| Maximum Speed: | 116 mph (214 km/h) |
| Ceiling: | 18,000 ft (5,486 m) |
| Endurance: | 2 hours |
| Engine: | One 180-hp Mercedes D.IIIa six-cylinder, in-line, water-cooled |
| Armament: | Twin Spandau machine guns |

## Albatros D.VII

| | |
|---|---|
| Wingspan: | 30 ft 7 in (9.3 m) |
| Length: | 21 ft 8½ in (6.6 m) |
| Height: | 8 ft 9½ in (2.7 m) |
| Weight Empty: | 1,386 lb (630 kg) |
| Weight Loaded: | 1,947 lb (885 kg) |
| Maximum Speed: | 127 mph (204 km/h) |

Ceiling:              18,000 ft (5,486 m)
Endurance:            2 hours
Engine:               One 195-hp Benz Bz IIIb six-cylinder, in-line, water-cooled
Armament:             Twin Spandau machine guns

## Albatros D.IX

Wingspan:             34 ft 1½ in (10.3 m)
Length:               21 ft 10 in (6.6 m)
Height:               9 ft 1 in (2.7m)
Weight Empty:         1,489 lb (677 kg)
Weight Loaded:        1,973 lb (897 kg)
Maximum Speed:        97 mph (155 km/h)
Ceiling:              18,000 ft (5,486 m)
Endurance:            2 hours
Engine:               One 180-hp Mercedes D IIIa six-cylinder, in-line, water-cooled
Armament:             Twin Spandau machine guns

## Albatros D.X

Wingspan:             32 ft 3½ in (9.8 m)
Length:               20 ft 3¼ in (6.2 m)
Height:               9 ft 1 in (2.7 m)
Weight Empty:         1,465 lb (666 kg)
Weight Loaded:        1,991 lb (905 kg)
Maximum Speed:        106 mph (170 km/h)
Ceiling:              18,000 ft (5,486m)
Endurance:            1½ hours
Engine:               One 195-hp Benz IIIb
Armament:             Twin Spandau machine guns

## Albatros D.XI

Wingspan:             26 ft 3 in (8.0 m)
Length:               18 ft 3½ in (5.5 m)
Height:               9 ft 4½ in (2.8 m)
Weight Empty:         1,087 lb (494 kg)
Weight Loaded:        1,516 lb (689 kg)
Maximum Speed:        118 mph (190 km/h)
Ceiling:              18,000 ft (5,486 m)
Endurance:            1½ hours
Engine:               One 160-hp Siemens-Halske Sh III
Armament:             Twin Spandau machine guns

## Albatros D.XII

Wingspan:             26 ft 11 in (8.2 m)
Length:               18 ft 11½ in (5.7 m)
Height:               9 ft 2¼ in (2.8 m)
Weight Empty:         1,276 lb (580 kg)
Weight Loaded:        1,672 lb (760 kg)
Maximum Speed:        112 mph (180 km/h)
Ceiling:              28,000 ft (8,534 m)

Endurance:        1 hour
Engine:           One 160-hp Mercedes D III
Armament:         Twin Spandau machine guns

## Albatros G.I

Wingspan:         89 ft 6½ in (27.2 m)
Length:           39 ft 4¼ in (11.9 m)
Height:           9 ft 9¼ in (2.9 m)
Weight Empty:     7,610 lb (3,452 kg)
Weight Loaded:    9,522 lb (4,319 kg)
Maximum Speed:    123 mph (76.4 km/h)
Ceiling:          18,000 ft (5,486 m)
Endurance:        2 hours
Engine:           Four 120-hp Mercedes D.II

## Albatros G.III

Wingspan:         59 ft 0½ in (18.0 m)
Length:           39 ft 0¼ in (11.8 m)
Height:           9 ft 9¼ in (2.9 m)
Weight Empty:     4,541 lb (2,064 kg)
Weight Loaded:    6,930 lb (3,150 kg)
Maximum Speed:    93 mph (150 km/h)
Ceiling:          18,000 ft (5,486 m)
Endurance:        2 hours
Engine:           Two 220-hp Benz IV

## Albatros J.II

Wingspan:         44 ft 5½ in (13.5 m)
Length:           27 ft 8 in (8.4 m)
Height:           11 ft 2 in (3.4 m)
Weight Empty:     2,259 lb (1,027 kg)
Weight Loaded:    4,239 lb (1,927 kg)
Maximum Speed:    87 mph (140 km/h)
Ceiling:          18,000 ft (5,486 m)
Endurance:        2 hours
Engine:           One 220-hp Benz IVa
Armament:         Two fixed forward-firing Spandau machine guns
                  One manually operated Parabellum in the observer's cockpit

## Albatros W.I

This was a seaplane version of the Albatros B.II

## Albatros W.2

The same specifications as the B.II but with a 160-hp Mercedes D.III engine

## Albatros W.3 & 5

Wingspan:         74 ft 6 in (22.7 m)

Length:                   43 ft 0 in (13.1 m)
Height:                   14 ft 0 in (4.2 m)
Weight Empty:             4,979 lb (2,263 kg)
Weight Loaded:            8,063 lb (3,665 kg)
Maximum Speed:            83 mph (133 km/h)
Ceiling:                  18,000 ft (5,486 m)
Endurance:                4 hours
Engine:                   Two 150-hp Benz III
Armament:                 Two manually operated Parabellum in the observer's cockpit
                          One torpedo

## Albatros W.4

Wingspan:                 31 ft 2 in (9.5 m)
Length:                   27 ft 11 in (8.5 m)
Height:                   11 ft 11½ in (3.6 m)
Weight Empty:             1,738 lb (790 kg)
Weight Loaded:            2,354 lb (1,070 kg)
Maximum Speed:            100 mph (160 km/h)
Ceiling:                  9,800 ft (3,000 m)
Endurance:                3 hours
Engine:                   One 160-hp Mercedes D III
Armament:                 Two fixed forward-firing Spandau machine guns

## Albatros W.8

Wingspan:                 37 ft 7¼ in (11.4 m)
Length:                   31 ft 5½ in (9.5 m)
Height:                   11 ft 1½ in (3.4 m)
Weight Empty:             2,640 lb (1,200 kg)
Weight Loaded:            4,026 lb (1,830 kg)
Maximum Speed:            93 mph (150 km/h)
Ceiling:                  18,000 ft (5,486 m)
Endurance:                4 hours
Engine:                   One 195-hp Benz IIIb
Armament:                 One manually operated Parabellum in the observer's cockpit
                          One fixed forward-firing Spandau machine gun

# Automobil und Aviatik AG &
# Hannoversche Waggonfabrik AG

The Aviatik Company was a well-known German aircraft manufacturer before the First World War, but in January 1912 the company was almost put out of business by Otto Weiner of the Albatros Company. In an attempt to monopolise the aviation market, the Albatros Company sent the Inspectorate of Military Aviation copies of letters they claimed came from Deutsche Flugzeugwerke (DFW) and Rumpler, claiming that Aviatik was in fact a French firm staffed by Frenchmen. It was claimed that the French automobile company Peugeot held 900,000 marks of Aviatik's 1,000,000 marks capital and so controlled every aspect of the company.

A week prior to releasing the 'incriminating' letters, Albatros had proposed to the War Ministry that they could produce a minimum of twenty-four aircraft if the Army would subsidise them on an increasing scale to 40,000 marks for any order less than six aircraft. The Ministry had been contemplating the offer of such a large order from a single factory, when news broke about the 'incriminating letters'. General von Lyncker and Colonel Messing, who had been considering the offer, assumed the information correct and decided that they would only deal with Albatros. However, General von Lyncker was concerned about the overall control that Albatros was having over military aviation and amended the contract by limiting the subsidy for five years, stating that repairs to the aircraft would be carried out in military workshops, and that the subsidy would be withheld if any of the aircraft did not meet the requirements laid down.

The Head of the War Department, Generalmajor von Wandel, and Colonel Schmiedecke were suspicious of the claims made by the Albatros company and carried out their own investigation. They discovered that all Aviatik's shareholders were in fact Alsatians. To further their investigation, they contacted the general commanding the 14th Army Corps stationed in Alsace, where the company was located, but he considered all the people involved in the company to be beyond reproach.

Generalmajor von Wandel was furious; he rejected Albatros' offer to build another factory and refused to eliminate Aviatik from all future contracts, which would have inevitably resulted in the collapse of the company, on the trumped up charges that had been levelled against them. Von Wandel also reprimanded the General Inspectorate for believing the allegations without substantiating them first, and warned them to be on their guard against the obviously questionable methods being used by the Albatros Company.

The Inspectorate felt control of aviation procurement was being slowly taken away from them, and so put forward a proposal that the War Ministry should allocate funds from their budget to buy aircraft, while leaving the selection of type and allocation to them. The War Ministry, who felt that it was time that both departments accepted the necessity of maintaining closer ties with each other, immediately rejected this.

At the beginning of the war, a number of Aviatik B.I and IIs, built before the war, were pressed into service with the Imperial German Air Service as unarmed reconnaissance aircraft. Like most of the early aircraft, the pilot flew the aircraft from the rear cockpit, while the observer sat in front. Powered by a 100-hp Mercedes D.I engine, both the B.I and B.II had a top speed of 85 mph and endurance of 2½ hours.

Early in 1915, the Aviatik Company produced the C.I reconnaissance aircraft, in which the observer was armed with a Parabellum machine gun that was mounted on rails either side of the cockpit. This unusual arrangement was not the best as it gave a very restricted line of fire when it was necessary to use the machine gun and also when carrying out observation duties. Thoughts turned to reversing the seating arrangements, but this idea had already been pre-empted by other aircraft manufacturers like Albatros, Rumpler and LVG (Luft-Verkehrs Gesellschaft), who were mass-producing far superior designs.

The design of the Aviatik C.I was of the conventional box girder construction, made up of four spruce longerons held together with stranded steel cables. The fuselage was covered with curved aluminium panels over the engine area, while fabric covered the remainder of the fuselage. The wings had a span of 41 feet and were of the normal rectangular shape, covered with fabric.

Powered by a six-cylinder in-line, water-cooled, 160-hp Mercedes D.III engine, the aircraft had a top speed of 88 mph, a ceiling of 11,480 feet and endurance of 3 hours. Originally the radiators were mounted on either side of the fuselage, but an improved model was mounted just below the leading edge of the top wing, on the front section struts. The manifold exhaust was led over the top wing, which restricted the pilot's view considerably.

The undercarriage was of the normal V-type, the struts being joined by a short horizontal tube that also served as an anchorage for the rubber cord shock absorbers. It was additionally strengthened with stranded steel cables that cross-braced the undercarriage between the front legs.

A C.Ia model was produced with the seating arrangement of pilot and observer reversed, but when the C.II appeared shortly afterwards the seating was as before, with the pilot sat in the back. Orders for forty-three of this type were made before it was superseded by the C.III, which appeared at the beginning of 1916. The airframe of the C.III was the same as the C.I and C.II, but with a few additional refinements. The manifold exhaust system was changed so that it ejected horizontally to starboard instead of directly over the top. A new aerofoil-shaped radiator was installed in the starboard side of the upper wing centre-section. The nose-section was streamlined and a large nose cone fitted. The pilot's cockpit was fitted with a streamlined headrest, which provided him with an extra degree of comfort. These refinements added a further 11 mph to the aircraft's top speed.

The brief appearance early in 1917 of the Aviatik C.V showed an excursion into a new way of thinking. The gull-shaped wings of the aircraft provided the crew with an excellent upward and uninterrupted field of vision. The aircraft was powered by the 180-hp Argus As.III engine, which was neatly cowled and streamlined into the fuselage. Surprisingly, only one of the aircraft was built.

The Aviatik C.VI model was, in fact, one that was built under licence by DFW (Deutsche Flugzeug-Werke). This was one of the most successful of all the two-seat, reconnaissance/artillery, observation/photographic aircraft produced by Germany during the First World War, and large numbers of the aircraft were made. The C.VI was powered by a six-cylinder in-line, water-cooled, 200-hp Benz

Bz.IV engine, which gave a top speed of 96 mph, a climb rate of 340 feet per minute and a flight duration of 3½ hours.

If there was a C.VII model then it was probably only on the drawing board, because the next model to make an appearance was the Aviatik C.VIII. Looking very much like the Halberstadt CL.II, the C.VIII had a plywood-covered fuselage tapering down to a narrow tail.

This was quickly followed by three C.IX prototypes that were built for test purposes. One of the prototypes had ailerons on all four wingtips; another had ailerons on the top wing only. The remaining aircraft's airframe was tested to destruction.

The first of the fighter aircraft appeared late in 1916, in the shape of the Aviatik D.II. The whole forward section of the fuselage was a steel tube, while the aft section was of plywood. It was fitted with a 160-hp Mercedes D.III engine. Only one of the aircraft was built. One year later, two prototype Aviatik D.IIIs appeared to take part in the D-type competition at Aldershof. They were powered by the 195-hp Benz Bz.IIIb V-8 engine, giving the aircraft a top speed of 108 mph.

An Aviatik D.IV appeared soon afterwards, but there is virtually no information on this aircraft available. In mid-1918, Aviatik produced another fighter, the D.VI. This also took part in the D competitions that were held at Aldershof and like the D.IIIs, performed extremely well. Powered by a 195-hp Benz IIIb V-8 engine and with a large car-type radiator on the nose, the D.VI was fitted with a four-bladed propeller. Only one D.VI was built, and the information gained was passed to the next generation fighter, the Aviatik D.VII.

There was very little difference between the Aviatik D.VI and the D.VII, except for the re-designing of the tail surfaces. The aircraft was armed with twin Spandau machine guns.

The Aviatik company incursion into the fighter world was not a very successful one, but their development of the two-seat reconnaissance/artillery-spotting aircraft was second to none, and large numbers of these aircraft became the mainstays of the Flieger-Abteilung of the German Imperial Air Service.


## SPECIFICATIONS

### Aviatik C.I

| | |
|---|---|
| Wingspan: | 41 ft 0¼ in |
| Length: | 26 ft |
| Height: | 9 ft 8¼ in |
| Weight Empty: | 1,650 lb |
| Weight Loaded: | 2,732 lb |
| Maximum Speed: | 88 mph |
| Ceiling: | 11,480 ft |
| Endurance: | 3 hours |
| Engine: | One 160-hp Mercedes D.IIIa six-cylinder, in-line, water-cooled |
| Armament: | One manually operated Parabellum machine gun mounted on rails |

### Aviatik C.III

| | |
|---|---|
| Wingspan: | 38 ft 5¼ in (11.8 m) |
| Length: | 26 ft 6¼ in (8.0 m) |
| Height: | 9 ft 8¼ in (2.9 m) |

| Weight Empty: | 2,156 lb (980 kg) |
|---|---|
| Weight Loaded: | 2,948 lb (1,340 kg) |
| Maximum Speed: | 100 mph (160 km/h) |
| Ceiling: | 14,760 ft (4,600 m) |
| Endurance: | 3 hours |
| Engine: | One 160-hp Mercedes D.IIIa six-cylinder, in-line, water-cooled |
| Armament: | Two manually operated Parabellum machine guns mounted on rails |

## Aviatik C.V

No information available on this gull-winged experimental model

## Aviatik C.VI

| Wingspan: | 43 ft 7½ in (13.2 m) |
|---|---|
| Length: | 25 ft 10¼ in (7.8 m) |
| Height: | 10 ft 8 in (3.2 m) |
| Weight Empty: | 2,178 lb (990 kg) |
| Weight Loaded: | 3,234 lb (1,470 kg) |
| Maximum Speed: | 97 mph (155 km/h) |
| Ceiling: | 16,400 ft (5,000 m) |
| Endurance: | 3½ hours |
| Engine: | One 200-hp Benz Bz IV six-cylinder, in-line, water-cooled |
| Armament: | One manually operated Parabellum machine gun and one fixed, forward-firing Spandau machine gun |

## Aviatik C.VII

None built

## Aviatik C.VIII

| Wingspan: | 35 ft 4 in (10.7 m) |
|---|---|
| Length: | 23 ft 11½ in (7.3 m) |
| Height: | 9 ft 0¼ in (2.7 m) |
| Weight Empty: | 1,701 lb (773 kg) |
| Weight Loaded: | 2,493 lb (1,166 kg) |
| Maximum Speed: | 103 mph (165 km/h) |
| Ceiling: | 16,800 ft (5,000 m) |
| Endurance: | 3 hours |
| Engine: | One 160-hp Mercedes D.III six-cylinder, in-line, water-cooled |
| Armament: | One manually operated Parabellum machine gun and one fixed, forward-firing Spandau machine gun |

## Aviatik C.IX

| Wingspan: | 35 ft 4 in (10.7 m) |
|---|---|
| Length: | 23 ft 11½ in (7.3 m) |
| Height: | 9 ft 0¼ in (2.7 m) |
| Weight Empty: | 2,156 lb (980 kg) |
| Weight Loaded: | 2,948 lb (1,340 kg) |

| | |
|---|---|
| Maximum Speed: | 100 mph (160 km/h) |
| Ceiling: | 14,760 ft (5,000 m) |
| Endurance: | 3 hours |
| Engine: | One 200-hp Benz IV six-cylinder, in-line, water-cooled |
| Armament: | One manually operated Parabellum machine gun and one fixed forward-firing Spandau machine gun |

## Aviatik D.II (Only one built)

| | |
|---|---|
| Wingspan: | 35 ft 4 in (10.7 m) |
| Length: | 20 ft 0¼ in (6.1 m) |
| Height: | 9 ft 0¼ in (2.7 m) |
| Weight Empty: | Not known |
| Weight Loaded: | Not known |
| Maximum Speed: | 90 mph (145 km/h) |
| Ceiling: | Not known |
| Endurance: | 1 hour |
| Engine: | One 160-hp Mercedes D III six-cylinder, in-line, water-cooled |
| Armament: | None |

## Aviatik D.III (Only one built)

| | |
|---|---|
| Wingspan Upper: | 29 ft 6½ in (9.0 m) |
| Wingspan Lower: | 26 ft 4½ in (8.0 m) |
| Length: | 20 ft 0¼ in (6.1 m) |
| Height: | 9 ft 0¼ in (2.7 m) |
| Weight Empty: | 1,399 lb (636 kg) |
| Weight Loaded: | 1,901 lb (864 kg) |
| Maximum Speed: | 90 mph (145 km/h) |
| Ceiling: | Not known |
| Endurance: | 1 hour |
| Engine: | One 195-hp Benz IIIb six-cylinder, in-line, water-cooled |
| Armament: | None |

## Aviatik D.IV

No information available

## Aviatik D.VII

| | |
|---|---|
| Wingspan: | 31 ft 8½ in (9.6 m) |
| Length: | 20 ft 0¼ in (6.1 m) |
| Height: | 8 ft 2½ in (2.5 m) |
| Weight Empty: | 1,639 lb (745 kg) |
| Weight Loaded: | 2,079 lb (945 kg) |
| Maximum Speed: | 120 mph (192 km/h) |
| Ceiling: | 19,680 ft (6,000 m) |
| Endurance: | 1 hours |
| Engine: | One 195-hp Benz IIIb six-cylinder, in-line, water-cooled |
| Armament: | Twin forward-firing synchronised Spandau machine guns |

# Hansa-Brandenburgische Flugzeugwerke GmbH

The Hansa-Brandenburg Company started life as the Brandenburgische Flugzeugwerke. It was created by Igo Etrich but when it was taken over by the Austrian millionaire entrepreneur Camillo Castiglioni, the name was changed to Hansa-Brandenburgische Flugzeugwerke GmbH. With the company came the Chief Designer and Technical Director Ernst Heinkel, who was not only to lead the company into the forefront of First World War aviation, but was to leave his mark on the world of aviation after the Second World War.

The company was better known for the production of seaplanes than for land-based aircraft. One of their first aircraft, however, was the Brandenburg D, a two-seat observation aircraft that was built specifically for the German Army in 1914. Just twelve aircraft were delivered to the German Army.

A few months later came the Brandenburg FD (BI) designed by Ernst Heinkel. Four of the aircraft were sent to flying schools at Hanseatische Flugzeug-Werke and Caspar Hamburg-Fuhlsbüttel, three to the Austrian Army and five to the German Army. During their short but active roles, they contributed greatly to the development of the German Air Arm.

The fuselage was constructed of a steel tube with a plywood sheet covering; the wings were made of ash covered in fabric. The engine, with its rhino horn manifold exhaust, was a 110-hp Benz Bz.III. The wings of the Brandenburg FD were distinctive inasmuch as the interplane struts were inward sloping, a feature that was to be seen later on nearly all Austro-Hungarian Brandenburg C types.

Prior to the First World War, the Brandenburg Company had been working on a design for a floatplane, resulting, just after the war had started, in the Brandenburg W. With a wingspan of 54 ft 2 in and a fuselage length of 30 ft 10 in, the floatplane was powered by a 150-hp Benz Bz.III engine which gave it a top speed of only 56 mph. The floats of the aircraft were extremely crude and looked more like modified dinghies, but a total of twenty-seven were supplied to the Imperial German Naval Air Arm.

In 1915, the Brandenburg NW appeared, designed for reconnaissance duties and fitted with radio. Some were fitted with bomb racks that carried 5 kg bombs. Based on the design of the Brandenburg W, the NW model showed a great deal of refinement and, whether deliberately or by accident, showed a remarkable resemblance to Heinkel's three-bay Albatros seaplanes. The floats on the NW model were of an elongated wedge shape and had a greater stabilising effect on the aircraft while taxiing. The W model was powered by a 160-hp Mercedes D.III engine, which gave the aircraft a top speed of only 56 mph. The floatplane carried no armament but had an endurance of 4 hours. Thirty-two Brandenburg NWs were supplied to the German Navy.

Later the same year the development of the NW model was taken a step further by the creation of the Brandenburg GNW. This two-seater, unarmed reconnaissance floatplane had an improved climbing performance, although the aircraft's top speed was almost the same. Sixteen of the aircraft were delivered to the German Navy at the end of 1915.

The delivery in May 1916 of the Brandenburg LW caused a slight stir; its designer Ernst Heinkel claimed that it was the first reconnaissance floatplane to be armed with a defensive weapon. Based on the design of the C.I land aircraft designed and built for the Austro-Hungarian Army, only one was ever constructed. Toward the end of 1916, a new model appeared, the Brandenburg KW. Powered by the 200-hp Benz Bz.IV engine, which gave the aircraft a top speed of 83 mph, it was deemed to be underpowered and relegated to training duties.

One floatplane that was not relegated was the Brandenburg GW. It had been designed as a torpedo-carrying strike aircraft, and carried a single torpedo weighing 1,595 lb. Twenty-six aircraft were supplied to the Navy, all of which operated from the seaplane station at Angernsee in Courland. Each was powered by two 160-hp Mercedes D.III engines, which gave the aircraft a top speed of 64 mph. It had a wingspan of 70 ft 9 in, a wing area of 1,103 sq. ft and a length of 41 ft 3 in. The GW carried a single Parabellum machine gun as armament.

The decision to build another large flying boat resulted from the success of the torpedo trials with the GW, and heralded the arrival of the Brandenburg GDW. With a wingspan of 80 ft 4 in, a length of 51 ft 10 in, a height of 16 ft 4½ in and weighing 10,672 lb when loaded, the GDW was indeed a very large aircraft. It was powered by two 200-hp Benz Bz.IV engines, which gave the aircraft a top speed of 81 mph. The torpedo it had been designed to carry weighed 4,015 lb, but bigger does not necessarily mean better and only one of the aircraft was ever built, and after initial tests that was relegated to training duties.

The next aircraft from Brandenburg Werkes was in complete contrast to the GDW. This was the Brandenburg CC, a small single-seater floatplane fighter that had initially been built for the Austro-Hungarian Navy. The CC stood for Camillo Castiglioni, an extremely wealthy Austrian/Italian with strong connections to the Austro-Hungarian monarchy, who was the financier behind Brandenburg Werkes. As stated earlier, Castiglioni already owned two aircraft manufacturing plants, the M otorluftfahrzeuggesellschaft (MLG) and the Hungarian Airship and Flying Machine Company in Budapest, which was the cause of some concern for the military.

The small Brandenburg CC floatplane was powered by a 150-hp Benz Bz.III engine, which gave the aircraft a top speed of 109 mph, and a climb rate of 650 feet per minute. It had a wingspan of 30 ft 6 in, a length of 25 ft 3 in and was armed with two Spandau machine guns. The Austro-Hungarian ace Leutnant Gottfried Banfield had a great deal of success while flying this little fighter. A large number of the aircraft were supplied to the Austro-Hungarian Navy, and twenty-six were supplied to the German Navy.

A slightly larger version of the Brandenburg CC model appeared in the middle of 1916, the Brandenburg FB 1915. With a wingspan of 52 ft 6 in, a length of 33 ft 2 in and powered by a 165-hp Austro-Daimler engine, this fighter, although enthusiastically received by the Austro-Hungarians, was not liked by the German Navy. Only six were supplied to the German Navy, but a considerable number were supplied to the Austro-Hungarian Navy, who were delighted with the aircraft and used them extensively during operations in the Adriatic.

In 1916, Ernst Heinkel designed a single-seat scout aircraft for the Austrian Army, which featured an unusual wing bracing system. The struts were in the form of four V-struts that were joined in the centre of the wing. This gave a star-effect configuration. Built under licence by the Phönix and Ufag factories, the Brandenburg KDW (Kampf Doppeldecker Werke), the aircraft was converted to a seaplane after a demand for a seaplane-station fighter. There were handling problems due in the main to the blanketing of the small rudder by the deep fuselage. Like previous fighter aircraft, the fuselage consisted of four spruce longerons with plywood formers and spruce spacers. The fuselage was then covered with plywood. The tail surfaces were constructed of steel tubing covered in fabric. The wings were of wooden construction covered in fabric.

Powered by a six-cylinder, in-line, water-cooled, 160-hp Maybach Mb.III engine, it gave the fighter a top speed of 106 mph. Fifty-eight of the aircraft were built; thirty-eight were fitted with a single Spandau machine gun and the last twenty fitted with twin Spandau machine guns.

While the development of the KDW was taking place, Ernst Heinkel had been working on a replacement. The seaplane fighters at the time were vulnerable to attack from the rear as all their guns were forward-firing, and Heinkel was asked to come up with a design for a two-seat fighter that had both forward and rearward firing capabilities. The result was the Brandenburg W.12. The elevated rear machine gun gave a superb field of fire all round the aircraft, including over the top of the wing. Based on the fuselage of the KDW, it tapered upward from behind the engine mountings to give the rear gun the improved field of fire. The wings were made of spruce covered in fabric with plywood ribs. The upper wing was a one-piece structure, while the lower was of two pieces with heavy spruce struts between. The ailerons were of steel tubing covered in fabric. Powered by either a six-cylinder, in-line, water-cooled 160-hp Mercedes engine or a six-cylinder, in-line, water-cooled 150-hp Benz Bz.III engine, the W.12 had a top speed of 100 mph and an endurance of 3½ hours.

It was in a W.12, on 17 December 1917, that Oberleutnant Christiansen attacked and destroyed the British non-rigid airship C.27.

With the need for seaplanes firmly established in the expansion of the German naval flying services, an aircraft with a longer endurance was required. The Brandenburg W.12 had served well but a larger aircraft was needed. What developed was the Brandenburg W.19, with a wingspan of 45 ft 3½ in (10 feet longer than W.12), a fuselage length of 34 ft 11½ in (3½ feet longer than the W.12) and powered by a six-cylinder, in-line, water-cooled 260-hp Maybach Mb.IV engine. The aircraft's endurance was around 5 hours and the first three of the fifty-five delivered aircraft were fitted with one fixed forward-firing Spandau machine gun and one manually operated Parabellum machine gun in the rear cockpit. The remaining fifty-two aircraft were fitted with twin fixed forward-firing Spandau machine guns and one Parabellum in the rear cockpit.

The respect that some German and Allied fliers had for one another was never more apparent than on 4 June 1918, when a patrol of British F2A flying boats from Felixstowe and Yarmouth were attacked by German Brandenburg W.19 and W.29 seaplanes. In the ensuing fight a number of aircraft on either side were shot down and one of them, flown by Lieutenant Robertson, was floating wrecked and upside down on the water. One of the German seaplanes alighted alongside and the pilot asked Robertson, who was clinging to the wreckage, whether he wanted to be picked up and taken as a prisoner-of-war to Zeebrugge or to take his chance on being picked up by the Royal Navy. Robertson politely declined the offer of assistance, and with that the German pilot saluted his fallen adversary, took a picture of him and took off. The Royal Navy later rescued Robertson.

Two more land-based aircraft were produced during 1917, both of which were prototypes. The Brandenburg L.14 was a single-seat fighter produced as a development for the Austrian-built Brandenburg D.I. Powered by a 200-hp Hiero engine, with a wingspan of 33 ft 6 in, a fuselage length of 23 ft 1½ in and a top speed of 102 mph, only one of this type was built. The Brandenburg L.16 was a purely experimental model triplane. It was developed to test a variety of radiators and their positions for the 185-hp Austro-Daimler engine.

Friedrich Christiansen, now firmly established as one of Germany's top seaplane commanders, approached Ernst Heinkel suggesting that an even faster and more manoeuvrable seaplane fighter was needed. Heinkel looked at the success of the W.12 and decided to produce a monoplane version of the aircraft. To all intents and purposes, the W.29 was just a W.12 with the top wing removed. The wing was extended by another nine feet and differed in thickness. The bracing struts were almost twice as thick at the roots, as the wing had been turned from a high-speed section to a high-lift section. Construction of the aircraft was the same as the W.12 – spruce longerons for the fuselage covered in fabric, and the wing constructed of spruce main spars with plywood ribs covered with fabric. Seventy-eight of the aircraft were built and supplied to the German Navy; the first forty were fitted with only one fixed forward-firing machine gun, but were fitted with radios. The remaining aircraft were fitted with twin, fixed, forward-firing Spandau machine guns and one manually operated machine gun in the rear cockpit, but the radios were removed. Powered by a six-cylinder, in-line, water-cooled, 150-hp Benz Bz.III engine, the W.29 was capable of a maximum speed of 109 mph, could operate at a height of 16,400 feet and had an endurance of around 4 hours.

In one incident, Christiansen's W.29s attacked two F2a flying boats from Felixstowe, shooting both down. The first crashed into the sea; the second was destroyed as it lay helplessly on the water after making an emergency landing.

In 1916, Hansa-Brandenburg took over the Oertz Company, which was a subsidiary of the Hamburg Yacht Company. The Oertz Company, like many other boat-builders, saw the opportunity to move into a different field of transport using their existing skills. Very few made the transition, as they found the technical side far too difficult, but Oertz did, albeit only briefly. The company's owner, Dipl.Ing Max Oertz, created four different designs, from which were produced a total of twelve flying boats. They were the Oertz W.4, W.5, W.6 and W.8, all of which were powered by the Maybach IV engines, which were mounted inside the hull. The pusher propellers were connected to the engine by means of a series of gears. All were biplanes, with the exception of the W.6, which was a tandem-wing biplane. The beam of the hull was slightly wider than normal, which gave an extra stability to the hull.

The Brandenburg Werke produced a number of the finest reconnaissance and fighter aircraft (predominantly seaplanes) of the First World War, but was also one of the least recognised manufacturing companies.

## SPECIFICATIONS

### Brandenburg BI (FD)

| | |
|---|---|
| Wingspan: | 43 ft 1 in (13.2 m) |
| Length: | 27 ft 9 in (8.4 m) |
| Height: | 9 ft 8½ in (3.0 m) |
| Weight Empty: | Not known |
| Weight Loaded: | Not known |
| Maximum Speed: | 62 mph |
| Ceiling: | 3,350 ft |
| Endurance: | 1 hour |
| Engine: | One 110-hp Benz Bz II |
| Armament: | None |

## Brandenburg D

| | |
|---|---|
| Wingspan: | 43 ft 1 in (13.2 m) |
| Length: | 27 ft 9 in (8.4 m) |
| Height: | 9 ft 8½ in (3.0 m) |
| Weight Empty: | Not known |
| Weight Loaded: | Not known |
| Maximum Speed: | 62 mph |
| Ceiling: | 3,350 ft |
| Endurance: | 1 hour |
| Engine: | One 110-hp Benz Bz II |
| Armament: | None |

## Brandenburg W.11

| | |
|---|---|
| Wingspan: | 32 ft 9½ in (8.2 m) |
| Length: | 26 ft 11 in (8.2 m) |
| Height: | 10 ft 10½ in (3.3 m) |
| Weight Empty: | 2,057 lb (935 kg) |
| Weight Loaded: | 2,673 lb (1,215 kg) |
| Maximum Speed: | 110 mph (176 km/h) |
| Ceiling: | 3,290 ft (1,112 m) |
| Endurance: | 1½ hours |
| Engine: | One 200-hp Benz Bz IV |
| Armament: | Two fixed forward-firing Spandau machine guns |

## Brandenburg W.13

| | |
|---|---|
| Wingspan: | 66 ft 9¼ in (20.4 m) |
| Length: | 44 ft 11½ in (13.7 m) |
| Height: | 13 ft 10½ in (4.3 m) |
| Weight Empty: | 3,410 lb (1,550 kg) |
| Weight Loaded: | 6,270 lb (2,850 kg) |
| Maximum Speed: | 110 mph (176 km/h) |
| Ceiling: | 3,290 ft (1,112m) |
| Endurance: | 3 hours |
| Engine: | One 350-hp Austro-Daimler |
| Armament: | One Schwarzlöse manual machine gun |

## Brandenburg W.16

| | |
|---|---|
| Wingspan: | 30 ft 4¼ in (9.3 m) |
| Length: | 24 ft 1½ in (7.35 m) |
| Height: | 9 ft 7½ in (2.9 m) |
| Weight Empty: | 1,399 lb (636 kg) |
| Weight Loaded: | 1,971 lb (896 kg) |
| Maximum Speed: | 107 mph (170 km/h) |
| Ceiling: | 3,290 ft (1,112 m) |
| Endurance: | 2 hours |
| Engine: | One 160-hp Oberursel U.III |
| Armament: | Two Spandau forward-firing machine guns |

## Brandenburg W.17 – 18

| | |
|---|---|
| Wingspan: | 35 ft 1¼ in (10.7 m) |
| Length: | 26 ft 9 in (8.2 m) |
| Height: | 11 ft 4 in (3.4 m) |
| Weight Empty: | 1,925 lb (875 kg) |
| Weight Loaded: | 2,519 lb (1,145 kg) |
| Maximum Speed: | 100 mph (160 km/h) |
| Ceiling: | 10,290 ft (3,136 m) |
| Endurance: | 2 hours |
| Engine: | One 150-hp Benz Bz III |
| Armament: | Two Spandau forward-firing machine-guns |

## Brandenburg W.25

| | |
|---|---|
| Wingspan: | 34 ft 1½ in (10.4 m) |
| Length: | 28 ft 10½ in (8.8 m) |
| Height: | 11 ft 4 in (3.4 m) |
| Weight Empty: | 2,221 lb (918 kg) |
| Weight Loaded: | 2,600 lb (1,182 kg) |
| Maximum Speed: | 100 mph (160 km/h) |
| Ceiling: | 3,290 ft (1,002 m) |
| Endurance: | 2½ hours |
| Engine: | One 150-hp Benz Bz III |
| Armament: | Two fixed forward-firing Spandau machine guns |

## Brandenburg W.26

| | |
|---|---|
| Wingspan: | 61 ft 8¼ in (18.8 m) |
| Length: | 42 ft 8½ in (13.0 m) |
| Height: | 13 ft 4 in (4.1 m) |
| Weight Empty: | 3,685 lb (1,675 kg) |
| Weight Loaded: | 5,478 lb (2,490 kg) |
| Maximum Speed: | 85 mph (135 km/h) |
| Ceiling: | 3,290 ft (1,002 m) |
| Endurance: | 8 hours |
| Engine: | One 260-hp Mercedes D.IVa |
| Armament: | Two fixed forward-firing Spandau machine-guns |

## Brandenburg W.20 (Three examples built)

| | |
|---|---|
| Wingspan (1): | 19 ft 0½ in (5.8 m) |
| Wingspan (2/3): | 22 ft 4 in (6.8 m) |
| Length (1): | 19 ft 4½ in (5.9 m) |
| Length (2/3): | 19 ft 5¼ in (5.92 m) |
| Height: | 11 ft 0½ in |
| Weight Empty: | 871 lb (396 kg) |
| Weight Loaded: | 1,250 lb (568 kg) |
| Maximum Speed: | 100 mph (160 km/h) |
| Ceiling: | 3,290 ft |
| Endurance: | 1½ hours |
| Engine: | One 80-hp Oberursel U.O |
| Armament: | None |

## Brandenburg L.16 (Triplane)

| | |
|---|---|
| Wingspan: | 29 ft 6½ in |
| Length: | 23 ft 8 in |
| Height: | 12 ft 2 in |
| Weight Empty: | 1,628 lb |
| Weight Loaded: | 2,057 lb |
| Maximum Speed: | 118 mph |
| Ceiling: | 9,290 ft |
| Endurance: | 1½ hours |
| Engine: | One 185-hp Austro-Daimler |
| Armament: | Two fixed forward-firing Spandau machine-guns |

## Brandenburg W.29

| | |
|---|---|
| Wingspan: | 44 ft 3½ in |
| Length: | 30 ft 8½ in |
| Height: | 9 ft 10¼ in |
| Weight Empty: | 2,200 lb |
| Weight Loaded: | 3,286 lb |
| Maximum Speed: | 109 mph |
| Ceiling: | 16,400 ft |
| Endurance: | 4 hours |
| Engine: | One 150-hp Benz Bz III six-cylinder, in-line, water-cooled |
| Armament: | One fixed forward-firing Spandau machine-gun (the first 40) |
| | Two fixed forward-firing Spandau machine-guns (the last 38) |

## Brandenburg W.32

| | |
|---|---|
| Wingspan: | 36 ft 9 in (15.9 m) |
| Length: | 30 ft 3½ in (9.2 m) |
| Height: | 10 ft 8 in (3.4 m) |
| Weight Empty: | 2,339 lb (1,063 kg) |
| Weight Loaded: | 3,397 lb (1,544 kg) |
| Maximum Speed: | 108 mph (173 km/h) |
| Ceiling: | 3,290 ft |
| Endurance: | 2 hours |
| Engine: | One 160-hp Mercedes D.III |
| Armament: | Two fixed forward-firing Spandau machine guns and one manually operated Parabellum machine gun mounted in the observer's cockpit |

## Brandenburg W.33

| | |
|---|---|
| Wingspan: | 52 ft 0 in (15.9 m) |
| Length: | 36 ft 5¼ in (11.10 m) |
| Height: | 11 ft 0½ in (3.4 m) |
| Weight Empty: | 3,124 lb (1,420 kg) |
| Weight Loaded: | 4,510 lb (2,050 kg) |
| Maximum Speed: | 108 mph (173 km/h) |
| Ceiling: | 3,290 ft |
| Endurance: | 1½ hours |
| Engine: | One 245-hp Maybach Mb.IV |

Armament:                 Two fixed forward-firing Spandau machine guns and
                          one manually operated Parabellum machine gun mounted
                          in the observer's cockpit

## Brandenburg W

Wingspan:                 54 ft 2 in (16.5 m)
Length:                   30 ft 10¼ in (9.4 m)
Height:                   11 ft 0½ in (3.4 m)
Weight Empty:             2,640 lb (1,200 kg)
Weight Loaded:            4,026 lb (1,830 kg)
Maximum Speed:            56 mph (90 km/h)
Ceiling:                  3,290 ft
Endurance:                1½ hours
Engine:                   One 150-hp Benz Bz III
Armament:                 None

## Brandenburg LW

Wingspan:                 40 ft 8¼ in (12.4 m)
Length:                   31 ft 2¼ in (9.5 m)
Height:                   11 ft 0½ in (3.4 m)
Weight Empty:             2,187 lb (944 kg)
Weight Loaded:            3,421 lb (1,555 kg)
Maximum Speed:            81 mph (130 km/h)
Ceiling:                  3,290 ft
Endurance:                3 hours
Engine:                   One 160-hp Mercedes D.III
Armament:                 One Parabellum machine gun

## Brandenburg NW

Wingspan:                 54 ft 2 in (16.5 m)
Length:                   30 ft 10¼ in (9.4 m)
Height:                   8 ft 4 in (2.4 m)
Weight Empty:             2,244 lb (1,020 kg)
Weight Loaded:            3,630 lb (1,650 kg)
Maximum Speed:            56 mph (90 km/h)
Ceiling:                  3,290 ft
Endurance:                4 hours
Engine:                   One 160-hp Mercedes D.III
Armament:                 None

## Brandenburg GNW

Wingspan:                 53 ft 2 in (16.2 m)
Length:                   32 ft 5 in (9.8 m)
Height:                   8 ft 4½ in (2.5 m)
Weight Empty:             2,420 lb (1,100 kg)
Weight Loaded:            3,835 lb (1,743 kg)
Maximum Speed:            72 mph (116 km/h)
Ceiling:                  3,290 ft
Endurance:                4 hours

Engine:                  One 160-hp Mercedes D.III
Armament:                None

## Brandenburg KW

Wingspan:                53 ft 10 in (16.4 m)
Length:                  36 ft 8 in (11.1 m)
Height:                  13 ft 4 in (4.5 m)
Weight Empty:            3,183 lb (1,447 kg)
Weight Loaded:           4,633 lb (2,106 kg)
Maximum Speed:           84 mph (134 km/h)
Ceiling:                 3,290 ft
Endurance:               6 hours
Engine:                  One 200-hp Benz Bz IV
Armament:                One Parabellum machine gun

## Brandenburg GW

Wingspan:                70 ft 9 in (21.5 m)
Length:                  41 ft 3 in (12.5 m)
Height:                  13 ft 7¼ in (4.1 m)
Weight Empty:            5,135 lb (2,334 kg)
Weight Loaded:           9,506 lb (3,928 kg)
Maximum Speed:           64 mph (102 km/h)
Ceiling:                 3,290 ft
Endurance:               6 hours
Engine:                  Two 160-hp Mercedes D.III
Armament:                One Parabellum machine gun
                         One Torpedo

## Brandenburg GDW

Wingspan:                80 ft 4½ in (24.5 m)
Length:                  51 ft 10¼ in (15.8 m)
Height:                  16 ft 5 in (5.0 m)
Weight Empty:            6,459 lb (2,936 kg)
Weight Loaded:           10,672 lb (4,851 kg)
Maximum Speed:           81 mph (130 km/h)
Ceiling:                 3,290 ft
Endurance:               5 hours
Engine:                  Two 200-hp Benz Bz IV
Armament:                None

## Brandenburg CC

Wingspan:                30 ft 6¼ in (9.3 m)
Length:                  25 ft 3 in (7.7 m)
Height:                  11 ft 5 in (3.5 m)
Weight Empty:            1,575 lb (716 kg)
Weight Loaded:           2,268 lb (1,031 kg)
Maximum Speed:           109 mph (175 km/h)
Ceiling:                 3,290 ft
Endurance:               1½ hours

Engine:                One 150-hp Benz Bz III
Armament:              Two Spandau machine guns

## Brandenburg FB

Wingspan:              52 ft 6 in (16.0 m)
Length:                33 ft 2 in (10.1 m)
Height:                11 ft 5 in (3.5 m)
Weight Empty:          2,508 lb (1,140 kg)
Weight Loaded:         3,564 lb (1,620 kg)
Maximum Speed:         109 mph (175 km/h)
Ceiling:               3,290 ft
Endurance:             1½ hours
Engine:                One 165-hp Austro-Daimler
Armament:              One Parabellum machine gun

## Oertz W.5

Wingspan:              59 ft 1 in (18.0 m)
Length:                38 ft 4½ in (11.7 m)
Height:                11 ft 5 in (3.5 m)
Weight Empty:          4,440 lb (2,018 kg)
Weight Loaded:         5,804 lb (2,638 kg)
Maximum Speed:         78 mph (125 km/h)
Engine:                One 240-hp Maybach Mb.IV
Armament:              One Parabellum machine gun

## Oertz W.6

Wingspan:              65 ft 7½ in (20.0 m)
Length:                47 ft 8½ in (14.5 m)
Height:                15 ft 8 in (4.7 m)
Weight Empty:          8,316 lb (3,780 kg)
Weight Loaded:         11,066 lb (5,030 kg)
Maximum Speed:         78 mph (125 km/h)
Engine:                Two 240-hp Maybach Mb.IV
Armament:              One Parabellum machine gun

## Oertz W.8

Wingspan:              64 ft 4 in (19.6 m)
Length:                35 ft 1¼ in (10.7 m)
Height:                11 ft 8 in (3.5 m)
Weight Empty:          3,484 lb (1,584 kg)
Weight Loaded:         4,895 lb (2,225 kg)
Maximum Speed:         87 mph (140 km/h)
Engine:                One 240-hp Maybach Mb.IV
Armament:              One Parabellum machine gun

# Deutsche Flugzeug-Werke GmbH (DFW)

One of the first pure military aircraft produced by the DFW factory was the DFW B.I biplane or, to give it its correct designation, the DFW Type MD14 B.I. Developed in 1914 as a reconnaissance and training aircraft, it originally had a welded steel tube fuselage and was powered by a 100-hp Mercedes D.I engine. Later versions had an all-wood plywood-covered fuselage and were fitted with the more powerful 180-hp Benz III engines. The B.I had a wingspan of 45 ft 11½ in, a length of 27 ft 6½ in and a top speed of 75 mph.

The B.II, which was powered by the 120-hp Mercedes D.II engine, was produced at the beginning of 1915 and had a wingspan of 41 ft 4½ in – some 4½ in shorter than that of the B.I, but with the same length of fuselage. Like the B.I, the B.II was used as a reconnaissance aircraft as well as for training purposes. The German fighter ace and holder of the Order *Pour le Mérite* ('Blue Max'), Oberleutnant Kurt Wüsthoff, trained in one of the B.II training aircraft at the Leipzig-Lindenthal flying training school near Berlin.

An incursion into the single-seater fighter market with the DFW *Floh* ('Flea') ended when the tiny aircraft crashed on its initial test flight early in 1915. One of the reasons given for the accident was the appalling lack of visibility from the cockpit. Powered by a 100-hp Mercedes D.I engine, with a wingspan of 20 ft 4 in, and a fuselage length of 14 ft 9½ in, the DFW *Floh* looked completely out of proportion.

At a request of Idflieg (Inspektion der Fliegertruppen – Inspectorate of Aviation Troops), DFW were asked to join the R-plane programme and develop a heavy bomber. Their first bomber was the DFW R.I, designed by Hermann Dorner, which took a year to make. They were unique in their construction inasmuch as the four eight-cylinder, in-line 220-hp Mercedes D.IV engines were internally mounted, each driving a separate propeller. They were mounted in an unusual manner: the two tractor-types were fitted above and slightly ahead on the two pusher-type engines. The first radiators were triangular shaped and were mounted between the centre-section struts, but these were soon replaced by four Windhoff radiators fitted to the fuselage in the centre section gap.

The first flight took place on 5 September 1916, the first of twelve flights before the aircraft was delivered to the Army Air Park at Döberitz. After further testing by Army pilots, the R.I was flown via Königsberg to Alt-Auz to join Rfa 500. On 13 June 1917, the R.I carried out its one and only mission, when it dropped 680 kg of bombs on Schlok, in retaliation for an earlier Russian attack.

Departing on its second mission in September 1917, the R.I experienced a problem when one of its four engines failed. The pilots, instead of continuing on three engines, turned the aircraft round to return to the field. Overheating of a gearbox caused the second engine to be stopped, the result being that the aircraft was now too heavy to be kept in the air. Searching for a place to land, the crew of the giant aircraft, which was now running on the two remaining engines, spotted a training field and put the aircraft down. Unfortunately they failed to spot a deep trench running across the field and the aircraft crashed as the wheels plunged down into the trench. The aircraft spilled its load of bombs and fuel onto the field then exploded. One of the crew was killed.

In September 1916, the prototype DFW C Type was produced. This was the forerunner of what was to be one of the most successful of all the two-seater German reconnaissance aircraft of the First World War, the DFW C.V. Only one C Type was built, and it was powered by a 150-hp Benz Bz III engine. This was quickly followed by the DFW C.I and C.II, and the only difference between the two aircraft was that the pilot flew the aircraft from the rear cockpit in the C.I, but in the C.II flew it from the front seat. Otherwise they were identical in every other detail and a number of these aircraft were built and delivered to the German Army. Powered by 150-hp Benz Bz.III, the C.I and C.II had a wingspan of 36 ft 9 in, a fuselage length of 23 ft 7½ in, an operating ceiling of 13,120 feet and a top speed of 87 mph. There was only one gun, a manually operated Parabellum machine gun mounted in the rear cockpit.

A second DFW R.II was built at the end of 1916 after an order from Idflieg. Basically the same as the R.I, except that the overall dimensions were increased slightly, the R.II was powered by four eight-cylinder, in-line Mercedes D.IVa engines. The fuselage of the first R.I was made up of spruce longerons covered in plywood, but because of the twisting forces that the fuselage was subjected to during flight, the R.II longerons were reinforced with steel tube frames and cables.

The first of the R.IIs made its maiden flight on 17 September 1917, and although the flight was very successful, there were still problems with vibration despite the strengthened engine mounts. Encasing the transmission shafts with stiffener tubes later solved this problem. A second of six R.IIs ordered was built in February 1918, but there were problems and modifications that had to be made before it was accepted by the Army. A third was built later, but none ever saw active service.

An attempt to develop a pusher aircraft, a DFW C.III pusher biplane powered by a 150-hp Benz Bz.III, amounted to nothing. The aircraft looked almost identical to the French Breguet pusher biplane.

The DFW C.IV was developed at the end of 1916 and featured single-bay wings. A 150-hp Benz Bz.III engine powered the C.IV, which had the radiator mounted beneath the upper leading edge. The aircraft was armed with two machine guns, a fixed forward-firing Spandau and a manually operated Parabellum mounted in the rear cockpit. A number of these aircraft were developed for the German Army.

There was another attempt to develop a single-seat fighter in 1917, with the DFW D.I. The prototype was very similar to the DFW *Floh*, the only difference being there was a 160-hp Mercedes D.III engine with a car-type radiator mounted at the nose. Only one was built. A second modified prototype appeared some months later fitted with twin Spandau machine guns. Again only one was built. A third DFW D.I modified prototype appeared at the end of 1917. Almost identical to the second modified D.I, only the ailerons were removed from the lower wingtips. The development of these models led to the production of the DFW Dr.I triplane. It was designed for the D Type competition at Aldershof, Berlin, in January 1918, but was not a success.

Another model, the DFW F.34, appeared in April 1918. Looking very similar to the Albatros fighter, it was powered by a 160-hp Mercedes D.III engine that gave it a top speed of 110 mph and a climb rate of 1,100 feet per minute. It was armed with twin, fixed, forward-firing Spandau machine guns, but very little is known of its whereabouts after its sudden appearance.

A third DFW heavy bomber, the R.III, was on the drawing boards at the end of September 1918. The aircraft had a separate navigator's steering section in front of the wings, while the dual cockpit was situated directly under the trailing edge of the wings. It had a double-decked fuselage capable of carrying 2,500 kg of bombs, eight machine guns, a wireless cabin, a bomb-aimer's position and eight sleeping bunks. One unusual feature was the replacing of the normal tailskid with a faired tail wheel, but before production could begin the war came to an end.

## SPECIFICATIONS

### DFW B.I

| | |
|---|---|
| Wingspan: | 45 ft 11¼ in (14.0 m) |
| Length: | 27 ft 6½ in (8.4 m) |
| Height: | 9 ft 3 in (2.8 m) |
| Weight Empty: | 1,430 lb (650 kg) |
| Weight Loaded: | 2,233 lb (1,105 kg) |
| Maximum Speed: | 75 mph (120 km/h) |
| Ceiling: | 13,100 ft (4,000 m) |
| Endurance: | 2 hours |
| Engine: | One 100-hp Mercedes D.I six-cylinder, in-line, water-cooled |
| Armament: | One manually operated Parabellum machine gun mounted in the observer's cockpit |

### DFW B.II

| | |
|---|---|
| Wingspan: | 41 ft 4¼ in (12.6 m) |
| Length: | 27 ft 6½ in (8.4 m) |
| Height: | 9 ft 3 in (2.8 m) |
| Weight Empty: | 1,644 lb (747 kg) |
| Weight Loaded: | 2,618 lb (1,190 kg) |
| Maximum Speed: | 75 mph (120 km/h) |
| Ceiling: | 13,100 ft (4,000 m) |
| Endurance: | 2 hours |
| Engine: | One 100-hp Mercedes D.I six-cylinder, in-line, water-cooled |
| Armament: | One manually operated Parabellum machine gun mounted in the observer's cockpit |

### DFW C.I & II

| | |
|---|---|
| Wingspan: | 36 ft 9 in (11.2 m) |
| Length: | 23 ft 7½ in (7.2 m) |
| Height: | 9 ft 3 in (2.7 m) |
| Weight Empty: | 1,595 lb (725 kg) |
| Weight Loaded: | 2,717 lb (1,235 kg) |
| Maximum Speed: | 87 mph (140 km/h) |
| Ceiling: | 13,100 ft (4,000 m) |
| Endurance: | 2 hours |
| Engine: | One 150-hp Benz Bz III six-cylinder, in-line, water-cooled |

Armament:                One manually operated Parabellum machine gun mounted
                         in the observer's cockpit

## DFW C.IV

Wingspan:                43 ft 6½ in (13.2 m)
Length:                  25 ft 10½ in (7.8 m)
Height:                  10 ft 8 in (3.2 m)
Weight Empty:            2,134 lb (967 kg)
Weight Loaded:           3,146 lb (1,427 kg)
Maximum Speed:           97 mph (156 km/h)
Ceiling:                 16,400 ft (5,000 m)
Endurance:               3½ hours
Engine:                  One 150-hp Benz Bz III six-cylinder, in-line, water-cooled
Armament:                One fixed forward-firing Spandau machine gun
                         One manually operated Parabellum machine gun mounted
                         in the observer's cockpit

## DFW C.V

Wingspan:                43 ft 6½ in (13.2 m)
Length:                  25 ft 10½ in (7.8 m)
Height:                  10 ft 8 in (3.2 m)
Weight Empty:            2,134 lb (967 kg)
Weight Loaded:           3,146 lb (1,427 kg)
Maximum Speed:           97 mph (156 km/h)
Ceiling:                 16,400 ft (5,000 m)
Endurance:               3½ hours
Engine:                  One 200-hp Benz Bz IV six-cylinder, in-line, water-cooled
Armament:                One fixed forward-firing Spandau machine gun
                         One manually operated Parabellum machine gun mounted
                         in the observer's cockpit

## DFW C.VI

Wingspan:                44 ft 7½ in (13.6 m)
Length:                  24 ft 7½ in (7.5 m)
Height:                  10 ft 8 in (3.2 m)
Weight Empty:            2,134 lb (967 kg)
Weight Loaded:           3,146 lb (1,427 kg)
Maximum Speed:           97 mph (156 km/h)
Ceiling:                 16,400 ft (5,000 m)
Endurance:               3½ hours
Engine:                  One 200-hp Benz Bz IV six-cylinder, in-line, water-cooled
Armament:                One fixed forward-firing Spandau machine gun
                         One manually operated Parabellum machine gun mounted
                         in the observer's cockpit

## DFW Dr.I

Wingspan Upper:          No details available
Wingspan Middle:         No details available
Wingspan Lower:          No details available

| | |
|---|---|
| Length: | No details available |
| Height: | No details available |
| Weight Empty: | No details available |
| Weight Loaded: | No details available |
| Maximum Speed: | No details available |
| Ceiling: | No details available |
| Endurance: | Not known |
| Engine: | One 160-hp Mercedes D.III six-cylinder, in-line, water-cooled |
| Armament: | Two forward-firing Spandau synchronised machine guns |

## DFW F.34

| | |
|---|---|
| Wingspan: | 29 ft 9½ in (9.8 m) |
| Length: | 18 ft 0½ in (5.5 m) |
| Height: | 9 ft 2¼ in (2.8 m) |
| Weight Empty: | 1,760 lb (800 kg) |
| Weight Loaded: | 2,706 lb (1,230 kg) |
| Maximum Speed: | 110 mph (177 km/h) |
| Ceiling: | 16,400 ft (5,000 m) |
| Endurance: | 3 hours |
| Engine: | One 160-hp Mercedes D.III six-cylinder, in-line, water-cooled |
| Armament: | Two Spandau forward-firing machine guns |

## DFW F.37 (C.VII)

| | |
|---|---|
| Wingspan: | 44 ft 7½ in (13.6 m) |
| Length: | 22 ft 1½ in (7.0 m) |
| Height: | 9 ft 2¼ in (2.8 m) |
| Weight Empty: | 1,760 lb (800 kg) |
| Weight Loaded: | 2,706 lb (1,230 kg) |
| Maximum Speed: | 100 mph (160 km/h) |
| Ceiling: | 16,400 ft (5,000 m) |
| Endurance: | 3½ hours |
| Engine: | One 200-hp Benz Bz IV six-cylinder, in-line, water-cooled |
| Armament: | None |

## DFW D.I

| | |
|---|---|
| Wingspan: | 20 ft 4¼ in (6.2 m) |
| Length: | 14 ft 9¼ in (4.5 m) |
| Height: | 8 ft 2¼ in (2.4 m) |
| Weight Empty: | 924 lb (420 kg) |
| Weight Loaded: | 1,430 lb (650 kg) |
| Maximum Speed: | 100 mph (160 km/h) |
| Ceiling: | Not known |
| Endurance: | 1½ hours |
| Engine: | One 100-hp Mercedes D.I six-cylinder, in-line, water-cooled |
| Armament: | None |

## DFW R.I

| | |
|---|---|
| Wingspan: | 96 ft 9½ in (29.5 m) |
| Length: | 57 ft 9 in (17.6 m) |

Height:              21 ft 4 in (6.0 m)
Weight Empty:        12,462 lb (5,652 kg)
Weight Loaded:       18,478 lb (8,380 kg)
Maximum Speed:       75 mph (120 km/h)
Ceiling:             16,400 ft (5,000 m)
Endurance:           6 hours
Engine:              Four 220-hp Mercedes D.IV six-cylinder, in-line,
                     water-cooled
Armament:            Bombs

## DFW R.II

Wingspan:            115 ft (35.06 m)
Length:              68 ft 8 in (20.93 m)
Height:              21 ft (6.4 m)
Weight Empty:        19,038 lb (8,634 kg)
Weight Loaded:       25,783 lb (11,693 kg)
Maximum Speed:       83.8 mph (135 km/h)
Endurance:           6 hours
Engine:              Four 260-hp Mercedes D.IVa
Armament:            One dorsal, one ventral and two nose-mounted machine guns

## DFW R.III

Wingspan:            175 ft 6 in (53.5 m)
Length:              82 ft 0½ in (25 m)
Height:              28 ft 2½ in (8.6 m)
Weight Empty:        19,038 lb (8,634 kg)
Weight Loaded:       25,783 lb (11,693 kg)
Maximum Speed:       83.8 mph (135 km/h)
Endurance:           6 hours
Engine:              Eight 260-hp Mercedes D.IVa
                     Two 120-hp Mercedes D.II to drive superchargers
Armament:            One dorsal, one ventral and two nose-mounted
                     machine guns

# Euler-Werke, Frankfurt-am-Main

The first German manufacturer of aircraft appeared in 1908 in a field near Darmstadt. The Euler Works, as it was originally known, had been founded by August Euler, who made bicycles and automobiles. It was the manufacture of these forms of transport that brought him into contact with other German and French metal firms, among whom were Delagrange, Blériot and Farman, all of which were aircraft manufacturers. August Euler had learned to fly some years earlier and held licence No.1 in Germany. He approached the French company Voisin with an offer to build the Voisin aircraft in Germany under licence, but the French Government stepped in and prevented it. It is possible they had already seen signs of an impending conflict between the two countries.

August Euler had built and flown one of the first powered aircraft in Germany. He had also devised a method of aiming a machine gun without special sights, which was effected by the aircraft's controls. He applied to the Imperial Patent Office for a patent, which was accepted and was awarded the patent No. 248601. Euler offered his patent to the German War Ministry, who turned it down almost out of hand. In a memorandum, after seeing the patent, Major Siegert of the General Staff wrote:

> One of the major disadvantages of the biplane with the engine at the nose is using an automatic weapon. The guns are prevented from firing forward by the propeller, to the sides by the rigging wires, to the rear by the pilot, above and below by the wings.

Undaunted, August Euler went ahead with his plans to build an aircraft, and it was discovered later that, encouraged by the German Army, he built a factory on the field. It has to be remembered that aircraft manufacture was at the time in its infancy, and the factory consisted of a design office fitted with two drawing boards, a workshop fitted out with lathes, sanders and benches and an assembly shop measuring 50 metres long, 20 metres wide and 9 metres high. Euler had obtained the field after writing to General von Eichhorn, commander of the 18th Army Corps in Darmstadt, offering to train some of his officers as pilots in exchange for a field and hangar. The German War Ministry agreed, on the condition that he pay for the construction of the hangar and that he allow the Army unlimited access to the field. In return, he could have the field rent-free for five years and a promise that other aircraft manufacturers would not be allowed to build aircraft on the field during this period.

August Euler drew up plans for the hangar, and realised that he was unable to obtain enough labour to construct it without importing labour from nearby towns. He wrote to General von Eichhorn explaining the problem and suggested using the Army, for payment of course, to build the hangar and its workshops. Von Eichhorn agreed and arranged for the 21st Nassau Pioneer Battalion to be sent to the field. In return, Euler had to provide all the material, transportation and housing for the battalion and pay the battalion 2,400 marks. In less than four months the building was completed, and the manufacture of the first aircraft begun.

On 15 December 1911, August Euler opened up a new factory in Frankfurt-am-Main, which had five large hangars and accompanying workshops capable of producing thirty aircraft at one time. This was a welcome announcement to the German military machine because of the Moroccan crisis the previous summer that had sent warning bells of unrest throughout the Middle East. The first aircraft produced by the company was a two-seat pusher known as the *Gelber Hund* ('Yellow Dog'), which was fitted with a revolutionary machine gun installation in the nose. At the same time, a proposal had been put forward regarding mounting a machine gun that would fire through the propeller hub. It was not the success Euler hoped for and it failed to impress the German War Department and gain any contracts. Again it was Major Siegert who, in another of his memorandums, wrote:

> The idea of mounting a machine gun within the propeller hub is an affectation, as is the alternative of coupling the firing mechanism to the propeller's rotation, which would make it possible to fire bullets between the propeller blades when they are in the correct position. The objection to mounting the gun barrel within the hub of the propeller is the same as to any gun position which is fixed along the longitudinal axis of the aircraft: the pilot is forced to fly directly at the enemy in order to fire. Under the circumstances this is highly undesirable. With this form of gun installation any superiority in speed will be nullified when weapons are activated.

Once again this kind of comment only highlighted the resistance to change by the military hierarchy which was placing a stranglehold on German military aviation. It was to take a war to release it and, 'necessity being the mother of invention,' enormous strides were made within a very short time.

The German aircraft manufacturers found it easier in the early stages to copy existing designs of aircraft and August Euler was no exception. He copied the successful Voisin model. He did this by buying one of the models, and infuriated the French company because he had no licence to do so. Problems arose because the German engineers lacked the detailed knowledge required for the construction and the use of the materials. The copy produced was substantially inferior to the original.

In April 1912, August Euler suggested to one of his former pupils, Prince Heinrich of Prussia, that the creation of a National Aviation Fund would help the development of the German aircraft industry, which in turn would help develop German military aviation. Prince Heinrich, who was the patron of German aviation, welcomed the suggestion and under his patronage a committee was formed with high-ranking members of the banking and political fields. Despite the influential support of Prince Heinrich, over the next two years the development of the German aircraft industry was notably slower than that of the Army manufacturers.

Euler, unlike many of his counterparts and because of the various positions he had held in the National Aviation Fund and the Aviators Association, was in a strong financial position. He also had an overestimation of his own importance and it was this that brought him into conflict with the Army, the very people to whom he was trying to sell his aircraft.

In a letter to Major-General Messing of the General Inspectorate, Euler accused them of refusing to buy the Gnome engines he was building under licence from the French company, while encouraging another German manufacturer, Oberursel, to obtain a production licence from the Gnome Company to build the engine. This acrimony had started some time earlier, when one of Euler's aircraft had crashed, killing the two Army officers on board. The Army tried to get Euler to admit that there were problems with the aircraft, which he refused to do, resulting in Captain Job von Dewall, the commanding officer of the air station at Darmstadt, carrying out exhaustive examinations of all the aircraft that came out of the Euler factory there.

Accusing von Dewall of carrying out a vendetta against him, Euler was prompted to write a letter to Messing and attempted to use his influential friends to resolve the matter. However, his money and powerful friends cut no ice with the Prussian Army, and Euler was forced to lower his price for the fourteen aircraft he had supplied, from 348,750 marks to 247,300 marks. In fact, he had no choice: he was about to lose over half his workforce, and was even thinking of selling his factories. Euler's pride was shattered, and such was the power of the Prussian Army that it forced Euler to carry out licensed production.

During the First World War, Euler continued to design and produce aircraft, but he was now way down the order of manufacturers and being overtaken by Rumpler, Aviatik and Albatros. He joined forces with an Austro-Hungarian engineer by the name of Julius Hromadnik and together they designed a number of different types of aircraft, including four triplanes. The first of these was the Euler Dreidecker Type 2, powered by a 160-hp Oberursel U.III engine and designed primarily as a trainer, which appeared in March 1917. One month later the Euler Dreidecker Type 3 appeared, this time powered by a 160-hp Mercedes D.III engine. A move to using a rotary engine produced the Euler Dreidecker Type 4, powered by a 180-hp Goebel Goe.III rotary engine. None of these triplanes attracted the military and only one of each was built.

In September 1917 the Euler Vierdecker, a quadruplane, appeared. It was powered by a 100-hp Oberursel U.I rotary engine, but lacked any sort of performance that would have attracted the German military into placing an order. Using some of the better points of the Dreideckers, Euler produced a biplane version, the Doppledecker Type 2, powered by a 160-hp Siemens-Halske Sh.III counter-rotating engine. There had been a Type 1, but it had been purely experimental and amounted to nothing, as did the Type 2.

The end of the war brought about the demise of the Euler-Werke and the company disappeared, like many others, into obscurity.


## SPECIFICATIONS

### Euler B.II

| | |
|---|---|
| Wing Span: | 39 ft 9¼ in (12.12 m) |
| Length: | 27 ft 2½ in (8.30 m) |
| Height: | 9 ft 8 in (2.9 m) |
| Weight (Empty): | 1,655 lb (757 kg) |
| Weight (Loaded): | 2,578 lb (1,172 kg) |
| Speed: | 65 mph (105 km/h) |
| Endurance: | 4 hours |
| Engine: | 100 hp Mercedes D.I |

## Euler B.III

| | |
|---|---|
| Wing Span: | 41 ft 0¼ in (12.5 m) |
| Length: | 25 ft 10½ in (7.89 m) |
| Height: | 9 ft 8 in (12.12 m) |
| Weight (Empty): | 1,655 lb (757 kg) |
| Weight (Loaded): | 2,578 lb (1,172 kg) |
| Speed: | 75 mph (120 km/h) |
| Endurance: | 3 hours |
| Engine: | 120 hp Mercedes D.II |

## Euler C.I

| | |
|---|---|
| Wing Span: | 48 ft 7 in (14.8 m) |
| Length: | 30 ft 6 in (9.3 m) |
| Height: | 10 ft 6 in (3.2 m) |
| Weight (Empty): | 1,082 lb (492 kg) |
| Weight (Loaded): | 2,578 lb (1,172 kg) |
| Speed: | 95 mph (120 km/h) |
| Endurance: | 4 hours |
| Engine: | 160 hp Mercedes D.III |

## Euler D.I (Nieuport Copy)

| | |
|---|---|
| Wing Span: | 26 ft 7 in (8.1 m) |
| Length: | 19 ft 0¼ in (5.80 m) |
| Height: | 8 ft 8½ in (2.66 m) |
| Weight (Empty): | 838 lb (380 kg) |
| Weight (Loaded): | 1,323 lb (600 kg) |
| Speed: | 87 mph(140 km/h) |
| Endurance: | 4 hours |
| Engine: | 80 hp Oberursel U.O |
| Armament: | One synchronised, fixed forward-firing machine gun |

## Euler D.II

| | |
|---|---|
| Wing Span: | 24 ft 6¼ in (7.47 m) |
| Length: | 19 ft 6 in (5.94 m) |
| Height: | 9 ft 0¼ in (2.75 m) |
| Weight (Empty): | 836 lb (380 kg) |
| Weight (Loaded): | 1,353 lb (615 kg) |
| Speed: | 90.6 mph (145 km/h) |
| Endurance: | 1½ hours |
| Engine: | 100 hp Oberursel U.I |
| Armament: | None |

## Euler Triplane

| | |
|---|---|
| Wing Span: | 32 ft 10 in (10 m) |
| Length: | 26 ft 3 in (8 m) |
| Height: | 10 ft 2 in (3.1 m) |
| Weight: | Not known |
| Area: | 405 sq ft (37.5 sq m) |

Engine:          220-hp Mercedes D.IV
Armament:        None

## Euler Dr.4

Wing Span:       32 ft 10 in (10 m)
Length:          26 ft 3 in (8.0 m)
Height:          10 ft 2 in (3.1 m)
Weight:          Not known
Area:            405 sq ft (37.5 sq m)
Engine:          220-hp Mercedes D.IV
Armament:        None

There were other models claimed but although there are some photographs available, they were almost all-experimental models.

# Flugzeubau Friedrichshafen GmbH, Manzell

The Friedrichshafen FF.29 was one of the first aircraft built by the Flugzeubau Friedrichshafen GmbH firm and was a seaplane used for coastal patrol work. It was powered by a 120-hp Mercedes D.II engine and carried no armament, but on the odd occasion carried a very small bomb load. It was superseded by the FF.29a, which had modified floats and tail surfaces. The FF.29a was also the first and last winged German aircraft to ever be carried on a submarine.

During the early stages of the First World War, the German Army quickly overran Belgium, and the port of Zeebrugge was soon in German hands, becoming a base well suited to operations by U-boats. A handful of officers in the Imperial German Navy based at Zeebrugge began to look into the possibilities of operating aircraft from submarines, although at that time there was no operational requirement to do so. Rather it was a case of personal initiative, circumstance and the availability of a Friedrichshafen FF.29a twin-float, single-engined seaplane.

The base commander and U-boat captain, Oberleutnant zur See Friedrich von Arnauld de la Periere, who also, unusually, happened to be an aviator, together with Oberleutnant zur See Walter Forstman, commander of the U-12, both later to become 'Ace' U-boat commanders, were seized with the offensive spirit, and were determined to find out whether the radius of action of a seaplane could be usefully extended by using the submarine as a seaplane transporter. The nearest point on the enemy coast, North Foreland in Kent, lay some 73 miles away.

Despite it being midwinter, on 6 January 1915, the seaplane, with its 57-ft wingspan, was lashed down athwartships to the foredeck of the U-12 and the unlikely pair sailed out into the harbour to carry out trials. The bows were trimmed down and the aircraft was subsequently floated off and taxied away, all within the protection afforded by the long breakwater of the Zeebrugge Mole. It was decided to continue with the trials immediately. The strange and vulnerable combination, with the aircraft lashed athwartships and the U-12's two heavy Korting oil engines leaving a telltale plume of smoke, headed for the open sea. Despite a heavy swell, the situation was just about manageable. Some 30 miles offshore, the U-boat's commander flooded the forward tanks and floated the aircraft off, which was able to take off successfully. With von Arnauld de la Periere and his observer Herman Mall aboard, they flew along the coast of Kent undetected before returning to Zeebrugge direct, rather than making the agreed rendezvous with the U-12 in weather which had deteriorated further. At the debrief, Forstman and von Arnauld considered the whole exercise a complete success but agreed that after the difficulties in getting the aircraft launched, the seas needed to be calmer and the aircraft more secure on the deck.

This remarkable trial, conducted in wartime, and virtually in the Allies' backyard, was designed to establish a strike capability with small bombs, if not at the heartland then at least the coastal towns of the enemy. Soon the Friedrichshafen FF.29 had been adapted to carry 12-kg bombs, and during the year, twenty-six raids were flown against British and French targets. On Christmas Day 1915, a Friedrichshafen FF.29 flew along the River Thames to Erith on the outskirts of London and dropped two bombs. It was fortunate that they fell without causing injury and damage. Three British aircraft chased the FF.29 without success and it returned safely. The German airmen, or 'Zeebrugge Flers' as they were called, had more problems from their aircraft than they did from the British. On many occasions their seaplanes were forced to land with fouled ignitions or fuel line stoppages and because of the limited range of their aircraft, many of the more important targets were beyond reach. Understandably, the frustrations of the aircraft crews created morale problems, but the U-boat officers recognised the problems because they also shared the dangers of operating relatively new and untried weapons and, because of this, a bond sprang up between them.

Combined trials of aircraft and submarine had continued sporadically, but high-level support was not forthcoming. No doubt this was a correct decision, given the vulnerability of the combination and the unreliability endemic in these early aeroplanes. A report to the German High Command on the future of submarine-launched aircraft was thoroughly investigated, and the decision was made that the project be dropped. Von Arnauld was told: 'U-boats operate in the sea, aircraft in the air; there is no connection between the two.' The days of experimenting with aircraft and submarine were over.

At the beginning of 1915, the Friedrichshafen Company, in response to a request for a heavy bomber, produced the Friedrichshafen G.I. This was a twin pusher-engined bomber with a biplane tail that carried a crew of three, a pilot, a gunner and bombing officer/gunner. Only a limited number were built, but it paved the way for further models.

Within a couple of months it was followed by the G.II, which was almost identical but had a single tail. One additional modification was to put flaps behind the wheels so as to prevent stones being flung up into the pusher airscrew. The engines were two Benz Bz.IV pusher types, and the aircraft had a wingspan of 66 ft 7½ in, a fuselage length of 36 ft 3 in and a height of 11 ft 10 in. It was a reasonably successful aircraft, and a number were built to join the Gotha bombers of the Bombengeschwader force. The information and results that came back from the Front later helped create the G.III.

The company continued to develop the flying boat, and in May 1915, produced the Friedrichshafen FF.31. Only two of these aircraft were built, and were of the pusher type. Looking very similar to a floatplane version of the British D.H.2 Gunbus, the FF.31 carried a single manually operated Parabellum machine gun. The two aircraft, Nos 274 and 275 had a wingspan of 55 ft 3½ in, a length of 33 ft 4 in and a top speed of 61 mph. They were powered by a 150-hp Benz Bz.III engine and used by the German Navy.

One of the most successful of all of Friedrichshafen's seaplanes was the FF.33. There were seven variants of this aircraft, the 33e being the most memorable. The seven were split into two categories, the FF.33b, 33e, 33j, and 33s were unarmed reconnaissance patrol seaplanes. The remaining three, 33f, 33h and 33l were armed patrol fighters that were used for escort purposes. The FF.33/33a was designed so that the pilot sat in the rear cockpit. However, the design of the FF.33b reversed the seating positions, placing the pilot in the forward cockpit. A 160-hp Maybach engine was fitted in the 33b, with the radiators placed either side of the fuselage adjacent to the front cockpit. Only five of these variants were built.

The FF.33e was almost identical with the exception of the floats; the tail float had been removed, and the remaining floats were considerably longer. A 150-hp

Benz Bz.III engine powered the FF.33e, with the radiator system located against the leading edge of the upper wing. Around 188 of the FF.33e seaplanes were delivered to the German Navy, the most famous of these being the *Wölfchen* that was carried aboard the German auxiliary cruiser SMS *Wolf*.

From November 1916 to December 1918, the SMS *Wolf* and her 'cub' scoured the Indian and Pacific Oceans looking for prey. The FF.33e *Wölfchen* would be lowered onto the water and would take off on a reconnaissance flight, sending back information by radio. If a likely merchant ship was found, the pilot of the *Wölfchen* would identify the nationality and drop a message printed in English onto the deck, ordering the vessel to alter course and steam toward the German cruiser *Wolf*. The underlying threat was that if she didn't do what she was told, she would be bombed. Then, as if to drive the point home, the *Wölfchen* would drop a bomb about 20 yards from the bow of the merchant ship. A number of ships were captured in this manner and prize crews put aboard. The Armistice put an end to the raider's roaming of the sea.

Experimentation with the pusher engine continued with the Friedrichshafen FF.34. With twin fuselages, and powered by a 240-hp Maybach Mb.IV engine, the aircraft had a 60 ft 4½ in wingspan, a length of 35 ft 8 in and a height of 13 ft 5½ in, and carried a single manually operated Parabellum machine gun. It was also one of the first German aircraft to carry a radio transmitter. Only one of the aircraft was built. The fuselage was later retained and re-modelled as the FF.44.

In 1915, Friedrichshafen built a twin-engined torpedo aircraft, the FF.35. Powered by two 160-hp Mercedes D.III engines that drove pusher airscrews, it had a 77 ft 10 in wingspan, a fuselage length of 44 ft 3½ in, had a top speed of 71 mph and carried an armament of one torpedo and two manually operated Parabellum machine guns. Again only one was ever built.

One of the first land versions of the FF.31, the FF.37, appeared at the beginning of 1915 and once again only one was built. Like most of the aircraft manufacturers at the time, the company was always experimenting with variations of production models seeking to improve performance figures.

Another variation that came from the FF.33c was the FF.39, a two-seat, single-engined reconnaissance seaplane that carried a radio transmitter. Powered by a 200-hp Benz Bz.IV engine, the FF.39 had a wingspan of 56 ft 1½ in and a fuselage length of 38 ft 1 in. It had a top speed of 85 mph, an endurance of five hours and carried one machine gun, a manually operated Parabellum in the rear cockpit. Fourteen of these aircraft were supplied to the German Navy.

An experiment with a three-seater reconnaissance seaplane resulted in the Friedrichshafen FF.40. It had a single 240-hp Maybach engine mounted in the fuselage, which turned two tractor airscrews between the wings. It had a wingspan of 68 ft 11 in, a length of 40 ft 9½ in and a height of 14 ft 5½ in, and carried one manually operated Parabellum machine gun mounted in the nose section. Only one of the aircraft was built.

The tests of the FF.40 resulted, in February 1916, in the production of nine FF.41s. This was a twin-engined, three-seater, reconnaissance seaplane of which two versions were built: a single tail and a compound tail. Encased in metal housings, the two 150-hp Benz Bz.III engines drove tractor airscrews. With a wingspan of 72 ft 1 in, a fuselage length of 43 ft 6½ in and a height of 15 ft 5½ in, the FF.41 had a top speed of 78 mph and a range of 360 miles. It was armed with one torpedo and a single, manually operated Parabellum machine gun in the front cockpit. It is not known if it carried a radio transmitter.

A deviation from the large reconnaissance seaplanes resulted in the appearance of the Friedrichshafen FF.43, a single-seat fighter. With a top speed of 101 mph and a climb rate of over 500 feet per minute, this little fighter seemed destined to be put into major production, but for some unknown reason only one was ever built. Another single-seat fighter appeared shortly afterwards, the Friedrichshafen D.I, powered by a 160-hp Mercedes D.III engine. Again, like its stable mate, the FF.43, only one was built.

When the Friedrichshafen G.III appeared, it formed, together with the Gotha, the backbone of the German bomber force that carried out bombing raids on Paris and London. The G.III had a wingspan of 77 ft 9½ in, a fuselage length of 42 ft and was powered by two six-cylinder, in-line, water-cooled, 260-hp Mercedes D.IVa engines, which gave the aircraft a maximum speed of 84 mph and an endurance of 5 hours. It carried three manually operated Parabellum machine guns mounted in the nose and rear cockpits. The bomb load was sometimes as high as 3,300 lb.

Information gained from previous aircraft resulted in the FF.44, a two-seat reconnaissance aircraft, which in reality was the FF.34 re-built with a normal fuselage. It was powered by a 240-hp Maybach Mb.IV engine fitted with reduction gears. The FF.44 had a wingspan of 60 ft 4½ in, a fuselage length of 35 ft 7½ in and a height of 13 ft 11½ in. It had a flight endurance of 5 hours and carried a single manually operated Parabellum machine gun mounted in the rear cockpit.

In 1917, in an attempt to take the offensive, Friedrichshafen built the FF.48. This two-seater fighter seaplane was fitted with machine guns for both the pilot and the observer. For a fighter it was quite a large machine, with a wingspan of 54 ft 4 in, a length of 36 ft 9 in and a height of 14 ft 5½ in. It was powered by a direct-drive 240-hp Maybach engine, which gave the fighter a surprising top speed of 95 mph and a climb rate of over 500 feet per minute. Only three examples of this aircraft were built.

May 1917 saw the appearance of the FF.49c, the successor to the FF.33j. The FF.49c was fitted with a 200-hp Benz Bz.IV engine. The FF.49c was probably one of the most reliable and rugged of all the German seaplanes, and on a number of occasions had made open sea landings to rescue other crews. It was equipped with both a radio transmitter and receiver and was armed with one fixed, forward-firing Spandau machine gun and a manually operated Parabellum machine gun in the rear cockpit.

A number of these seaplanes were carried on the German seaplane carriers like the SMS *Santa Helena* and one incident concerning an FF.49c from the ship was to lay testament to its strength and durability. The aircraft, flown by Hans Sommermann with his observer Georg Pätzold, took off on a reconnaissance patrol over the English Channel/North Sea together with another seaplane. During the flight they discovered a new minefield and set to the task of plotting its position. When they realised that their fuel gauges were showing low, they proceeded to go back to their mother ship, but were unable to locate her. After six hours in the air, both aircraft ran out of fuel and put down on the water. Putting out their sea anchors, the two aircraft waited to be rescued, but during the night freshening winds and a heavy sea caused one of the aircraft to slip her anchor.

Sommermann and Pätzold struggled through stormy seas for the next five days; on the sixth day, close to collapse from hunger and thirst, they spotted some fishing boats and fired red flares. These were ignored, so in desperation they hacked away a wing panel, to which they tied a piece of white fabric, and waved it desperately in the direction of the trawlers. Suddenly, one of the trawlers moved in their direction and sped toward them. The trawler, a Swedish vessel, took the two immensely grateful aviators aboard and took them to Sweden. They owed their lives to the ruggedness and strength of the FF.49c that, even after the terrific battering it took in the storm tossed seas of the North Sea, still remained afloat.

Their companions had been rescued two days earlier by a Dutch ship, after they had attracted its attention by ingeniously signalling SOS with their machine gun.

The success of the FF.49c prompted the designers to modify one of them as a single-engined bomber. Powered by a 200-hp Benz Bz.IV engine, the FF.49b, as it was re-designated, carried no armament other than bombs, but it was fitted with a radio transmitter and receiver. With a wingspan of 56 ft 11 ½ in, a fuselage length of 37 ft 10 in and a height of 14 ft, the aircraft had a top speed of 95 mph and a flight endurance of 5½ hours. The pilot's position was also reversed with him flying the aircraft from the rear cockpit. Twenty-five of these models were built.

Another land-based fighter appeared in June 1917, the Friedrichshafen D Type Vierdecker (quadruplane). Looking very much like the Albatros, and built purely as an experimental model, the aircraft, powered by a 160-hp Mercedes D.III, crashed on its first flight.

Soon after, the Friedrichshafen C.I, another land-based aircraft, arrived. Although it appeared as a new model, it was in fact an FF.33L seaplane fitted with a conventional undercarriage. Only one was built. At the same time as the appearance of the C.I, a new model did actually appear, the Friedrichshafen N.I. This was a single-engined, two-seater night bomber powered by a 260-hp Mercedes D.IVa engine. The design was such that the wings were swept back considerably; this resulted in the pilot having to try and look over a highly extended nose. This made night landings in the aircraft an absolute nightmare, and consequently only one of the aircraft was built.

At the end of June 1917, three twin-engined torpedo-carrying seaplanes were built, powered by two 260-hp Mercedes C.IVa engines. Designated the Friedrichshafen FF.53, they were not the success hoped for and so the information gathered was used to built the FF.59a. There were two versions of this aircraft, the FF.59a and FF.59b, which eventually resulted in the production of the FF.59c.

When the 59c appeared at the beginning of 1918, it was obvious that it was little more than a modified FF.39. True, the inboard bracing cabled had been removed, which enabled the rear gunner to shoot forward, albeit somewhat riskily, and a 200-hp Benz engine fitted, but to all intents and purposes it was still an FF.39. It was fitted with a radio transmitter and receiver, now becoming more and more a normal part of aircraft equipment. The FF.59c had a wingspan of 58 ft 5 in, a fuselage length of 37 ft 1 in, a height of 13 ft 11½ in, a top speed of 88 mph and a flight endurance of over 5 hours.

Friedrichshafen having been spurred on by the success of the FF.33 model (especially that of the FF.33e *Wölfchen*, which showed the ease with which a seaplane could be carried and operated from a ship), the FF.64 was produced. Designed as a two-seat reconnaissance aircraft, the wings could be folded back without compromising its structural strength for easy storage aboard a ship. It was powered by a 160-hp Mercedes D.III engine and carried a manually operated Parabellum machine gun in the rear cockpit. The FF.64 was fitted with a radio transmitter and receiver. Only three of this model was built.

At the same time as the FF.64 was being developed, an experimental single-wing seaplane was being designed. Based loosely on the Brandenburg W.29, the FF.63, as it was known, had only two test flights before it was scrapped.

Another G-class bomber was built at the end May 1918, the Friedrichshafen G.IV (FF.55). Based on the design of the previous G bombers, the G.IV had the front cockpit removed, giving it a 'sawn-off' look. It had a twin tail and was armed with only one rear gun. It had a wingspan of 74 ft 2 in, a fuselage length of 39 ft 4½ in and was powered by two 260-hp Mercedes D.IVa engines. An unknown number were built. There was a G.V (FF.62) built, but no details of the aircraft can be found.

An extremely large experimental triplane was built during 1918 and was one of the first seaplanes to have an enclosed cockpit. Powered by four 160-hp

Mercedes D.III engines, the Friedrichshafen FF.60, as it was designated, carried a crew of four: two pilots, an observer/gunner and a gunner. It had been designed for long-distance patrols but only one was built before the Armistice came. No specifications are available.

The Friedrichshafen Company was one of the major manufacturers of seaplanes during the First World War and produced some of the world's finest naval aircraft of that period.

## SPECIFICATIONS

### Friedrichshafen FF.31

| | |
|---|---|
| Wingspan: | 55 ft 4 in (16.8 m) |
| Length: | 33 ft 3½ in (10.1 m) |
| Height: | 12 ft 9½ in (3.9 m) |
| Weight Empty: | 2,288 lb (1,040 kg) |
| Weight Loaded: | 3,366 lb (1,530 kg) |
| Maximum Speed: | 74 mph (119 km/h) |
| Ceiling: | 13,100 ft (4,000 m) |
| Endurance: | 5-6 hours |
| Engine: | One 150-hp Benz Bz.III six-cylinder, in-line, water-cooled |
| Armament: | One manually operated Parabellum machine gun mounted in the observer's cockpit |

### Friedrichshafen FF.33e

| | |
|---|---|
| Wingspan: | 54 ft 11½ in (16.7 m) |
| Length: | 34 ft 3½ in (10.5 m) |
| Height: | 12 ft 2½ in (3.7 m) |
| Weight Empty: | 2,217 lb (1,008 kg) |
| Weight Loaded: | 3,636 lb (1,635 kg) |
| Maximum Speed: | 74 mph (119 km/h) |
| Ceiling: | 13,100 ft (4,000 m) |
| Endurance: | 5-6 hours |
| Engine: | One 150-hp Benz Bz.III six-cylinder, in-line, water-cooled |
| Armament: | One manually operated Parabellum machine gun mounted in the observers cockpit |

### Friedrichshafen FF.34

| | |
|---|---|
| Wingspan: | 60 ft 4 in (18.4 m) |
| Length: | 35 ft 7¼ in (10.8 m) |
| Height: | 13 ft 5½ in (4.1 m) |
| Weight Empty: | Not known |
| Weight Loaded: | Not known |
| Maximum Speed: | 74 mph (119 km/h) |
| Ceiling: | 13,100 ft (4,000 m) |
| Endurance: | 5-6 hours |
| Engine: | One 240-hp Maybach Mb.IV six-cylinder, in-line, water-cooled |
| Armament: | One manually operated Parabellum machine gun mounted in the observer's cockpit |

## Friedrichshafen FF.35

| | |
|---|---|
| Wingspan: | 77 ft 11 in (23.7 m) |
| Length: | 44 ft 3½ in (13.5 m) |
| Height: | 13 ft 5½ in (4.1 m) |
| Weight Empty: | 5,042 lb (2,292 kg) |
| Weight Loaded: | 7,795 lb (3,543 kg) |
| Maximum Speed: | 71 mph (114 km/h) |
| Ceiling: | 13,100 ft (4,000 m) |
| Endurance: | 5-6 hours |
| Engine: | Two 160-hp Mercedes D.III six-cylinder, in-line, water-cooled |
| Armament: | One manually operated Parabellum machine gun mounted in the observer's cockpit |
| | One torpedo |

## Friedrichshafen FF.39

| | |
|---|---|
| Wingspan: | 56 ft 1½ in (17.1 m) |
| Length: | 38 ft 1 in (11.6 m) |
| Height: | 14 ft 1 in (4.3 m) |
| Weight Empty: | 3,164 lb (1,438 kg) |
| Weight Loaded: | 4,624 lb (2,102 kg) |
| Maximum Speed: | 85 mph (137 km/h) |
| Ceiling: | 13,100 ft (4,000 m) |
| Endurance: | 5 hours |
| Engine: | One 200-hp Benz Bz.IV six-cylinder, in-line, water-cooled |
| Armament: | One manually operated Parabellum machine gun mounted in the observer's cockpit |

## Friedrichshafen FF.40

| | |
|---|---|
| Wingspan: | 68 ft 11 in (21 m) |
| Length: | 40 ft 9½ in (12.4 m) |
| Height: | 14 ft 5¼ in (4.4 m) |
| Weight Empty: | 4,024 lb (1,829 kg) |
| Weight Loaded: | 5,586 lb (2,539 kg) |
| Maximum Speed: | 85 mph (137 km/h) |
| Ceiling: | 13,100 ft (4,000 m) |
| Endurance: | 5 hours |
| Engine: | One 240-hp Maybach six-cylinder, in-line, water-cooled |
| Armament: | One manually operated Parabellum machine gun mounted in the observer's cockpit |

## Friedrichshafen FF.41

| | |
|---|---|
| Wingspan: | 72 ft 1 in (22.0 m) |
| Length: | 43 ft 6½ in (13.2 m) |
| Height: | 15 ft 5¼ in (4.7 m) |
| Weight Empty: | 5,060 lb (2,300 kg) |
| Weight Loaded: | 8,074 lb (3,670 kg) |
| Maximum Speed: | 78 mph (125 km/h) |
| Ceiling: | 13,100 ft (4,000 m) |
| Endurance: | 3 hours |

| Engine: | Two 150-hp Benz Bz.III six-cylinder, in-line, water-cooled |
| Armament: | One manually operated Parabellum machine gun mounted in the front observer's cockpit<br>One torpedo |

## Friedrichshafen FF.43

| Wingspan: | 32 ft 6½ in (9.9 m) |
| Length: | 27 ft 11 in (8.5 m) |
| Height: | 11 ft 1½ in (3.4 m) |
| Weight Empty: | 1,756 lb (798 kg) |
| Weight Loaded: | 2,372 lb (1,078 kg) |
| Maximum Speed: | 102 mph (164 km/h) |
| Ceiling: | 13,100 ft (4,000 m) |
| Endurance: | 3 hours |
| Engine: | One 160-hp Mercedes D.III six-cylinder, in-line, water-cooled |
| Armament: | Two fixed forward-firing Spandau machine guns |

## Friedrichshafen FF.44

| Wingspan: | 60 ft 4½ in (18.4 m) |
| Length: | 35 ft 7¼ in (10.8 m) |
| Height: | 13 ft 11½ in (4.2 m) |
| Weight Empty: | 3,436 lb (1,562 kg) |
| Weight Loaded: | 5,071 lb (2,305 kg) |
| Maximum Speed: | 102 mph (164 km/h) |
| Ceiling: | 13,100 ft (4,000 m) |
| Endurance: | 5 hours |
| Engine: | One 240-hp Maybach Mb.IV six-cylinder, in-line, water-cooled |
| Armament: | One manually operated Parabellum machine gun in the observer's cockpit |

## Friedrichshafen FF.48

| Wingspan: | 53 ft 4 in (16.2 m) |
| Length: | 36 ft 9 in (11.2 m) |
| Height: | 14 ft 5¼ in (4.4 m) |
| Weight Empty: | 3,500 lb (1,591 kg) |
| Weight Loaded: | 4,885 lb (2,216 kg) |
| Maximum Speed: | 96 mph (154 km/h) |
| Ceiling: | 13,100 ft (4,000 m) |
| Endurance: | 5-6 hours |
| Engine: | One 240-hp Maybach Mb.IV six-cylinder, in-line, water-cooled |
| Armament: | One manually operated Parabellum machine gun in the observer's cockpit<br>One fixed forward-firing Spandau machine gun |

## Friedrichshafen FF.49b

| Wingspan: | 56 ft 11½ in (17.3 m) |
| Length: | 37 ft 9½ in (11.5 m) |

Height:               13 ft 11½ in (4.2 m)
Weight Empty:         3,150 lb (1,432 kg)
Weight Loaded:        4,613 lb (2,097)
Maximum Speed:        95 mph (152 km/h)
Ceiling:              13,100 ft (4,000 m)
Endurance:            5-6 hours
Engine:               One 200-hp Benz Bz.IV six-cylinder, in-line, water-cooled
Armament:             None

## Friedrichshafen FF.49c

Wingspan:             56 ft 3¼ in (17.1 m)
Length:               38 ft 3 in (11.7 m)
Height:               14 ft 9¼ in (4.5 m)
Weight Empty:         3,333 lb (1,515 kg)
Weight Loaded:        4,723 lb (2,147 kg)
Maximum Speed:        87 mph (138 km/h)
Ceiling:              13,100 ft (4,000 m)
Endurance:            5-6 hours
Engine:               One 200-hp Benz Bz.IV six-cylinder, in-line, water-cooled
Armament:             One manually operated Parabellum machine gun in
                      the observer's cockpit
                      One fixed forward-firing Spandau machine gun

## Friedrichshafen FF.59c

Wingspan:             58 ft 5 in (17.8 m)
Length:               37 ft 1 in (11.3 m)
Height:               13 ft 11½ in (4.2 m)
Weight Empty:         3,494 lb (1,588 kg)
Weight Loaded:        4,946 lb (2,248 kg)
Maximum Speed:        88 mph (141 km/h)
Ceiling:              13,100 ft (4,000 m)
Endurance:            5-6 hours
Engine:               One 200-hp Benz Bz.IV six-cylinder, in-line, water-cooled
Armament:             One manually operated Parabellum machine gun in
                      the observer's cockpit

## Friedrichshafen G.II

Wingspan:             66 ft 7½ in (20.3 m)
Length:               36 ft 3 in (11.0 m)
Height:               11 ft 9½ in (3.6 m)
Weight Empty:         4,840 lb (2,200 kg)
Weight Loaded:        6,934 lb (6,934 kg)
Maximum Speed:        95 mph (152 km/h)
Ceiling:              16,100 ft (4,900 m)
Endurance:            5-6 hours
Engine:               Two 200-hp Benz Bz.IV six-cylinder, in-line, water-cooled
Armament:             One manually operated Parabellum machine gun in
                      the nose, a second in section aft of the cockpit

## Friedrichshafen G.III

| | |
|---|---|
| Wingspan: | 77 ft 9¼ in (23.7 m) |
| Length: | 42 ft 0 in (12.8 m) |
| Height: | 11 ft 9½ in (3.6 m) |
| Weight Empty: | 5,929 lb (2,695 kg) |
| Weight Loaded: | 8,646 lb (3,930 kg) |
| Maximum Speed: | 95 mph (152 km/h) |
| Ceiling: | 16,100 ft (4,900 m) |
| Endurance: | 5-6 hours |
| Engine: | Two 200-hp Benz Bz.IV six-cylinder, in-line, water-cooled |
| Armament: | One manually operated Parabellum machine-gun in the nose, a second in section aft of the cockpit |

## Friedrichshafen G.IV

| | |
|---|---|
| Wingspan: | 74 ft 2 in (22.6 m) |
| Length: | 39 ft 4½ in (12 m) |
| Height: | 11 ft 9½ in (3.6 m) |
| Weight Empty: | 5,929 lb (2,695 kg) |
| Weight Loaded: | 8,646 lb (3,930 kg) |
| Maximum Speed: | 95 mph (152 km/h) |
| Ceiling: | 16,100 ft (4,900 m) |
| Endurance: | 5-6 hours |
| Engine: | Two 260-hp Mercedes D.IVa six-cylinder, in-line, water-cooled |
| Armament: | One manually operated Parabellum machine gun in the aft section of the cockpit |

## Friedrichshafen C.I

| | |
|---|---|
| Wingspan: | 43 ft 8 in (13.3 m) |
| Length: | 26 ft 3 in (8.0 m) |
| Height: | 12 ft 2½ in (3.7 m) |
| Weight Empty: | 2,217 lb (1,008 kg) |
| Weight Loaded: | 3,636 lb (1,635 kg) |
| Maximum Speed: | 74 mph (119 km/h) |
| Ceiling: | 13,100 ft (4,000 m) |
| Endurance: | 5-6 hours |
| Engine: | One 150-hp Benz Bz III. six-cylinder, in-line, water-cooled |
| Armament: | One manually operated Parabellum machine gun mounted in the observer's cockpit |

## Friedrichshafen N.I

No details available

# Fokker Flugzeug-Werke GmbH

During the First World War, the name Fokker became synonymous with military aviation and the company produced some of Germany's finest aircraft. Anthony Fokker, a Dutchman, produced the first of his many aircraft, the Spin (Spider), in 1910. This was followed by variations of the Spin until April 1914, when the first of his military aircraft appeared. This was the Fokker M.5, which consisted of two types, the M.5K and M.5L, both powered by a 50-hp Gnôme engine. The K stood for the short wingspan version, the L for the long-span model. Performance was disappointing, so a reconditioned 70-hp Gnôme engine was purchased and installed in the M.5L. The difference in performance was immediately noticeable and together with the new comma-shaped rudder, which was to make the early Fokker aircraft instantly recognisable, the aircraft became an attractive proposition to the Army. A number of both the M.5K and L models were purchased by the military and were in operation as reconnaissance aircraft when the war began. There was one further 'M' model, the Fokker M.5K/MG, which mounted a Parabellum machine gun for testing synchronisation gear.

The Fokker Company, Fokker Aviation Ltd, first officially appeared on 22 February 1912, when it was entered in the Berlin Trade Register with a capital of 20,000 marks. The following year saw the orders for which Fokker had been looking, when the German Army ordered four Fokker M.2s, complete with their Daimler trucks and equipment, at a cost of 47,000 marks each. One month later the Army ordered a further six aircraft at a cost of 19,500 marks each.

The authorities were not happy with the Fokker Company sharing the airfield at Johannisthal with other aircraft manufacturers, so they suggested that Fokker should move his entire operation to Schwerin-Görries in Mecklenburg. As an incentive to do so, they offered to guarantee him thirty pupils a year for his newly-created flying school. He was also offered the chance to build a factory at 10 per cent of the building cost, with the right to buy at a later date, plus an airfield at a very low rental.

This was an offer he could not refuse, so he persuaded his father and brother to invest in the company to the tune of 300,000 guilders. This enabled extensions to the factory to be built and the latest manufacturing equipment to be installed. Six months later another cash injection of 100,000 guilders was put into the company.

Three years later, the name of the company was changed to the Fokker Aircraft Factory Ltd. During this period, Anthony Fokker's father and brother continued to support the company financially.

Fokker had developed a number of aircraft prior to the First World War, but on the day that war was declared against Britain, all German aircraft manufacturers were informed by telegram that their aviation material was under the control of the Army. Fokker was immediately inundated with requests by the German Navy and various other operational units to buy his existing aircraft. In fact, had the Allies offered to buy his aircraft, there is no doubt that Fokker would have sold them to the highest bidder. Fokker off-loaded all of his aircraft, spare parts and junk, with the exception of an M.5L Grüner Vogel (Green Bird) belonging to Leutnant von Buttlar's squadron. He also accepted orders for aircraft from the Army, Navy and Austria – orders that he had no hope of fulfilling, and for this he received a severe reprimand from the IdFlieg (Inspektion der Fliegertruppen – Inspectorate of Aviation Troops).

The Fokker works consisted of a number of tumbledown shacks and huts, so Fokker and his staff set to work to repair, enlarge and equip these workshops for production. The one main factor against Anthony Fokker was that he was an alien in a country that was at war, and as such could expect no special entitlements.

The IdFlieg approached Fokker with the suggestion of developing a two-seat aircraft for the purposes of artillery spotting. What developed was the Fokker M.6. Based on the airframe of the M.5, the M.6 had a wingspan of 36 feet and a fuselage length of 22 feet 6 inches and was powered by an 80-hp Oberursel U.O rotary engine. The aircraft completed its initial tests and was then sent to Schwerin to be evaluated by military pilots. On its second flight, the pilot, Oberleutnant Kolbe, with an observer by the name of Hauptmann Ruff, got confused with the fuel cocks. The result was that the engine stopped in mid-air, and the aircraft crashed while Kolbe was attempting to land. The aircraft was completely destroyed and Kolbe killed. The observer was lucky to escape with just minor injuries. This was the only example of the M.6 aircraft.

The M.6 was followed some months later by an unusual model, the Fokker M.7 sesquiplane (1½ wings). With the exception of the wings, the rest of the aircraft was that of an M.5, with the fuselage adapted to carry an observer in tandem with the pilot. An 80-hp Oberursel U.O engine powered the M.7. Production started in January 1915 and twenty were built, all going to German Naval Air Stations for reconnaissance purposes.

While at one of the seaplane stations, Fokker sought permission from the Reichsmarineamt to convert one of the M.7s into a twin-float seaplane. The wingspan was increased and the interplane struts were inclined inwards to provide stronger bracing bays of equal length.

The floats were taken from the unsuccessful W.2 and were made of wood. They were fitted to the aircraft by a strut system that was far stronger than that of the W.2. The M.7, now designated the Fokker W.3, underwent a series of trials, none of which were successful. The aircraft appeared to be extremely reluctant to leave the water, so the whole project was abandoned. The aircraft reverted back to an M.7 and was sent to the Marine-Landflieger Abteilung at Johannisthal for training purposes.

Back at the Fokker workshops, Colonel von Eberhardt of the Idflieg was delighted with Fokker's progress. After seeing a design for a new aircraft, the Fokker M.8, Eberhardt ordered a number of aircraft to form the nucleus of an observation squadron, and within days Fokker and his staff were at work developing the Fokker M.8.

The first aircraft came off the production line in July 1914 and within days was in action on reconnaissance duties. This was the first truly successful aircraft built by Fokker and was the production model of the recently aborted M.6. There were a number of modifications, including large apertures with side windscreens cut into the sides of the fuselage under the wings. This was done to give both the pilot and the observer a good downward field of vision. The tandem seating favoured in the M.6 was replaced by side-by-side seating in a single large cockpit, which was ideal for observation and artillery spotting purposes but no good in an attacking or defensive role.

In September, a Fokker M.8 was forced to land near St Omer and was captured intact. A number of Allied pilots flew the aircraft and were very impressed with its handling qualities.

Two Fokker squadrons, Feldflieger-Abteilungen (Field Aviation Unit) 40 and 41, consisting of six aircraft each, were formed for the purposes of artillery spotting and reconnaissance. Designated the Fokker A.I, the M.8 was flown by selected pilots only, one of them being Leutnant Otto Parschau, who was later to be awarded the *Pour le Mérite*. Another of the pilots was Leutnant Oswald Boelcke, destined to be one of the top aces of the German Army Air Service. Powered by the 80-hp Oberursel rotary engines, over thirty of the aircraft were supplied to the Army.

The Fokker factory was not only supplying aircraft to the German Army, but also to the Austro-Hungarian Air Service. In September 1915, Fokker supplied two aircraft, the Fokker M.10E, a single seat artillery spotter powered by 80-hp Oberursel U.O rotary engine, and the Fokker M.10Z, a two-seat reconnaissance/ trainer powered by a 100-hp Oberursel U.I rotary engine.

The addition of a machine gun to the aircraft meant it became a fighting machine. No longer the observer or the 'carrier-pigeon', the aircraft was now recognised as an essential part of the war machinery. One of the major problems that faced the pilots was the fitting of forward-firing guns. This was easily the most effective method of attacking a foe, although invariably the propeller got in the way. Many Allied aircraft were of the pusher type, meaning the engine and propeller were at the rear. This gave the pilot an unobstructed view of his opponent and enabled his observer, who sat in front of the pilot, to carry out an attack without the fear of hitting the propeller and shooting themselves down.

One of the first Allied aircraft to be designed for offensive missions was a two-seat biplane with a pusher engine, the Vickers FB5, or Gunbus as it was more commonly known. The first of these aircraft began to arrive at the beginning of 1915 and were issued to 5 Squadron, Royal Flying Corps in France. A well known pre-war French aviator and stunt pilot, Roland Garros, a member of Escadrille MS.23, realised the problems facing pilots and gunner alike and designed a forward-facing gun mounting on his own Morane Parasol. He had a Hotchkiss machine gun mounted directly in front of the cockpit and wedges of armoured steel screwed to the backs of each blade to deflect any bullets fired that did not pass between them. It worked to a certain degree, and in the first part of April he shot down and destroyed three German aircraft.

On 18 April 1915, Garros was attacking the railway station at Courtrai when his aircraft was hit by a rifle bullet from the gun of a German soldier by the name of Schlenstedt, who was on guard at the time. The bullet severed the fuel line and the aircraft was forced to crash land behind German lines. That bullet was to become the catalyst behind of one of the most important influences in the art of aerial fighting during the First World War. Although Garros tried to destroy his aircraft he was unsuccessful and, together with his aircraft, was captured.

It did not take the Germans long to realise who they had captured and the prize they had in his aircraft. The wreckage of his Morane Parasol was passed to a Hauptmann Foerster, who took it to Doeberitz, where a Simon Brunnhuber was ordered to make a working copy of the interrupter firing mechanism. This he did, and high ranking officers watched with great interest as the engine and propeller were set up and the machine gun was fired. It is not certain whether or not the steel of the deflecting plates was of armoured-plated quality, or whether the armour-piercing bullets used were of superior quality, but the propeller disintegrated and the whole test bed was shattered. All those who were watching were lucky to escape without injury. It was then decided to pass the whole project over to Anthony Fokker, who, after examining the method used to fire the machine gun, recognised its limitations and decided that instead of making copies of it, he would improve upon it.

A synchronised machine gun with an interrupter mechanism had earlier been designed by a Franz Schneider, who was a Swiss engineer working with LVG (Luft-Verkehrs Gesellschaft), and the gun mechanism was patented on 15 July 1913, under patent No. 276396.

Two years later, when Anthony Fokker patented his interrupter mechanism, patent No. 310396, Franz Schneider questioned the patent, saying it was based on his design. Fokker maintained that Schneider's design was based on the blocking of the machine gun when a propeller blade was in front of the barrel. A two-bladed propeller revolved at 1,200 times a minute, which meant that it passed in front of a gun muzzle 2,400 times in a minute. Fokker's design was worked by a camshaft and lever, which fired the machine-gun the instant there was no blade in front of the gun barrel. The Parabellum gun fired 600 times in a minute, so his design was based on a method by which the propeller shaft fired the gun when there was no blade in the way. In all probability, the actual design was more than likely conceived by another member of Fokker's design team, Heinrich Luebbe.

Fokker and his engineers, Luebbe, Leinberger and Heber, got to work and 72 hours later they had designed and built the mechanism. Every time the propeller blade lined up with the muzzle in front of the firing machine gun, a cam, actuated by the engine, stopped the gun firing. The system was tested and fitted to a Fokker M.5K monoplane for final testing. A young Leutnant Oswald Boelcke was assigned to carry out the testing, and after normal tests he took it on a mission. After the third mission, Boelcke had scored a victory (the first M.5K victory was by Leutnant Wintgens on 1 July 1915). The Germans were delighted and ordered not only the interrupter firing gear system, but the Fokker M.5K aircraft, which was re-designated the E.I (Eindecker).

In 1916, LVG and Schneider sued Fokker for patent infringement; the battle continued until 1933 and although the courts repeatedly found in Schneider's favour, Fokker refused to acknowledge the rulings.

The arrival of the Fokker Eindecker and its interrupter firing mechanism meant a new threat for the Allies. By the end of the summer of 1915, the German pilots were attacking the British and French aircraft with devastating results. They had acquired air supremacy.

Anthony Fokker at this time was under a great deal of criticism not from only his own countrymen, but from the Allies about his close ties with Germany. Fokker's defence was that at the onset of the war, the German Army had requisitioned his aircraft, together with the entire stock of spare engines and equipment. He said he was blamed for not placing himself at the disposal of the Allies, but argued that his own country, Holland, preferred to buy French aircraft, and England and Italy never even bothered to respond to his proposals. Russia was so corrupt that it would have been impossible to deal with them, and the only country that even offered to respond to him (although it was not entirely with open arms) was Germany. It is said the British Government later even offered him a substantial sum of money to work for them.

The need to arm reconnaissance aircraft prompted Fokker to carry out a most unusual experiment. He took two M.7 fuselages, each with its own tail section, and in between fitted a nacelle with two 80-hp Oberursel rotary engines, one pusher and one tractor. In the nacelle between the engines sat the pilot. The two fuselages and the nacelle were joined together by a biplane structure. In the front of the fuselage sat two gunners, which made it ideal for a frontal attack, but made no provision for defence if attacked from the rear. After a number of test flights carried out by Anthony Fokker himself, the idea was scrapped because there were too many problems to make it a worthwhile project.

Fokker brought out another experimental aircraft at the end of 1915, the Fokker M.16E. This was a single-bay two-seater aircraft with the top wing level with the top of the fuselage. Powered by a 120-hp Mercedes D.II engine, the aircraft was a model for the next version, the two-seater Fokker M.16Z. This was a complete re-design of the M.16E and was powered by a 200-hp Austro-Daimler engine. It was fitted with a forward-firing Schwarzlose machine gun for the pilot and a single, manually operated Schwarzlose machine gun for the observer. Thirty of these aircraft were built and sold to the Austro-Hungarian Air Force.

A single-seater version was also built at the end of 1915, the Fokker M.17E/1. Powered by a 100-hp Oberursel U.I rotary engine, the M.17E/1 was armed with a fixed forward-firing Spandau machine gun. Only one was ever built. A modified version of the E/1, the E/2, appeared shortly after and a small number were sold to the Austro-Hungarians with a designation of Fokker B.III, for unarmed scouting roles. Three more experimental versions were developed at the end of 1915 and the beginning of 1916: the Fokker M.17Z, M.18Z and M.20Z. The only differences between the three models were modifications to the tail surfaces and the testing of new engines.

There appeared to be a period at the end of 1915 and the beginning of 1916 in which a number of experimental aircraft made appearances. The Fokker M.22 was fitted with a re-designed cowling, followed by the W.4, a floatplane version of the Fokker M.7. Neither was put into production. At the beginning of 1916, Fokker decided that all his experimental aircraft would carry the prefix of 'V'.

The first of these, the Fokker V.1, designed by Reinhold Platz, was a revolutionary model that had a steel-tube fuselage that was rounded out to the cowling. The wings, although appearing to be of an orthodox structure, had all moving surfaces and had no fin surfaces. The deep section wings were fully cantilevered and covered in plywood. The conventional ailerons were replaced by one metre long differentially moving wingtips giving lateral control. A lifting surface fairing was fitted between the axle, a characteristic that was to persist with virtually all subsequent Fokker aircraft. Powered by a 100-hp Oberursel U.I rotary engine, the V.1 was fitted with twin forward-firing Spandau machine guns.

One of the finest aircraft series produced by Fokker was the Fokker D. However, its beginning was hardly auspicious for when the first of the series, the Fokker D.I, was presented to the military for evaluation, it came in for some scathing reports. This infuriated Anthony Fokker, but unfortunately for him the reports came from two German Flying Corps officers, who besides carrying out their normal duties were both eminent aeronautical engineers. A number of recommendations were made and after all had been implemented, three of the aircraft were ordered. After further evaluation by the air force there followed an additional order for twenty-five Fokker D.Is with the 120-hp Mercedes engine. Some minor modifications were made and a further eighty were delivered.

The Austro-Hungarian Air Force also purchased a number of aircraft from Fokker, but then the Ungarische Allgemeine Maschinefabrik AG (MAG) of Budapest started to build the Fokker D.I under licence. A number of the aircraft were also used in Turkey and Mesopotamia. Tragedy struck the Fokker factory on 27 June 1916, when chief designer Martin Kreutzer took a Fokker D.I on an acceptance flight. Shortly after taking off the aircraft crashed and Kreutzer was dragged from the wreckage. Barely conscious, the mortally injured Kreutzer managed to explain to his rescuers that a jammed rudder had caused the crash, but that didn't stop Anthony Fokker turning up and verbally berating the dying man.

Reinhold Platz, who was instrumental in designing and producing the Fokker D.II, took Kreutzer's place. The Fokker D.III closely followed this at the end of August 1916. Almost immediately one of the aircraft was given to Oberleutnant Oswald Boelcke, one of Germany's top aces. On the day after receiving the aircraft, 2 September 1916, Boelcke claimed his twentieth victim when he shot down a D.H.2 flown by Captain R. Wilson. Encouraged by this, Boelcke retained the aircraft and during the next two weeks he claimed five more victims.

Although the aircraft was easy to fly and very manoeuvrable, it was noticeably slower than the Nieuport and no faster than the Sopwith 1½-Strutter. This was not good enough for Boelcke so when the Albatros D.I appeared (a considerably better aircraft), Boelcke quickly switched aircraft. The Fokker D.III, on Boelcke's recommendation, became a home-defence fighter.

The Fokker D.IV, also known as the Fokker M.20, was one of the aircraft designed by Anthony Fokker himself. German aeronautical engineers at Aldershof carried out structural tests on the wings and serious weaknesses were found. Idflieg insisted on improvements, and again the structure of the wings became suspect. After a series of tests, it became apparent to Idflieg that Fokker and his engineers relied heavily on guesswork when designing new aircraft. With the problems ironed out, an initial order for twenty of the aircraft was placed, which was later increased to thirty.

The Fokker D.IV had some initial success but the front-line pilots did not like the aircraft and when a new engine became available, the 160-hp Mercedes D.IIIa, priority was given to the Albatros and Pfalz fighters. To add insult to injury, Anthony Fokker was ordered to build 400 AEG C.IV two-seater aircraft under licence. Complaining that the complexity of the aircraft's design would prevent him making any profit, Anthony Fokker was told to study the soundness of the aircraft's structural design and learn from it. During construction of the AEG C.IV, the whole Fokker factory was under the supervision of Dr Koner, an expert on materials and production control. One wonders if the reason for that was a deliberate move to enable the Idflieg to keep a watchful eye on Fokker.

The Fokker V.1 was re-designed and fitted with conventional tail surfaces and an improved 120-hp Mercedes water-cooled engine. The differentially moving wingtips for lateral control were retained, however. The new model was designated the Fokker V.2.

At the beginning of 1917 a new design of aircraft appeared – the Fokker V.3. The new design had three wings; the middle and bottom spans were of identical length, while the top span was longer. A 110-hp Oberursel U.II engine powered the aircraft. The V.3 was to be the forerunner of the famous Fokker Dr.I. This was followed by the V.4, which had hollow inter-plane struts between the wings to cure the wing vibration suffered by the V.3. Then came the V.5, V.6 and V.7, all of which were variations of the V.3. The V.8, however, was of a most unusual design and said to have been built expressly on the instructions of Anthony Fokker. It was a triplane with an extended fuselage, with a pair of wings mounted just aft of the cockpit. Powered by a 120-hp Mercedes D.II engine, the aircraft had two very short test flights but was totally impracticable and soon scrapped.

The V.9, V.10 and V.11 that followed reverted back to biplanes. The V.11 was judged at the first of the D-type competitions to be the best in its class and although it was just the prototype, very little modification was required before the aircraft was put into production. The aircraft was powered by a 160-hp Mercedes D.III engine and had a climb rate of nearly 600 feet per minute.

The appearance of two Fokker F.I fighters, Nos 102/17 and 103/17, on 16 August 1917 at Manfred von Richthofen's fighter wing at Courtrai caused quite a stir. The leader of Jasta 10, Leutnant Werner Voss, visited the squadron on 29 August to test fly the aircraft and was delighted with the results. Making his first operational flight in 103/17 the following day, he shot down a British aircraft.

Between 30 August and 23 September, Voss claimed twenty-one aircraft shot down, but on the last day, while on patrol, he spotted a lone S.E.5a. Diving in to attack, he failed to notice two other S.E.5as of 'B' Flight, 56 Squadron, RFC, led by Captain James B. McCudden. Three aircraft now went after Voss and although he fought like a fury, Second Lieutenant Rhys-Davids, flying one of the other S.E.5as, shot down his aircraft. The British acknowledged the skill and daring of Voss, saying that such a foe should have been taken alive.

Richthofen, still recovering from a head wound received on 6 July, insisted on being one of the first of his Jasta to fly the aircraft. It was well known that he had very little faith in the reliability of the rotary engine, but he took to the F.I instantly. The following month six new Fokker Triplanes arrived, their designation having been changed to Fokker Dr.I.

One of the major problems that faced the pilots of the Fokker Dr.I was the cramped legroom in the tiny cockpit; as a result, the majority of the chosen pilots were relatively short. Nearly all the pilots of the Richthofen Jagdgeschwader flew the Fokker Dr.I until April 1918, when the Fokker D.VII biplane replaced it.

Throughout this period the all-red Fokker Dr.I Triplane of Manfred von Richthofen scoured the skies looking for opponents, and with his success created a legend. Some reports said that his aircraft was fitted with triple machine guns; others said he was invincible and in league with the devil. In fact, Richthofen's aircraft was a perfectly standard Fokker Dr.I, the only difference being that Richthofen had at least two spare aircraft available all the time. The aircraft was initially powered by a 110-hp Oberursel UR.II engine, which was later replaced by the Thulin-built Le Rhône nine-cylinder rotary engine.

The V.13 prototype was converted into the Fokker D.VI at the beginning of 1918. Powered by a 110-hp Oberursel UR.II engine, the aircraft underwent a series of tests, but was disappointing. Twenty-seven of the aircraft were ordered, but almost immediately they were relegated to home-defence duties. Seven aircraft, part of a later order, were sold to the Austro-Hungarian Air Force. A total of sixty Fokker D.VIs were supplied to the Army.

A number of 'V' models appeared during the year including the V.17, which was the first monoplane of the V series. The majority of the components cane from the now-defunct Dr.I. The wings were fitted mid-fuselage, which gave a poor downward/forward visibility. This was followed by the V.18, which was a biplane powered by a 160-hp Mercedes D.III engine. After a number of tests it was destroyed in an aerial collision with the V.13 during trials at Aldershof. There followed the V.20, V.21 and V.22, the latter becoming the production model D.VII. This was one of the most important German fighter aircraft of the war: over 1,000 were built and at least 800 of these were in operational use. It was one of those aircraft that lent itself to being open to variations and a large number were made, both experimental and production.

The V models continued to appear, the V.23, 24 25 26 and 27, all of which contributed to the development of the production aircraft. The V.26 went into production as the E.V model, which was later re-designated the Fokker D.VIII. By 1 November, eighty-five D.VIIIs were operational on the Western Front and a further twenty-five in service with the naval coast-defence units.

The remaining V series of aircraft, V.28, 29, 30, 31, 33, 34, 36 and 37, never went into production and were just experimental versions. The Fokker aircraft company was one of the most prolific of manufacturers of the First World War and left an indelible mark on the world of aviation.

As the end of the war appeared in sight, Anthony Fokker had a V.38 readied for his escape if it became necessary and kept under guard in a hangar. Unfortunately for Fokker, a number of the workers discovered this and they took it upon themselves to guard the aircraft, making sure that Fokker was not going to escape in it. Fokker was forced to flee to Berlin by train and in disguise. He paid a number of communist deserters to act as his bodyguard during the journey. After the Armistice, Anthony Fokker smuggled sixty of the V.38s and himself back to Holland.

## SPECIFICATIONS

### Fokker 'Spider'

| | |
|---|---|
| Wing Span: | 36 ft 0 in (11.0 m) |
| Length: | 25 ft 5 in (7.7 m) |
| Height: | 4 ft 3 in (1.3 m) |
| Weight Empty: | Unknown |
| Weight Loaded: | Unknown |
| Engine: | One 50-hp Argus |
| Maximum Speed: | Unknown |
| Endurance: | Unknown |
| Armament: | None |

### Fokker M.I

| | |
|---|---|
| Wing Span: | 43 ft 3 in (13.20 m) |
| Length: | 28 ft 2 in (8.60 m) |
| Height: | 9 ft 10 in (3.00 m) |
| Weight Empty: | Unknown |
| Weight Loaded: | Unknown |
| Engine: | One 95-hp Mercedes |
| Maximum Speed: | Unknown |
| Endurance: | Unknown |
| Armament: | None |

### Fokker M.2

| | |
|---|---|
| Wing Span: | 43 ft 3 in (13.2 m) |
| Length: | 27 ft 10 in (8.5 m) |
| Height: | 9 ft 10 in (3.0 m) |
| Weight Empty: | Unknown |
| Weight Loaded: | Unknown |
| Engine: | One 100-hp Mercedes |
| Maximum Speed: | 62 mph (100 km/h) |
| Endurance: | Unknown |
| Armament: | None |

## Fokker M.3/3a

| | |
|---|---|
| Wing Span: | 43 ft 3 in (13.2 m) |
| Length: | 27 ft 10 in (8.5 m) |
| Height: | 9 ft 10 in (3.0 m) |
| Weight Empty: | Unknown |
| Weight Loaded: | Unknown |
| Engine: | One 95-hp Mercedes (M.3) |
| | One 70-hp Renault (M.3a) |
| Maximum Speed: | 62 mph (100 km/h) |
| Endurance: | Unknown |
| Armament: | None |

## Fokker M.5L

| | |
|---|---|
| Wing Span: | 36 ft 1 in (11.0 m) |
| Length: | 22 ft 6 in (6.9 m) |
| Height: | 9 ft 10 in (3.0 m) |
| Weight Empty: | 770 lb (349 kg) |
| Weight Loaded: | 1,199 lb (544 kg) |
| Engine: | One 80-hp Oberursel U.O rotary |
| Maximum Speed: | 76 mph (122 km/h) |
| Service Ceiling: | 9,800 feet (3,000 m) |
| Endurance: | 1 hour |
| Armament: | None |

## Fokker M.6 (Prototype)

This had the same specifications as the M.5L, the only difference being the wing had been raised level with the top of the fuselage.

## Fokker M.7

| | |
|---|---|
| Wing Span Upper: | 38 ft 4½ in (11.7 m) |
| Wing Span Lower: | 23 ft 7½ in (7.2 m) |
| Length: | 26 ft 3 in (8.0 m) |
| Height: | 9 ft 8 in (2.9 m) |
| Weight Empty: | 838 lb (380 kg) |
| Weight Loaded: | 1,497 lb (679 kg) |
| Engine: | One 80-hp Oberursel U.O rotary |
| Maximum Speed: | 81 mph (130 km/h) |
| Service Ceiling: | 9,800 feet (3,000 m) |
| Endurance: | 1 hour |
| Armament: | None |

## Fokker M.8

Production model of the Fokker M.6

## Fokker M.9

This was a twin-fuselaged, twin-engined biplane that carried a crew of three. Only one was built. No specifications available.

## Fokker M.10

| | |
|---|---|
| Wing Span: | 37 ft 1 in (11.30 m) |
| Length: | 24 ft 7 in (7.50 m) |
| Height: | 8 ft 2 in (2.50 m) |
| Weight Empty: | 900 lb (409 kg) |
| Weight Loaded: | 1,570 lb (712 kg) |
| Engine: | One 80-hp Oberursel |
| Maximum Speed: | 81 mph (130 km/h) |
| Service Ceiling: | 9,800 ft (3,000 m) |
| Endurance: | Unknown |
| Armament: | None |

## Fokker M.10E

| | |
|---|---|
| Wing Span: | 37 ft 1 in (11.3 m) |
| Length: | 24 ft 7 in (7.5 m) |
| Height: | 8 ft 2 in (2.5 m) |
| Weight Empty: | 900 lb (409 kg) |
| Weight Loaded: | 1,570 lb (712 kg) |
| Engine: | One 80-hp Oberursel U.O rotary |
| Maximum Speed: | 81 mph (130 km/h) |
| Service Ceiling: | 9,800 ft (3,000 m) |
| Endurance: | 1 hour |
| Armament: | None |

## Fokker M.10Z

The 'Z', meaning *Zweistielig*, alluded to the aircraft being a two-bay model.

## Fokker M.16

| | |
|---|---|
| Wing Span: | 23 ft 7 in (7.20 m) |
| Length: | 20 ft 4 in (6.20 m) |
| Height: | 8 ft 11 in (2.71 m) |
| Weight Empty: | 604 lb (274 kg) |
| Weight Loaded: | 1,060 lb (481 kg) |
| Engine: | One 160-hp Mercedes |
| Maximum Speed: | 81 mph (130 km/h) |
| Endurance: | Unknown |
| Armament: | One Bergmann LMG 15nA machine gun |

## Fokker M.17

| | |
|---|---|
| Wing Span: | 28 ft 8 in (8.7 m) |
| Length: | 21 ft 0 in (6.4 m) |
| Height: | 9 ft 0 in (2.7 m) |
| Weight Empty: | 942 lb (427 kg) |
| Weight Loaded: | 1,398 lb (634 kg) |
| Engine: | One 100-hp Oberursel U.O |
| Maximum Speed: | 90 mph (145 km/h) |
| Endurance: | Unknown |

Armament:                One Schwarzlose machine gun synchronised to
                         fire through the propeller arc

## Fokker M.18

Wing Span:               29 ft 8 in (9.05 m)
Length:                  18 ft 8 in (5.70 m)
Height:                  8 ft 10 in (2.69 m)
Weight Empty:            975 lb (442 kg)
Weight Loaded:           1,540 lb (700 kg)
Engine:                  One 100-hp Mercedes D.I
Maximum Speed:           93 mph (150 km/h)
Endurance:               Unknown
Armament:                One Schwarzlose machine gun mounted on
                         the upper wing

## Fokker D.I

Wing Span:               29 ft 8 in (9.05 m)
Length:                  20 ft 8 in (6.30 m)
Height:                  8 ft 1 in (2.47 m)
Weight Empty:            1,020 lb (463 kg)
Weight Loaded:           1,480 lb (671 kg)
Engine:                  One 120-hp Mercedes D.II
Maximum Speed:           93 mph (150 km/h)
Endurance:               1½ hours. Later reduced to 1 hour
Armament:                One fixed forward-firing Spandau machine gun
                         synchronised to fire through the propeller

## Fokker D.II

Wing Span:               28 ft 8½ in (8.7 m)
Length:                  21 ft 0 in (6.4 m)
Height:                  8 ft 4½ in (2.2 m)
Weight Empty:            845 lb (384 kg)
Weight Loaded:           1,267 lb (576 kg)
Engine:                  One 100-hp Oberursel U.I rotary
Maximum Speed:           93 mph (150 km/h)
Endurance:               1½ hours. Later reduced to 1 hour
Armament:                One fixed forward-firing Spandau machine gun
                         synchronised to fire through the propeller

## Fokker D.III

Wing Span:               29 ft 8 in (9.05 m)
Length:                  20 ft 8 in (6.30 m)
Height:                  7 ft 5 in (2.25 m)
Weight Empty:            997 lb (452 kg)
Weight Loaded:           1,570 lb (710 kg)
Engine:                  One 160-hp Oberursel UR.III six-cylinder,
                         in-line, water-cooled
Maximum Speed:           100 mph (160 km/h)
Endurance:               1½ hours. Later reduced to 1 hour

Armament:                       Twin fixed forward-firing Spandau machine guns
                                synchronised to fire through the propeller

## Fokker D.IV

Wing Span:                      31 ft 10 in (9.7 m)
Length:                         20 ft 8 in (6.30 m)
Height:                         8 ft 1 in (2.47 m)
Weight Empty:                   1,340 lb (606 kg)
Weight Loaded:                  1,850 lb (841 kg)
Engine:                         One 160-hp Mercedes D.III six-cylinder,
                                in-line, water-cooled
Maximum Speed:                  100 mph (160 km/h)
Endurance:                      1½ hours
Armament:                       Twin fixed forward-firing Spandau machine guns
                                synchronised to fire through the propeller

## Fokker D.V

Wing Span:                      28 ft 8 in (8.75 m)
Length:                         19 ft 10 in (6.05 m)
Height:                         7 ft 6 in (2.30 m)
Weight Empty:                   800 lb (363 kg)
Weight Loaded:                  1,250 lb (566 kg)
Engine:                         One 100-hp Oberursel UR.I six-cylinder,
                                in-line, water-cooled
Maximum Speed:                  106 mph (170 km/h)
Endurance:                      1½ hours
Armament:                       One fixed forward-firing Spandau machine gun
                                synchronised to fire through the propeller

## Fokker D.VI

Wing Span:                      25 ft 1¼ in (7.6 m)
Length:                         20 ft 5½ in (6.2 m)
Height:                         8 ft 4½ in (2.5 m)
Weight Empty:                   865 lb (393 kg)
Weight Loaded:                  1,283 lb (583 kg)
Engine:                         One 110-hp Oberursel U.II 9-cylinder, rotary
Maximum Speed:                  122 mph (196 km/h)
Endurance:                      1½ hours
Armament:                       Two fixed forward-firing Spandau machine guns
                                synchronised to fire through the propeller

## Fokker D.VII

Wing Span:                      28 ft 6 in (8.70 m)
Length:                         22 ft 9 in (6.95 m)
Height:                         9 ft 8 in (2.95 m)
Weight Empty:                   1,540 lb (700 kg)
Weight Loaded:                  1,870 lb (850 kg)
Engine:                         One 160-hp Mercedes D.III six-cylinder,
                                in-line, water-cooled

| | |
|---|---|
| Maximum Speed: | 116 mph (186 km/h) |
| Endurance: | 2 hours |
| Armament: | Twin fixed forward-firing Spandau machine guns synchronised to fire through the propeller |

## Fokker E.V/D.VIII

| | |
|---|---|
| Wing Span: | 27 ft 4 in (8.34 m) |
| Length: | 19 ft 3 in (5.87 m) |
| Height: | 9 ft 3 in (2.82 m) |
| Weight Empty: | 890 lb (405 kg) |
| Weight Loaded: | 1,330 lb (605 kg) |
| Engine: | One 110-hp Oberursel UR.II six-cylinder, in-line, water-cooled |
| Maximum Speed: | 124 mph (200 km/h) |
| Service Ceiling: | 22,900 feet |
| Endurance: | 1 hour |
| Armament: | Twin fixed forward-firing Spandau machine guns synchronised to fire through the propeller |

## Fokker V.1

| | |
|---|---|
| Wing Span Upper: | 26 ft 5 in (8.0 m) |
| Wing Span Lower: | 21 ft 6 in (6.5 m) |
| Length: | 16 ft 5 in (5.0 m) |
| Height: | 9 ft 6 in (2.9 m) |
| Weight Empty: | Not known |
| Weight Loaded: | Not known |
| Engine: | One 100-hp Oberursel U.I six-cylinder, in-line, water-cooled |
| Maximum Speed: | 112 mph (180 km/h) |
| Service Ceiling: | 9,800 ft (3,000 m) |
| Endurance: | 1 hour |
| Armament: | None |

## Fokker V.2 and V.3

| | |
|---|---|
| Wing Span: | 26 ft 5 in (8.0 m) |
| Length: | 16 ft 5 in (5.0 m) |
| Height: | 9 ft 6 in (2.9 m) |
| Weight Empty: | Not known |
| Weight Loaded: | Not known |
| Engine: | One 160-hp Mercedes D.III |
| Maximum Speed: | 112 mph (180 km/h) |
| Service Ceiling: | 9,800 feet (3,000 m) |
| Endurance: | 1 hour |
| Armament: | None |

## Fokker V.4/Dr.1 Triplane

| | |
|---|---|
| Wing Span upper: | 23 ft 7 in (7.19 m) |
| Wing Span Middle: | 23 ft 7 in (7.19 m) |
| Wing Span Lower: | 23 ft 7 in (7.19 m) |

| | |
|---|---|
| Length: | 18 ft 11 in (5.77 m) |
| Height: | 9 ft 8 in (2.95 m) |
| Weight Empty: | 895 lb (406 kg) |
| Weight Loaded: | 1,290 lb (586 kg) |
| Engine: | One 110-hp Oberursel UR.II of Thulin-built Le Rhône 9-cylinder rotary |
| Maximum Speed: | 115 mph (185 km/h) |
| Service Ceiling: | 20,000 feet |
| Endurance: | 1½ hours. Later reduced to 1 hour |
| Armament: | Twin fixed forward-firing Spandau machine guns synchronised to fire through the propeller |

## Fokker V.5

| | |
|---|---|
| Wing Span: | 23 ft 7 in (7.19 m) – all three wings |
| Length: | 21 ft 0 in (6.4 m) |
| Height: | 9 ft 8 in (2.95 m) |
| Weight Empty: | 968 lb (440 kg) |
| Weight Loaded: | 1,397 lb (635 kg) |
| Engine: | One 160-hp Goebel Goe.III |
| Maximum Speed: | 115 mph (185 km/h) |
| Service Ceiling: | 20,000 feet |
| Endurance: | 1½ hours. Later reduced to 1 hour |
| Armament: | Twin fixed forward-firing Spandau machine guns synchronised to fire through the propeller |

## Fokker V.6

| | |
|---|---|
| Wing Span Upper: | 23 ft 7 in (7.19 m) |
| Wing Span Middle: | 21 ft 7 in (6.4 m) |
| Wing Span Lower: | 20 ft 0 in (6.0 m) |
| Length: | 23 ft 0 in (7.0 m) |
| Height: | 9 ft 8 in (2.95 m) |
| Weight Empty: | 968 lb (440 kg) |
| Weight Loaded: | 1,397 lb (635 kg) |
| Engine: | One 160-hp Mercedes D.III |
| Maximum Speed: | 115 mph (185 km/h) |
| Service Ceiling: | 20,000 feet |
| Endurance: | 1½ hours. Later reduced to 1 hour |
| Armament: | Twin fixed forward-firing Spandau machine guns synchronised to fire through the propeller |

## Fokker V.7

| | |
|---|---|
| Wing Span Upper: | 23 ft 7 in (7.19 m) |
| Wing Span Middle: | 23 ft 7 in (7.19 m) |
| Wing Span Lower: | 23 ft 7 in (7.19 m) |
| Length: | 23 ft 0 in (7.0 m) |
| Height: | 9 ft 8 in (2.95 m) |
| Weight Empty: | 1,080 lb (491 kg) |
| Weight Loaded: | 1,509 lb (686 kg) |
| Engine: | One 160-hp Siemens-Halske Sh.III |
| Maximum Speed: | 115 mph (185 km/h) |

| | |
|---|---|
| Service Ceiling: | 20,000 feet |
| Endurance: | 1½ hours. Later reduced to 1 hour |
| Armament: | Twin fixed forward-firing Spandau machine-guns synchronised to fire through the propeller |

## Fokker V.8

| | |
|---|---|
| Wing Span Upper: | 23 ft 7 in (7.19 m) |
| Wing Span Middle: | 23 ft 7 in (7.19 m) |
| Wing Span Lower: | 23 ft 7 in (7.19 m) |
| Wing Span Upper Fuselage: | 23 ft 7 in (7.19 m) |
| Wing Span Lower Fuselage: | 23 ft 7 in (7.19 m) |
| Length: | 23 ft 0 in (7.0 m) |
| Height: | 9 ft 8 in (2.95 m) |
| Weight Empty: | 968 lb (440 kg) |
| Weight Loaded: | 1,397 lb (635 kg) |
| Engine: | One 160-hp Mercedes D.III |
| Maximum Speed: | 115 mph (185 km/h) |
| Service Ceiling: | 20,000 feet (6,100 m) |
| Endurance: | 1½ hours. Later reduced to 1 hour |
| Armament: | None |

## Fokker V.9

| | |
|---|---|
| Wing Span Upper: | 25 ft 3¼ in (7.7 m) |
| Wing Span Lower: | 25 ft 3¼ in (7.7 m) |
| Length: | 19 ft 4½ in (5.9 m) |
| Height: | 9 ft 8 in (2.95 m) |
| Weight Empty: | 968 lb (440 kg) |
| Weight Loaded: | 1,276 lb (580 kg) |
| Engine: | One 110-hp Oberursel U.II |
| Maximum Speed: | 115 mph (185 km/h) |
| Service Ceiling: | 20,000 ft (6,100 m) |
| Endurance: | 1½ hours. Later reduced to 1 hour |
| Armament: | None |

## Fokker V.10

| | |
|---|---|
| Wing Span Upper: | 25 ft 3¼ in (7.7 m) |
| Wing Span Lower: | 25 ft 3¼ in (7.7 m) |
| Length: | 19 ft 4½ in (5.9 m) |
| Height: | 9 ft 8 in (2.95 m) |
| Weight Empty: | 968 lb (440 kg) |
| Weight Loaded: | 1,276 lb (580 kg) |
| Engine: | One 145-hp Oberursel U.III |
| Maximum Speed: | 115 mph (185 km/h) |
| Service Ceiling: | 31,160 ft (9,500 m) |
| Endurance: | 1½ hours. Later reduced to 1 hour |
| Armament: | None |

## Fokker V.11

| | |
|---|---|
| Wing Span Upper: | 25 ft 3¼ in (7.7 m) |
| Wing Span Lower: | 25 ft 3¼ in (7.7 m) |
| Length: | 19 ft 4½ in (5.9 m) |
| Height: | 9 ft 8 in (2.95 m) |
| Weight Empty: | 968 lb (440 kg) |
| Weight Loaded: | 1,857 lb (844 kg) |
| Engine: | One 160-hp Mercedes D.III |
| Maximum Speed: | 115 mph (185 km/h) |
| Service Ceiling: | 20,000 ft (6,100 m) |
| Endurance: | 1½ hours. Later reduced to 1 hour |
| Armament: | None |

## Fokker V.13

| | |
|---|---|
| Wing Span Upper: | 25 ft 3¼ in (7.7 m) |
| Wing Span Lower: | 22 ft 0 in (6.7 m) |
| Length: | 19 ft 4½ in (5.9 m) |
| Height: | 9 ft 8 in (2.95 m) |
| Weight Empty: | 968 lb (440 kg) |
| Weight Loaded: | 1,470 lb (668 kg) |
| Engine: | One 145-hp Oberursel U.III |
| | One 160-hp Siemens-Halske Sh.III |
| Maximum Speed: | 115 mph (185 km/h) |
| Service Ceiling: | 20,000 ft (6,100 m) |
| Endurance: | 1½ hours. Later reduced to 1 hour |
| Armament: | None |

## Fokker V.14, V.15 and V.16

Never built

## Fokker V.17

| | |
|---|---|
| Wing Span: | 23 ft 7 in (7.19 m) |
| Length: | 18 ft 11 in (5.77 m) |
| Height: | 9 ft 8 in (2.95 m) |
| Weight Empty: | 895 lb (406 kg) |
| Weight Loaded: | 1,290 lb (586 kg) |
| Engine: | One 110-hp Oberursel U.II |
| Maximum Speed: | 115 mph (185 km/h) |
| Service Ceiling: | 20,000 feet |
| Endurance: | 1½ hours. Later reduced to 1 hour |
| Armament: | None |

## Fokker V.18

| | |
|---|---|
| Wing Span Upper: | 28 ft 6 in (8.7 m) |
| Wing Span Lower: | 28 ft 6 in (8.7 m) |
| Length: | 22 ft 9 in (6.9 m) |
| Height: | 9 ft 8 in (2.9 m) |
| Weight Empty: | 1,540 lb (700 kg) |

| | |
|---|---|
| Weight Loaded: | 1,896 lb (861 kg) |
| Engine: | One 160-hp Mercedes D.III six-cylinder, in-line, water-cooled |
| Maximum Speed: | 116 mph (186 km/h) |
| Service Ceiling: | 20,990 ft (6,400 m) |
| Endurance: | 2 hours |
| Armament: | None |

## Fokker V.19

Not built.

## Fokker V.20

No details available except that it was powered by a 160-hp Mercedes D.III engine.

## Fokker V.21

No details available

## Fokker V 22

| | |
|---|---|
| Wing Span Upper: | 28 ft 2½ in (8.9 m) |
| Wing Span Lower: | 28 ft 2½ in (8.9 m) |
| Length: | 22 ft 11½ in (7.0 m) |
| Height: | 9 ft 0¼ in (2.75 m) |
| Weight Empty: | 1,540 lb (700 kg) |
| Weight Loaded: | 1,870 lb (850 kg) |
| Engine: | One 160-hp Mercedes D.III six-cylinder, in-line, water-cooled |
| Maximum Speed: | 116 mph (186 km/h) |
| Service Ceiling: | 20,990 ft (6,400 m) |
| Endurance: | 1½ hours |
| Armament: | Two fixed forward-firing Spandau machine guns |

## Fokker V.23

| | |
|---|---|
| Wing Span: | 27 ft 4 in (8.3 m) |
| Length: | 18 ft 11 in (5.7 m) |
| Height: | 9 ft 8 in (2.9 m) |
| Weight Empty: | 895 lb (406 kg) |
| Weight Loaded: | 1,866 lb (848 kg) |
| Engine: | One 160-hp Mercedes D.III |
| Maximum Speed: | 115 mph (185 km/h) |
| Service Ceiling: | 16,400 ft (5,000 m) |
| Endurance: | 1½ hours. Later reduced to 1 hour |
| Armament: | None |

## Fokker V.24

| | |
|---|---|
| Wing Span Upper: | 28 ft 2½ in (8.9 m) |
| Wing Span Lower: | 27 ft 4 in (8.3 m) |

| Length: | 22 ft 11½ in (7.0 m) |
| Height: | 9 ft 0¼ in (2.7 m) |
| Weight Empty: | 1,540 lb (700 kg) |
| Weight Loaded: | 2,213 lb (1,006 kg) |
| Engine: | One 200-hp Benz |
| Maximum Speed: | 115 mph (185 km/h) |
| Service Ceiling: | 16,400 ft (5,000 m) |
| Endurance: | 1½ hours. Later reduced to 1 hour |
| Armament: | None |

## Fokker V.25

No details available

## Fokker V.26/EV

| Wing Span: | 27 ft 4½ in (8.3 m) |
| Length: | 19 ft 3 in (5.8 m) |
| Height: | 9 ft 0¼ in (2.7 m) |
| Weight Empty: | 891 lb (405 kg) |
| Weight Loaded: | 1,241 lbs (605 kg) |
| Engine: | One 110-hp Oberursel U.II |
| Maximum Speed: | 127 mph (204 km/h) |
| Service Ceiling: | 16,400 ft (5,000 m) |
| Endurance: | 1½ hours |
| Armament: | Two fixed forward-firing synchronised Spandau machine guns |

## Fokker V.27

Specifications the same as the V.26 with the exception of the engine, which was a 195-hp V-8 Benz IIIb.

## Fokker V.28

The same specifications as the V.26. This model was used to test a variety of engines for the third of the D-type competitions.

## Fokker V.29

| Wing Span: | 31 ft 4½ in (9.5 m) |
| Length: | 22 ft 6 in (6.8 m) |
| Height: | 9 ft 0¼ in (2.7 m) |
| Weight Empty: | 891 lb (405 kg) |
| Weight Loaded: | 1,241 lb (605 kg) |
| Engine: | One 160-hp Mercedes D.III |
| Maximum Speed: | 127 mph (204 km/h) |
| Service Ceiling: | 16,400 ft (5,000 m) |
| Endurance: | 1½ hours |
| Armament: | Two fixed forward-firing synchronised Spandau machine guns |

## Fokker V.30

No details available

## Fokker V.31

No details available

## Fokker V.32

None built

## Fokker V.33

| | |
|---|---|
| Wing Span Upper: | 25 ft 3¼ in (7.7 m) |
| Wing Span Lower: | 21 ft 6 in (6.5 m) |
| Length: | 19 ft 4½ in (5.9 m) |
| Height: | 9 ft 8 in (2.95 m) |
| Weight Empty: | 968 lb (440 kg) |
| Weight Loaded: | 1,276 lb (580 kg) |
| Engine: | One 110-hp Oberursel U.II |
| Maximum Speed: | 115 mph (185 km/h) |
| Service Ceiling: | 20,000 ft (6,100 m) |
| Endurance: | 1½ hours. Later reduced to 1 hour |
| Armament: | None |

## Fokker V.34

| | |
|---|---|
| Wing Span Upper: | 28 ft 6 in (8.7 m) |
| Wing Span Lower: | 28 ft 6 in (8.7 m) |
| Length: | 22 ft 9 in (6.9 m) |
| Height: | 9 ft 8 in (2.9 m) |
| Weight Empty: | 1,540 lb (700 kg) |
| Weight Loaded: | 1,870 lb (850 kg) |
| Engine: | One 185-hp BMW IIIa |
| Maximum Speed: | 116 mph (186 km/h) |
| Endurance: | 2 hours |
| Armament: | Twin fixed forward-firing Spandau machine guns synchronised to fire through the propeller |

## Fokker V.35

None built

## Fokker V.36

| | |
|---|---|
| Wing Span Upper: | 28 ft 4 in (8.9 m) |
| Wing Span Lower: | 25 ft 6 in (7.7 m) |
| Length: | 21 ft 2½ in (6.5 m) |
| Height: | 9 ft 9½ in (3.0 m) |
| Weight Empty: | 1,401 lb (637 kg) |
| Weight Loaded: | 1,916 lb (871 kg) |
| Engine: | One 185-hp BMW IIIa |

| | |
|---|---|
| Maximum Speed: | 116 mph (186 km/h) |
| Service ceiling: | 19,680 ft (6,000 m) |
| Endurance: | 2 hours |
| Armament: | Twin fixed forward-firing Spandau machine guns synchronised to fire through the propeller |

## Fokker V.37

No details available, but believed to be based on the V.28 and powered by a 195-hp Benx IIIb engine.

## Fokker V.38

| | |
|---|---|
| Wing Span Upper: | 34 ft 8 in (10.6 m) |
| Wing Span Lower: | 34 ft 8 in (10.6 m) |
| Length: | 22 ft 9 in (6.95 m) |
| Height: | 9 ft 8 in (2.95 m) |
| Weight Empty: | 1,540 lb (700 kg) |
| Weight Loaded: | 1,870 lb (850 kg) |
| Engine: | One 160-hp Mercedes D.III six-cylinder, in-line, water-cooled |
| Maximum Speed: | 108 mph (175 km/h) |
| Endurance: | 2 hours |
| Armament: | Twin fixed forward-firing Spandau machine guns synchronised to fire through the propeller |

## Fokker E. III

| | |
|---|---|
| Wing Span: | 31 ft 2 in (9.5 m) |
| Length: | 23 ft 11 in (7.3 m) |
| Height: | 8 ft 2 in (2.49 m) |
| Weight Empty: | 770 lb (349 kg) |
| Weight Loaded: | 1,330 lb (604 kg) |
| Engine: | One 100\-hp Oberursel UR.I rotary |
| Maximum Speed: | 93 mph (150 km/h) |
| Service Ceiling: | 9,800 feet (3,000 m) |
| Endurance: | 1 hour |
| Armament: | One fixed forward-firing Spandau machine gun synchronised to fire through the propeller |

Close-up of the cockpit of an early Albatros.

Captured Albatros C.V.

Albatros C.VII.

Vzfw Reisch in his Albatros D.Va.

Albatros D.I taking off.

Albatros D.III of Jasta 30.

Leutnant Sachsenberg taking off in his Albatros D.III.

Leutnant von Tutschel leaning on an Albatros D.III.

Korporal August Schmid in his Albatros D.III.

Offizierstelvertreter Josef Kiss with his Albatros D.III.

Leutnant Julius Buckler standing in front of his Albatros.

Vzfw Martin Klein with his Albatros D.Va.

Early Aviatik monoplane outside the factory in 1911.

Oberleutnant Fritz Pisko with his Aviatik D.I after wing failure.

Forward section of an Aviatik D.I.

Aviatik D.I.

Frank Linke-Crawford's Aviatik D.I, in which he was later killed.

DFW Mars biplane under construction.

DFW Mars biplane in front of the factory.

Prince Heinrich of Prussia (centre) and August Euler (second from right) at the Euler Flying
School.

Alfons von Zeddelmann in his Euler B.

Baroness Leitner's crash in her Fokker Spin (Spider).

Fokker B.I of Flik 8.

Fokker D.II of the Austro-Hungarian Air Force.

Fokker D.III.

Fokker D.V.

Fokker D.VIIs of Jasta 40. The last two aircraft are an Albatros D.Va and a Pfalz D.IIIa.

Ground crew of Jasta 26 helping to dress pilots.

Fokker Dr.I triplane belonging to Leutnant Vallendor of Jasta B.

Fokker Dr.I triplane with 1914 crosses.

Leutnant Steinhäuser swinging the propeller of a Fokker triplane to start the engine.

Fokker Eindecker being started.

Fokker M.1.

Fokker M.9.

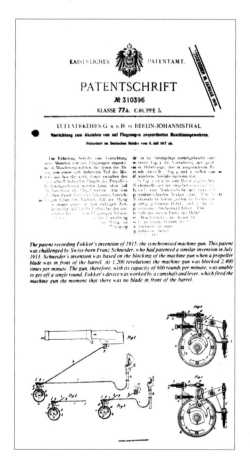

Anthony Fokker's patent for the synchronised machine gun.

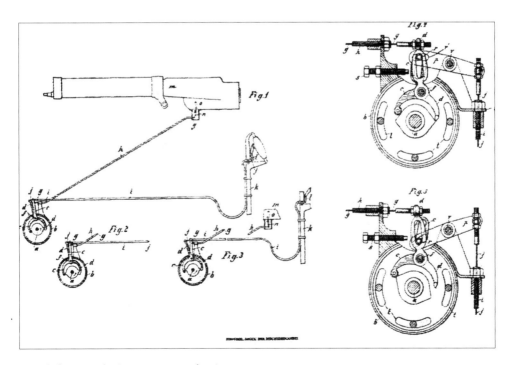

Detail showing the interrupter mechanism.

# Gothaer Waggonfabrik AG Gotha

One of the most famous German aircraft of the First World War was the twin-engined Gotha bomber built by the Gothaer Waggonfabrik Company. The origins of the company went way back before the war, when one of the first aircraft they built was of Taube (Dove) design and given the designation LE.3. Originally built for the civilian market, a number of these aircraft saw service as scouts at the beginning of the First World War after being requisitioned by the German Army. Powered by a 100-hp Mercedes D.I engine, the LE.3 had a wingspan of 47 ft 7 in, a fuselage length of 32 ft 9½ in, a top speed of 60 mph and a climb rate of 2,000 feet per minute. Only a small number of these aircraft were built.

Another of Gotha's aircraft that saw service at the beginning of the war was the LD.1a, which was developed from the civilian version, the LD.1. Manufactured specifically as an unarmed scouting and reconnaissance aircraft, the LD.1a was powered by a 100-hp Oberursel U.I engine, giving the aircraft a top speed of 71 mph. The aircraft had a wingspan of 47 ft 7 in, and a fuselage length of 24 ft 4 in. An unknown number were built.

Gotha also introduced a seaplane version of the reconnaissance aircraft, the WD.1. It was fitted with twin floats, with a small single float mounted under the tail section. Powered by a 100-hp Gnôme engine, the WD.1 had a wingspan of 46 ft 3½ in, a fuselage length of 33 ft 9½ in, a top speed of 61 mph and a maximum operating ceiling of 8,200 feet. Five WD.1s were supplied to the German Navy.

The development of the Gotha LD.2 in August 1914 brought another unarmed reconnaissance aircraft to the Gotha stable. Although similar in design and with almost the same specifications, it was powered by a 100-hp Mercedes engine with the radiators fixed either side of the fuselage, just in front of the cockpit. A small number were built and were used for a very short time at the Front, before being replaced by an improved model, the LD.6a. Just prior to the appearance of the LD.6a, Gotha produced a diminutive scout aircraft, the Gotha LD.5, which was almost half the size of the other models. Powered by a 100-hp Oberursel U.I engine, the aircraft was intended to be a fast reconnaissance model, but after testing it was realised that there were a number of stability problems and it was not a practical or viable proposition. Only one was built.

The LD.6a, on the other hand, was a standard size, long-distance reconnaissance aircraft, capable of carrying a small bomb load. It had balanced tail surfaces and was of the traditional wood and fabric construction. It was powered by a 150-hp Benz Bz.III engine that had the radiators mounted either side of the fuselage in front of the observer's cockpit. The LD.6a had a wingspan of 40 ft 8½ in, a fuselage length of 27 ft 7 in and a top speed of 78 mph.

At the beginning of March 1915, the last of the LD series was produced, the Gotha LD.7. Like all the previous LD models, this too was designed specifically for reconnaissance duties. Its specifications were almost identical to that of the LD.6a, with the exception of the engine, which was a 120-hp Mercedes D.II. An unknown number were produced, but it is thought that they numbered less than twenty.

A second seaplane version appeared during 1915, the Gotha WD.2. It was very similar in design to the LD.6a, and eleven of them were supplied to the Navy. The WD.2 was fitted with a 150-hp Benz Bz.III engine, which gave the aircraft a top speed of 70 mph and an operating ceiling of 9,840 feet. It had a wingspan of 51 ft 2½ in, a length of 34 ft 5½ in and carried no armament.

One version of the WD.2, however, was sent to Turkey, and was one of the first reconnaissance aircraft to be fitted with a machine gun, which was mounted on top of the centre section. To operate the gun, the observer had to stand up in his cockpit. A limited number were sent.

A radical new design, the Gotha WD.3, appeared in July 1915. It was a twin-boomed aircraft with a central nacelle that housed not only the 160-hp Mercedes D.III engine with a pusher airscrew, but also contained cockpits for the pilot and observer. The observer's position was in the extreme front of the nacelle and was fitted with a manually operated Parabellum machine gun. The WD.3 was also one of the first seaplanes to have a radio transmitter installed. With a wingspan of 51 ft 2½ in and a wing area of 583 square feet, the aircraft presented an unusual sight. A number of problems were discovered during tests and only one was built.

Another experimental seaplane was built at around the same time, the Gotha WD.5. This model was not a new variation, but a modified WD.2. The 150-hp Benz III engine was replaced with a 160-hp Mercedes engine that had the two narrow strip radiators attached to the front centre-section struts. This model was sent to the Haltenau Naval Air Station for tests, but was declined as a reconnaissance aircraft. The Commanding Officer, Kapitänleutnant Langfield, decided that he would keep the aircraft and use it as his personal transport.

A unique design by Oskar Ursinus was developed by Gotha at the beginning of 1915, the Gotha Ursinus GUH G.I. This was a landplane forerunner of what was to be a seaplane the following year. The design was unique, inasmuch as the fuselage was raised above both wings and engines. The aircraft carried a crew of three: pilot, observer and gunner. The gunner's position in the nose of the aircraft gave him an uninterrupted field of fire. The engines, two 150-hp Benz Bz.IIIs, were mounted so close together that the tips of the propellers were almost touching. The idea was that, should there be an engine failure on one of the engines during asymmetric flight, control of the aircraft could be maintained easily. Several of the land version models were built, but information on them is almost non-existent.

At the end of 1915, a twin-engined torpedo seaplane was built and designated the Gotha WD.7. Powered by two 120-hp Mercedes D.II engines, the WD.7 had a wingspan of 52 ft 6 in, a fuselage length of 37 ft 1 in, and a height of 11 ft 9½ in. It had a top speed of 85 mph and an operating ceiling of 13,120 feet. Eight of the aircraft were built and assigned to flying schools for training pilots and observers prior to their moving on to larger operational aircraft.

Another aircraft appeared at the same time, the Gotha WD.8. This, in reality, was a single-engined version of the WD.7, and was fitted with a 250-hp Maybach Mb.IV engine which gave the aircraft a top speed of 81 mph and an operating ceiling of 14,760 feet. It had been designed as an armed reconnaissance aircraft and was fitted with a manually operated Parabellum machine gun in the observer's rear cockpit. Only one was built.

In February 1916, Gotha constructed another armed reconnaissance seaplane, the Gotha WD.9. Only one of these aircraft was supplied to the German Navy and that was fitted with a 160-hp Mercedes D.III engine. A similar version, fitted with a 150-hp Benz engine, was supplied to the Turkish Government. The aircraft had a wingspan of 49 ft 2½ in, a fuselage length of 32 ft 2 in, a height of 12 ft 5½ in and a top speed of 85 mph. Both aircraft carried a manually operated Parabellum machine gun in the observer's rear cockpit.

With the relative success of the WD.7 model, Gotha produced another twin-engined torpedo-carrying reconnaissance aircraft, the Gotha WD.11. This model was considerably bigger and had a wingspan of 73 ft 10½ in, a fuselage length of 44 ft 1 in and a height of 15 ft 2 in. It was powered by two 160-hp Mercedes D.III engines, which drove two pusher airscrews and gave a top speed of 75 mph with a climb rate of nearly 300 feet per minute. The WD.11 carried one torpedo and had a manually operated Parabellum machine gun mounted in the observer's cockpit in the nose. Thirteen of these models were delivered to the German Navy.

Gotha continued to build seaplanes, and in 1916 produced the WD.12. This was an unarmed reconnaissance aircraft powered by a 160-hp Mercedes D.III engine, with a fuselage length of 32 ft 9½ in, a top speed of 88 mph and a flight endurance of 5½ hours. Only one WD.12 was supplied to the German Navy, although six were supplied to Turkey.

The seaplane version of the Gotha Ursinus GUH, the UWD appeared in 1916. It was almost identical, except that it was powered by two 160-hp Mercedes D.III engines and the undercarriage was replaced with floats. Only one of this model was built, and was not as successful as the land version.

The first of the prototype Gotha bombers appeared in 1916, the G.II and G.III. Both versions were identical externally and in specifications, the only difference being internal ones. They had a wingspan of 77 ft 9½ in, a fuselage length of 38 ft 8 in and a wing area of 967 square feet. They were powered by two 260-hp Mercedes D.IVa engines, which gave a top speed of 92.5 mph. Only a small number were built and flown on the Western Front, one unit being Boghol III based at Ghent, Belgium.

In September 1916 the first Gotha bomber appeared, the Gotha G.IV. Trials had earlier been carried out with the G.II and G.III, and the results that came back brought about the development of the bomber. There was one very unusual feature incorporated into the Gotha G.IV, known as the 'sting in the tail'. The rear gunner's position in the aircraft enabled him not only to fire upwards and backwards, but downwards as well. This was achieved by the gunner firing through a specially designed tunnel in the bottom of the fuselage. This defensive method was extremely effective, as a number of Allied fighter pilots were to find out to their cost.

The G.IV bomber arrived just as the German military hierarchy were about to phase out the use of Zeppelins for bombing raids. The Zeppelin had serious limitations. Because of their size they were easily spotted, they were slower and when hit with incendiary bullets invariably caught fire dramatically, unlike the Gotha G.IV.

In April 1917, thirty of the G.IV bombers were delivered to No. 3 Heavy Bomber Squadron, based at St Denis Westrem and Gontrode, which was under the command of Hauptmann Ernst Brandenburg. The first series of raids, carried out between 25 May and 22 August 1917, were relatively successful and the squadron suffered very few casualties. One of the reasons for their success was that the Gotha G.IV's Mercedes engines meant it was able to operate at a height of 15,000 feet. This allowed them to drop their bombs and, because of the inadequate British early warning system, be on their way back before Home Defence fighters could scramble and reach the Gotha's operating height.

The Gotha G.IV had a wingspan of 77 ft 9½ in, a fuselage length of 38 ft 11 in and a wing area of 966 square feet. Powered by two six-cylinder, in-line, water-cooled 260-hp Mercedes D.IVa engines, the G.IVa had a top speed of 87 mph with an operating ceiling of 21,320 feet and a range of 350 miles. Its armament consisted of two manually operated Parabellum machine guns mounted in the front and rear cockpits, and a bomb load that varied from 660 lb to 1,100 lb depending on the mission and whether it was a daylight or night time raid. The Gotha G.V, which followed shortly afterwards, was almost identical.

Another export model was the Gotha WD.13, an armed patrol seaplane which was an upgraded version of the WD.9. Although the German Navy carried out a series of trials with this aircraft, none were acquired; in 1917, however, the Turkish Government purchased over eight of the aircraft. Powered by a 150-hp Benz Bz.III engine, which gave the aircraft a top speed of 82 mph, it was armed with a manually operated Parabellum machine gun fitted in the observer's rear cockpit.

Of all the seaplanes designed by Gotha, only the WD.11 and the WD.14 were built with production numbers in mind. Thirteen WD.11 reconnaissance seaplanes were built, while sixty-nine models of the WD.14, which had been designed and developed as an attack torpedo aircraft, were produced. Developed from the WD.7 and WD.11 prototypes, the WD.14 had a wingspan of 83 ft 8 in, a fuselage length of 47 ft 4 in, and a height of 16 ft 5 in. It was powered by two 200-hp Benz Bz.IV engines which were mounted on the lower wings

The fuselage of the WD.14 consisted of a basic, rectangular braced box girder, made up of spruce longerons and spacers. The torpedo was slung beneath the fuselage and between the floats. The pilot's cockpit and the torpedo-man's cockpit were one and the same, and were situated under the wings. It was of a side-by-side configuration, with access available to the nose cockpit for the torpedo-man to enable him to aim and release the torpedo. Once the torpedo had been released, the torpedo-man's role reverted to that of gunner. There were two manually operated Parabellum machine guns mounted in the rear and nose cockpits.

Torpedo attacks using the WD.14 were carried out, but because the aircraft was substantially underpowered, the weight of the torpedo and the armament carried made it an extremely difficult aircraft to handle and only some of the top pilots were able to use it to its full capability. The attacks bore no fruit, and so the decision was made to use the aircraft for long-range reconnaissance missions over the North Sea in place of vulnerable airships. In place of the torpedo, jettisonable fuel tanks were fitted which enabled the aircraft to stay aloft for up to ten hours. Initially they were reasonably successful; then it was discovered that in the event of one of the engines failing, the WD.14 was unable to fly on one engine, and having to carry out emergency landings on rough seas proved disastrous. The aircraft were relegated to the role of minesweepers, but even at that they proved to be inadequate and ended up escorting coastal convoys.

Toward the end of 1917, another variation of an earlier model appeared, the Gotha WD.15. Derived from the WD.12, the WD.15 was an enlarged version with a plywood covered fuselage and fin. Only two of the aircraft were built, and both were powered by a 260-hp Mercedes D.IVa engine. The aircraft had a wingspan of 56 ft 5 in, a fuselage length of 36 ft 9 in, a top speed of 95 mph and an operating ceiling of 13,780 feet. These two WD.15s were the last single-engined aircraft that Gotha delivered to the German Navy.

The results acquired from using the Gotha WD.14 as a long range reconnaissance aircraft were put to use with the development of the Gotha WD.20. Only three of these aircraft were constructed and they were developed purely as long-range reconnaissance aircraft with additional fuel tanks in place of the torpedo carried by previous aircraft. The WD.20 had a wingspan of 73 ft 8½ in, a fuselage length of 47 ft 5 in, a top speed of 80 mph and a flight endurance of 10 hours. Its only armament were two manually operated Parabellum machine guns, one mounted in the nose, the other in the observer's cockpit just aft of the wings.

As the production of the G.V bomber series came to an end, a number of modified versions suddenly appeared. The G.Vb was a modified version of the G.Va, and was fitted with additional wheels on the undercarriage and a compound tail assembly. It was powered by two 260-hp Mercedes D.IVa engines that drove two pusher airscrews, giving the aircraft a top speed of 84 mph. A small number were built, but they were not successful. This was followed by a prototype model, the G.VI, probably the world's first asymmetric aircraft.

The G.VI's fuselage was offset to the portside and had a 260-hp Mercedes D.IVa engine mounted in the nose which drove a tractor airscrew. Another 260-hp Mercedes D.IVa engine, driving a pusher airscrew, was mounted in a nacelle in the starboard housing. A number of test flights were made but the aircraft crashed attempting to land and was destroyed. No more were made.

At the same time as the G.IV was making its test flights, another prototype came off the production line, the Gotha G.VII. This was a small twin-engined aircraft that had been developed for ultra-long-range photo-reconnaissance missions. When a special photographic unit, named the Reihenbildzug was formed, four of these aircraft were supplied. A month later, a production model based on the G.VII prototype was launched. The G.VII production model bore little or no resemblance to the prototype and was supplied to the military at the end of 1918, too late to make any significant difference to the outcome of the war. With a wingspan of 63 ft 3 in, a fuselage length of 31 ft 7½ in, and a wing area of 689 square feet, the G.VII had ailerons at all four wingtips and slightly swept wings compensated for the removal of the nose section.

Another version of the G.VII, the G.VIII, was built. The only difference was a longer wingspan of 71 ft 3½ in. There were a further two models built, the Gotha G.IX, which was built by LVG, and the Gotha G.X. The G.X was another twin-engined photo-reconnaissance aircraft but was powered by two 180-hp BMW (Bavarian Motor Werke) engines. Little is known about either aircraft as no details were made available.

Later, in 1918, a long-range reconnaissance aircraft was built, the Gotha WD.22. Similar in design and construction to the WD.14, the WD.22 was powered by four engines, two 160-hp Mercedes and two 100-hp Mercedes D.Is. The engines were mounted in tandem in twin nacelles, the two forward engines driving tractor airscrews and the two rear engines pusher airscrews. With a wingspan of 85 ft 3½ in, a fuselage length of 47 ft 3 in, a wing area of 1,588 square feet and a top speed of 82 mph, the WD.22 promised a lot but delivered very little.

Not to be deterred, Gotha, in 1918, came up with three of the largest aircraft built during the First World War, the Gotha WD.27. They were so large that they came into the category of the R aircraft, the *Riesen-Seeflugzeug* (Giant Seaplane). With a wingspan of 101 ft 8½ in, a fuselage length of 57 ft 9 in and a wing area of 2,084 square feet, the WD.27 was a giant of a seaplane. It was powered by four 160-hp Mercedes D.III engines, which were mounted in tandem in twin nacelles that turned spinnered pusher and tractor airscrews. The giant aircraft had a top speed of 84 mph.

## SPECIFICATION

### Gotha LE.3

| | |
|---|---|
| Wing Span: | 47 ft 7 in (14.5 m) |
| Length: | 32 ft 10 in (10.0 m) |
| Height: | 9 ft 8¼ in (3.0 m) |
| Weight Empty: | 1,518 lb (690 kg) |
| Weight Loaded: | 2,257 lb (1,026 kg) |
| Engine: | One 100-hp Mercedes D.I six-cylinder, in-line, water-cooled |
| Maximum Speed: | 60 mph (96 km/h) |
| Service Ceiling: | 2,900 feet (883 m) |

Endurance:          1½ hours. Later reduced to 1 hour
Armament:           None


## GOTHA LD.1A

Wing Span Upper:    47 ft 7 in (14.5 m)
Wing Span Lower:    47 ft 7 in (14.5 m)
Length:             24 ft 3½ in (7.4 m)
Height:             9 ft 8¼ in (3.0 m)
Weight Empty:       1,155 lb (525 kg)
Weight Loaded:      2,017 lb (917 kg)
Engine:             One 100-hp Oberursel U.I six-cylinder, in-line,
                    water-cooled
Maximum Speed:      72 mph (115 km/h)
Service Ceiling:    2,900 feet (883m)
Endurance:          1½ hours. Later reduced to 1 hour
Armament:           None

## Gotha LD.2

Wing Span Upper:    47 ft 7 in (14.5 m)
Wing Span Lower:    47 ft 7 in (14.5 m)
Length:             24 ft 7½ in (7.5 m)
Height:             9 ft 8¼ in (3.0 m)
Weight Empty:       1,617 lb (735 kg)
Weight Loaded:      2,479 lb (1,127 kg)
Engine:             One 100-hp Mercedes D.I six-cylinder, in-line,
                    water-cooled
Maximum Speed:      65 mph (105 km/h)
Service Ceiling:    2,900 feet (883 m)
Endurance:          1½ hours. Later reduced to 1 hour
Armament:           None

## Gotha LD 3 & 4    None built

## Gotha LD 5    No details available

## Gotha LD 6a

Wing Span Upper:    40 ft 8¼ in (12.4m)
Wing Span Lower:    40 ft 8¼ in (12.4m)
Length:             27 ft 7 in (8.4 m)
Height:             9 ft 8¼ in (3.0 m)
Weight Empty:       1,595 lb (725 kg)
Weight Loaded:      2,475 lb (1,125 kg)
Engine:             One 150-hp Benz Bz.III six-cylinder, in-line, water-cooled
Maximum Speed:      78 mph (125 km/h)
Service Ceiling:    2,900 feet (883 m)
Endurance:          1½ hours. Later reduced to 1 hour
Armament:           None

## Gotha LD.7

| | |
|---|---|
| Wing Span Upper: | 40 ft 8¼ in (12.4 m) |
| Wing Span Lower: | 40 ft 8¼ in (12.4 m) |
| Length: | 27 ft 7 in (8.4 m) |
| Height: | 9 ft 8¼ in (3.0 m) |
| Weight Empty: | 1,595 lb (725 kg) |
| Weight Loaded: | 2,475 lb (1,125 kg) |
| Engine: | One 120-hp Mercedes D.II six-cylinder, in-line, water-cooled |
| Maximum Speed: | 78 mph (125 km/h) |
| Service Ceiling: | 2,900 feet (883m) |
| Endurance: | 1½ hours. Later reduced to 1 hour |
| Armament: | None |

## Gotha WD.1

| | |
|---|---|
| Wing Span Upper: | 46 ft 3¼ in (14.1 m) |
| Wing Span Lower: | 46 ft 3¼ in (14.1 m) |
| Length: | 33 ft 9½ in (10.3 m) |
| Height: | 12 ft 8¼ in (3.8 m) |
| Weight Empty: | 1,980 lb (898 kg) |
| Weight Loaded: | 2,684 lb (1,220) |
| Engine: | One 100-hp Gnome |
| Maximum Speed: | 61 mph (90 km/h) |
| Service Ceiling: | 8,200 ft (2,500 m) |
| Endurance: | 5 hours |
| Armament: | None |

## Gotha WD.2

| | |
|---|---|
| Wing Span Upper: | 51 ft 2¼ in (15.6 m) |
| Wing Span Lower: | 51 ft 2¼ in (15.6 m) |
| Length: | 34 ft 5½ in (10.5 m) |
| Height: | 12 ft 8¼ in (3.8 m) |
| Weight Empty: | 2,343 lb (1,065 kg) |
| Weight Loaded: | 3,586 lb (1,630) |
| Engine: | One 150-hp Benz Bz.III |
| Maximum Speed: | 70 mph (112 km/h) |
| Service Ceiling: | 9,840 ft (3,000 m) |
| Endurance: | 5 hours |
| Armament: | None |

## Gotha WD.3

| | |
|---|---|
| Wing Span Upper: | 51 ft 2¼ in (15.6 m) |
| Wing Span Lower: | 51 ft 2¼ in (15.6 m) |
| Length: | 34 ft 5½ in (10.5 m) |
| Height: | 12 ft 8¼ in (3.8 m) |
| Weight Empty: | 2,431 lb (1,105 kg) |
| Weight Loaded: | 3,762 lb (1,710 kg) |
| Engine: | One 160-hp Mercedes D.III |
| Maximum Speed: | 62 mph (100 km/h) |

Service Ceiling:     9,840 ft (3,000 m)
Endurance:           5 hours
Armament:            One manually operated Parabellum machine gun mounted
                     in the nose

## Gotha WD.4          None built

## Gotha WD.5

Wing Span Upper:     41 ft 0¼ in (12.5 m)
Wing Span Lower:     41 ft 0¼ in (12.5 m)
Length:              33 ft 9½ in (10.3 m)
Height:              12 ft 8¼ in (3.8 m)
Weight Empty:        1,980 lb (900 kg)
Weight Loaded:       3,223 lb (1,465 kg)
Engine:              One 160-hp Mercedes D.III
Maximum Speed:       78 mph (126 km/h)
Service Ceiling:     9,840 ft (3,000 m)
Endurance:           5 hours
Armament:            None

## Gotha WD.6          None built

## Gotha WD.7

Wing Span Upper:     52 ft 6 in (16.0 m)
Wing Span Lower:     52 ft 6 in (16.0 m)
Length:              37 ft 1 in (11.3 m)
Height:              11 ft 9¼ in (3.5 m)
Weight Empty:        3,168 lb (1,440 kg)
Weight Loaded:       4,334 lb (1,970 kg)
Engines:             Two 120-hp Mercedes D.II
Maximum Speed:       85 mph (136 km/h)
Service Ceiling:     13,120 ft (4,000 m)
Endurance:           5 hours
Armament:            None

## Gotha WD.8

Wing Span Upper:     52 ft 6 in (16.0 m)
Wing Span Lower:     52 ft 6 in (16.0 m)
Length:              36 ft 9 in (11.2 m)
Height:              11 ft 9¼ in (3.5 m)
Weight Empty:        2,750 lb (1,250 kg)
Weight Loaded:       3,894 lb (1,770 kg)
Engine:              One 240-hp Maybach Mb.IV
Maximum Speed:       81 mph (130 km/h)
Service Ceiling:     14,760 ft (4,500 m)
Endurance:           5 hours
Armament:            One manually operated Parabellum machine gun mounted
                     in the rear observer's cockpit

## Gotha WD.9

| | |
|---|---|
| Wing Span Upper: | 49 ft 2½ in (15.0 m) |
| Wing Span Lower: | 49 ft 2½ in (15.0 m) |
| Length: | 32 ft 2 in (9.8 m) |
| Height: | 11 ft 9¼ in (3.5 m) |
| Weight Empty: | 2,288 lb (1,040 kg) |
| Weight Loaded: | 3,278 lb (1,490 kg) |
| Engine: | One 160-hp Mercedes D.III |
| Maximum Speed: | 85 mph (136 km/h) |
| Service Ceiling: | 14,760 ft (4,500 m) |
| Endurance: | 3 hours |
| Armament: | One manually operated Parabellum machine gun mounted in the rear observer's cockpit |

## Gotha WD.11

| | |
|---|---|
| Wing Span Upper: | 73 ft 10½ in (22.5 m) |
| Wing Span Lower: | 73 ft 10½ in (22.5 m) |
| Length: | 44 ft 1 in (13.4 m) |
| Height: | 15 ft 2 in (4.7 m) |
| Weight Empty: | 5,361 lb (2,437 kg) |
| Weight Loaded: | 7,883 lb (3,583 kg) |
| Engine: | Two 160-hp Mercedes D.III six-cylinder, in-line, water-cooled |
| Maximum Speed: | 75 mph (120 km/h) |
| Service Ceiling: | 22,900 feet (7,000 m) |
| Endurance: | 5 hours |
| Armament: | One manually operated Parabellum machine-gun mounted in the nose |
| | One torpedo carried under the fuselage between the floats |

## Gotha WD.12

| | |
|---|---|
| Wing Span: | 49 ft 2½ in (15.0 m) |
| Wing Span: | 49 ft 2½ in (15.0 m) |
| Length: | 32 ft 10 in (10.0 m) |
| Height: | 12 ft 6½ in (3.8 m) |
| Weight Empty: | 2,200 lb (1,000 kg) |
| Weight Loaded: | 3,140 lb (1,550 kg) |
| Engine: | One 160-hp Mercedes D.III water-cooled |
| Maximum Speed: | 88 mph (141 km/h) |
| Service Ceiling: | 22,900 feet |
| Endurance: | 5½ hours |
| Armament: | None |

## Gotha WD.13

| | |
|---|---|
| Wing Span Upper: | 47 ft 11 in (14.6 m) |
| Wing Span Lower: | 47 ft 11 in (14.6 m) |
| Length: | 33 ft 0½ in (10.0 m) |
| Height: | 12 ft 3¼ in (3.7 m) |
| Weight Empty: | 2,334 lb (1,061 kg) |

Weight Loaded:      3,219 lb (1,463 kg)
Engine:             One 150-hp Benz Bz.III water-cooled
Maximum Speed:      82 mph (131 km/h)
Service Ceiling:    22,900 feet
Endurance:          3 hours
Armament:           One manually operated Parabellum machine gun in
                    the observer's cockpit

## Gotha WD.14

Wing Span Upper:    83 ft 8 in (25.5 m)
Wing Span Lower:    83 ft 8 in (25.5 m)
Length:             47 ft 5 in (14.5 m)
Height:             16 ft 5 in (5.0 m)
Weight Empty:       6,930 lb (3,150 kg)
Weight Loaded:      10,212 lb (4,624 kg)
Engine:             Two 200-hp Benz Bz.IV six-cylinder, in-line, water-cooled
Maximum Speed:      84 mph (130 km/h)
Service Ceiling:    21,320 ft (6,500 m)
Endurance:          8 hours
Armament:           Two manually operated Parabellum machine gun mounted
                    in the nose and rear of the aircraft
                    Six 110 lb bombs

## Gotha WD.15

Wing Span Upper:    56 ft 5¼ in (17.2 m)
Wing Span Lower:    56 ft 5¼ in (17.2 m)
Length:             36 ft 9 in (11.2 m)
Height:             12 ft 3¼ in (3.7 m)
Weight Empty:       3,399 lb (1,545 kg)
Weight Loaded:      5,060 lb (2,300 kg)
Engine:             One 260-hp Mercedes D.IVa water-cooled
Maximum Speed:      95 mph (152 km/h)
Service Ceiling:    13,780 ft (4,200 m)
Endurance:          3 hours
Armament:           None

## Gotha WD.20

Wing Span Upper:    73 ft 8 in (25.5 m)
Wing Span Lower:    73 ft 8 in (25.5 m)
Length:             47 ft 5 in (14.5 m)
Height:             16 ft 5 in (5.0 m)
Weight Empty:       6,666 lb (3,030 kg)
Weight Loaded:      9,988 lb (4,540 kg)
Engine:             Two 200-hp Benz Bz.IV six-cylinder, in-line, water-cooled
Maximum Speed:      82 mph (130 km/h)
Service Ceiling:    21,320 ft (6,500 m)
Endurance:          8-10 hours
Armament:           Two manually operated Parabellum machine-guns
                    mounted in the nose and rear of the aircraft
                    Six 110 lb bombs

## Gotha WD.22

| | |
|---|---|
| Wing Span Upper: | 85 ft 4 in (26.0 m) |
| Wing Span Lower: | 85 ft 4 in (26.0 m) |
| Length: | 47 ft 3 in (14.4 m) |
| Height: | 16 ft 5 in (5.0 m) |
| Weight Empty: | 8,360 lb (3,800 kg) |
| Weight Loaded: | 11,374 lb (5,170 kg) |
| Engines: | Two 160-hp Mercedes D.III |
| | Two 100-hp Mercedes D.I |
| Maximum Speed: | 82 mph (130 km/h) |
| Service Ceiling: | 21,320 ft (6,500 m) |
| Endurance: | 8-10 hours |
| Armament: | Two manually operated Parabellum machine-guns mounted in the nose and rear of the aircraft |

## Gotha WD.27

| | |
|---|---|
| Wing Span Upper: | 101 ft 8½ in (31.0 m) |
| Wing Span Lower: | 101 ft 8½ in (31.0 m) |
| Length: | 57 ft 9 in (17.6 m) |
| Height: | 16 ft 5 in (5.0 m) |
| Weight Empty: | 9,900 lb (4,500 kg) |
| Weight Loaded: | 14,718 lb (6,690 kg) |
| Engines: | Four 160-hp Mercedes D.III |
| | Two 100-hp Mercedes D.I |
| Maximum Speed: | 84 mph (135 km/h) |
| Service Ceiling: | 21,320 ft (6,500 m) |
| Endurance: | 8-10 hours |
| Armament: | Two manually operated Parabellum machine-guns mounted in the nose and rear of the aircraft |

## Gotha UWD (Seaplane)

| | |
|---|---|
| Wing Span Upper: | 66 ft 7¼ in (20.3 m) |
| Wing Span Lower: | 66 ft 7¼ in (20.3 m) |
| Length: | 46 ft 7¼ in (14.2 m) |
| Height: | 13 ft 1½ in (4.5 m) |
| Weight Empty: | 4,268 lb (1,940 kg) |
| Weight Loaded: | 6,226 lb (2,830 kg) |
| Engine: | Two 160-hp Mercedes D.III |
| Maximum Speed: | 86 mph (138 km/h) |
| Service Ceiling: | 14,760 ft (4,500 m) |
| Endurance: | 5 hours |
| Armament: | Two manually operated Parabellum machine-guns mounted in the rear observer's cockpit |

## Gotha GUH G.I (Landplane)

| | |
|---|---|
| Wing Span Upper: | 66 ft 7¼ in (20.3 m) |
| Wing Span Lower: | 66 ft 7¼ in (20.3 m) |
| Length: | 46 ft 7¼ in (14.2 m) |
| Height: | 13 ft 1½ in (4.5 m) |

| | |
|---|---|
| Weight Empty: | 4,092 lb (1,860 kg) |
| Weight Loaded: | 6,226 lb (2,830 kg) |
| Engine: | Two 160-hp Mercedes D.III |
| Maximum Speed: | 86 mph (138 km/h) |
| Service Ceiling: | 14,760 ft (4,500 m) |
| Endurance: | 4 hours |
| Armament: | Two manually operated Parabellum machine guns mounted in the rear observer's cockpit |

## Gotha G.II & G.III

| | |
|---|---|
| Wing Span Upper: | 77 ft 9¼ in (23.7 m) |
| Wing Span Lower: | 77 ft 9½ in (23.7 m) |
| Length: | 38 ft 11 in (11.8 m) |
| Height: | 14 ft 1 in (4.3 m) |
| Weight Empty: | 4,800 lb (2,182 kg) |
| Weight Loaded: | 7,022 lb (3,192 kg) |
| Engine: | Two 260-hp Mercedes D.IVa six-cylinder, in-line, water-cooled |
| Maximum Speed: | 92 mph (148 km/h) |
| Service Ceiling: | 21,320 feet (6,500 m) |
| Endurance: | 5 hours |
| Armament: | Two manually operated Parabellum machine-guns mounted in the nose and rear of the aircraft Six 110 lb bombs |

## Gotha G.IV & G.V

| | |
|---|---|
| Wing Span Upper: | 77 ft 9¼ in (23.7 m) |
| Wing Span Lower: | 77 ft 9¼ in (23.7 m) |
| Length: | 38 ft 11 in (11.8 m) |
| Height: | 14 ft 1¼ in (4.3 m) |
| Weight Empty: | 6,028 lb (2,740 kg) |
| Weight Loaded: | 8,745 lb (3,975 kg) |
| Engine: | Two 260-hp Mercedes D.IVa six-cylinder, in-line, water-cooled |
| Maximum Speed: | 87 mph (140 km/h) |
| Service Ceiling: | 21,320 feet (6,500 m) |
| Endurance: | 3 hours |
| Armament: | Two manually operated Parabellum machine guns mounted in the nose and rear of the aircraft Six 110 lb bombs |

## Gotha G.Vb

| | |
|---|---|
| Wing Span Upper: | 77 ft 9¼ in (23.7 m) |
| Wing Span Lower: | 77 ft 9¼ in (23.7 m) |
| Length: | 40 ft 8¼ in (12.4 m) |
| Height: | 12 ft 1¼ in (3.6 m) |
| Weight Empty: | 6,490 lb (2,950 kg) |
| Weight Loaded: | 10,010 lb (4,550 kg) |
| Engine: | Two 260-hp Mercedes D.IVa six-cylinder, in-line, water-cooled |

Maximum Speed:     84 mph (135 km/h)
Service Ceiling:   21,320 feet (6,500 m)
Endurance:         3 hours
Armament:          Two manually operated Parabellum machine-guns
                   mounted in the nose and rear of the aircraft
                   Six 110 lb bombs

## Gotha G.VI

This aircraft had the same specifications as the Gotha G.V, but with minor modifications.

## Gotha G.VII

Wing Span Upper:   63 ft 3 in (19.3 m)
Wing Span Lower:   63 ft 3 in (19.3 m)
Length:            31 ft 7¼ in (9.6 m)
Height:            12 ft 1¼ in (3.6 m)
Weight Empty:      5,322 lb (2,419 kg)
Weight Loaded:     6,906 lb (3,139 kg)
Engine:            Two 260-hp Mercedes D.IVa six-cylinder, in-line,
                   water-cooled
Maximum Speed:     112 mph (180 km/h)
Service Ceiling:   21,320 feet (6,500 m)
Endurance:         3 hours
Armament:          One manually operated Parabellum machine gun
                   mounted in a dorsal position
                   Six 110 lb bombs

## Gotha G.VIII

Wing Span Upper:   71 ft 3½ in (21.7 m)
Wing Span Lower:   71 ft 3½ in (21.7 m)
Length:            32 ft 1½ in (9.8 m)
Height:            11 ft 6¼ in (3.5 m)
Weight Empty:      5,887 lb (2,676 kg)
Weight Loaded:     8,153 lb (3,706 kg)
Engine:            Two 245-hp Maybach Mb.IV
Maximum Speed:     112 mph (180 km/h)
Service Ceiling:   21,320 feet (6,500 m)
Endurance:         3 hours
Armament:          Not known

## Gotha G.X

No details available

# Halberstädter Flugzeug-Werke GmbH

One of the first aircraft built by the Halberstädt Company to be used in the war was the Halberstädt B. Powered by an 80-hp Oberursel U.O engine, this little biplane produced in 1914 was used purely for training purposes. It is thought only a handful was ever built.

A development of the B model was the two-seater Halberstädt B.I, the first of the purpose-built military aircraft to be constructed, used for reconnaissance purposes. Like most of the early aircraft, the pilot flew the aircraft from the rear cockpit, leaving the observer in the front cockpit to try and carry out his duties from a usually poor view. The B.II and B.III were almost identical to the B.I, the only difference being that different engines were tried. The B.I and B.II were fitted with a 100-hp Mercedes D.I engine, while the B.III was fitted with a 120-hp Mercedes D.II engine.

A new series appeared in late 1915: the Halberstädt C.I. This was a more compact version of the B.II and was fitted with a rotary engine. The crew positions were reversed and a manually operated Parabellum machine gun fitted in the observer's rear cockpit. Only a couple of these aircraft were built, as a weakness in the rudder was discovered.

The one and only twin-engined model appeared at the end of 1915, the Halberstädt G.I. Powered by two 160-hp Mercedes D.III engines, which gave it a top speed of 95 mph, the G.I had a flight endurance of four hours. It had a wingspan of 50 ft 10½ in, a fuselage length of 29 ft 6½ in, was armed with two manually operated Parabellum machine guns and carried a bomb load of 440 lb. Only one of the aircraft was built as it proved not to be satisfactory.

Another model appeared in February 1916, the Halberstädt D.I. Like the B series, the D.I was similar in most ways and differed only in not having staggered wings and having the radiators mounted on either side of the fuselage, just below the pilot's cockpit. The D.II and D.III models that followed were almost identical, with the exception of a change of engines from the 100-hp Mercedes D.I engine to the 120-hp Mercedes D.II engine.

Then came the first of the fighter aircraft, the Halberstädt D.IV. Powered by a 150-hp Benz Bz.III engine with its rhino horn exhaust, the D.IV had a top speed of 108 mph and a flight endurance of 1½ hours. It had a wingspan of 28 ft 10½ in, a fuselage length of 23 ft 11½ in, and a wing area of 259 square feet. It was capable of carrying one or two fixed, forward-firing Spandau machine guns. A small number were made, but it was the prototype for the Halberstädt D.V fighter that was to follow.

Based on a standard D.III airframe, the D.V was fitted with either a 120-hp Argus D.II or 120-hp Mercedes D.II engine. It had a wingspan of 28 ft 10½ in, a fuselage length of 23 ft 11½ in, a top speed of 108 mph and a climb rate of over 1,000 feet per minute. It was armed with one forward-firing, fixed Spandau machine gun. All the pilots that flew the aircraft were delighted with it. A large number of these aircraft were built and a number were supplied to the Turkish Government.

The first of the purpose-built, two-seat, long-range reconnaissance aircraft were built at the end of 1917. The Halberstädt C.III was constructed in the conventional manner of spruce wood and fabric and covered in plywood. It was powered by a 200-hp Benz Bz.IV engine that gave the aircraft a top speed of 103 mph. It carried an armament of one fixed, forward-firing Spandau machine gun and one manually operated Parabellum machine gun mounted on a scarf-type gun ring in the observer's rear cockpit.

The C.III had a wingspan of 40 ft and a fuselage length of 25 ft 3½ in. Only six of these machines were completed and supplied to the German Army.

The design of a two-seat fighter in May 1917 created another type of aircraft for the Halberstädt Company, the Halberstädt CL.II. It was created out of a need to protect the C-type photo-reconnaissance aircraft that were becoming increasingly more important for the success of German infantry. A new flight was created, the Schutzstaffeln (Escort Flights) and it was into this flight that the CL.II was introduced.

Powered by a 160-hp six-cylinder, in-line, water-cooled Mercedes D.III engine, that gave the aircraft a top speed of 103 mph, an operating ceiling of 16,700 feet and an endurance of 3 hours. With a wingspan of 35 ft 4 in, a fuselage length of 23 ft 11½ in and a wing area of 297 square feet, the CL.II was a relatively small aircraft for a two-seater. It carried a quite formidable armament in one fixed, forward-firing Spandau machine gun, a manually operated Parabellum machine gun which was mounted in the rear of the communal cockpit and 22 lb of bombs and a number of anti-personnel grenades.

A large number of Halberstädt CL.IIs were supplied to the German Army and were used during some of the major offensives. During a British court of inquiry into the success of the German counter-offensive during the Battle of Cambrai, evidence was produced that the appearance of German close-support aircraft, like the Halberstädt CL.II, flying at low-level and firing into both the front trenches and the rear sections, was a major cause of the British infantry being thrown into confusion. It was this confusion, the Court of Inquiry found, combined with the morale conferred on the German infantry by these aerial attacks that was one of the main contributors to the success of the German counter-offensive.

With these successes, the name Schutzstaffeln was changed to Schlachtstaffeln (Battle Flights) and the flight section expanded. With the expansion came the need for more aircraft, and the Halberstädt CL.IV was produced. Very similar to the CL.II, the CL.IV's fuselage was three inches shorter; the horizontal tail surfaces were of a larger span and had a higher aspect ratio. The engine was the same as the CL.II, but the aircraft was now more manoeuvrable, which was necessary for its new role. The success of the Schlachtstaffeln flights resulted in missions that went ahead of infantry advances, with the intention of 'softening up' the Allied lines with low-level strafing attacks. The fuselage of the CL.IV was covered in plywood which, because of the low-level attacks carried out by the crews, left them exposed to small-arms fire. A number of crews were wounded or killed in this way.

In March 1918, when the German Army made its final attempt to crush the Allies, thirty-eight Schlachtstaffeln had been created and were equipped with mostly Halberstadt CL.II and CL.IV aircraft. Some of the aircraft were fitted with two fixed, forward-firing Spandau machine guns, one manually operated

Parabellum machine gun in the rear of the large communal cockpit and a number of anti-personnel grenades mounted in boxes on the sides of the fuselage. There were a small number of flights that had been equipped with Hanover CL.IIIas. The failure of the offensive forced the CL.II and CL.IVs into a defensive role, a role they carried out with distinction.

Toward the end of 1918, with the Americans firmly established in the war, the need for photo-reconnaissance aircraft resulted in the production of the Halberstadt C.V. Earlier in the year the Halberstadt Company had developed a long-range, high-altitude reconnaissance aircraft and, unusually for manufacturers at this time, had carried out extensive tests on the prototype. They, in fact, tested it to destruction. The fuselage and tail section resembled that of the CL.IV, but that was the only resemblance. The communal cockpit was replaced by the conventional twin-cockpits and the dimensions of the aircraft were considerably larger than those of the CL.IV.

The aircraft had a wingspan of 44 ft 9 in, a fuselage length of 22 ft 8½ in, and was powered by a six-cylinder, in-line, water-cooled Benz Bz.IV engine. This gave the aircraft a top speed of 106 mph, an operating height of nearly 17,000 feet and an endurance of 3½ hours. With a crew of two, pilot and observer/gunner, the C.V carried one fixed forward-firing Spandau machine gun and one manually operated Parabellum machine gun in the rear cockpit.

The Halberstadt aircraft throughout the war performed as well as most other aircraft of their type, but never received the recognition with historians that they deserved.


## SPECIFICATIONS

### Halberstadt B.I

| | |
|---|---|
| Wing Span: | 39 ft 4 in (12.0 m) |
| Length: | 23 ft 11½ in (7.3 m) |
| Height: | 9 ft 0¼ in (2.7 m) |
| Weight Empty: | 1,410 lb (641 kg) |
| Weight Loaded: | 2,303 lb (1,047 kg) |
| Engine: | One 100-hp Mercedes D.I six-cylinder, in-line, water-cooled |
| Maximum Speed: | 103 mph (165 km/h) |
| Service Ceiling: | 16,700 feet (5,100 m) |
| Endurance: | 3 hours |
| Armament: | Two fixed forward-firing Spandau machine guns |
| | One manually operated Parabellum machine gun in rear observer's cockpit |
| | Four 22 lb bombs |

### Halberstadt B.II and B.III

Specifications are the same as those for the B.I.

### Halberstadt C.I

| | |
|---|---|
| Wing Span: | 31 ft 4 in (9.6 m) |
| Length: | 23 ft 6 in (7.1 m) |
| Height: | 9 ft 0¼ in (2.7 m) |
| Weight Empty: | Not known |

| | |
|---|---|
| Weight Loaded: | Not known |
| Engine: | One 110-hp Oberursel U.I rotary |
| Maximum Speed: | Not known |
| Service Ceiling: | Not known |
| Endurance: | 2 hours |
| Armament: | Two fixed forward-firing Spandau machine guns |
| | One manually operated Parabellum machine gun in rear |
| | observer's cockpit |

## Halberstadt C.III

| | |
|---|---|
| Wing Span: | 39 ft 4 in (12.0 m) |
| Length: | 23 ft 11½ in (7.3 m) |
| Height: | 9 ft 0¼ in (2.7 m) |
| Weight Empty: | 1,410 lb (641 kg) |
| Weight Loaded: | 2,303 lb (1,047 kg) |
| Engine: | One 100-hp Mercedes D.I six-cylinder, in-line, |
| | water-cooled |
| Maximum Speed: | 103 mph (165 km/h) |
| Service Ceiling: | 16,700 feet (5,100 m) |
| Endurance: | 3 hours |
| Armament: | Two fixed forward-firing Spandau machine guns |
| | One manually operated Parabellum machine gun in rear |
| | observer's cockpit |
| | Four 22 lb bombs |

## Halberstadt C.V

| | |
|---|---|
| Wing Span: | 44 ft 8½ in (13.6 m) |
| Length: | 22 ft 8½ in (6.9 m) |
| Height: | 11 ft 0¼ in (3.3 m) |
| Weight Empty: | 2,046 lb (930 kg) |
| Weight Loaded: | 2,730 lb (1,365 kg) |
| Engine: | One 220-hp Benx Bz.IV |
| Maximum Speed: | 106 mph (170 km/h) |
| Service Ceiling: | 16,400 feet (5,000 m) |
| Endurance: | 3 hours |
| Armament: | Two fixed forward-firing Spandau machine guns |
| | One manually operated Parabellum machine gun in rear |
| | observer's cockpit |
| | Four 22 lb bombs |

## Halberstadt C.VII

| | |
|---|---|
| Wing Span: | 44 ft 8½ in (13.6 m) |
| Length: | 22 ft 8½ in (6.9 m) |
| Height: | 11 ft 0¼ in (3.3 m) |
| Weight Empty: | 2,046 lb (930 kg) |
| Weight Loaded: | 2,730 lb (1,365 kg) |
| Engine: | One 245-hp Maybach Mb.IV |
| Maximum Speed: | 106 mph (170 km/h) |
| Service Ceiling: | 16,400 feet (5,000 m) |
| Endurance: | 3 hours |

| Armament: | One fixed forward-firing Spandau machine gun |
|---|---|
| | One manually operated Parabellum machine gun in rear observer's cockpit |
| | Four 22 lb bombs |

## Halberstadt C.VIII

| Wing Span: | 39 ft 4 in (11.9 m) |
|---|---|
| Length: | 24 ft 1½ in (7.3 m) |
| Height: | 9 ft 8¼ in (2.9 m) |
| Weight Empty: | 2,042 lb (928 kg) |
| Weight Loaded: | 2,999 lb (1,363 kg) |
| Engine: | One 245-hp Maybach Mb.IV |
| Maximum Speed: | 112 mph (180 km/h) |
| Service Ceiling: | 29,250 feet (9,000 m) |
| Endurance: | 3½ hours |
| Armament: | One fixed forward-firing Spandau machine gun |
| | One manually operated Parabellum machine gun in rear observer's cockpit |
| | Four 22 lb bombs |

## Halberstadt C.IX

| Wing Span: | 44 ft 8½ in (13.6 m) |
|---|---|
| Length: | 22 ft 8½ in (6.9 m) |
| Height: | 11 ft 0¼ in (3.3 m) |
| Weight Empty: | 2,090 lb (950 kg) |
| Weight Loaded: | 3,036 lb (1,380 kg) |
| Engine: | One 230-hp Hiero |
| Maximum Speed: | 106 mph (170 km/h) |
| Service Ceiling: | 16,400 feet (5,000 m) |
| Endurance: | 3 hours |
| Armament: | Two fixed forward-firing Spandau machine guns |
| | One manually operated Parabellum machine gun in rear observer's cockpit |
| | Four 22 lb bombs |

## Halberstadt CL.II, CL.III and CL.IIIa

| Wing Span: | 35 ft 4 in (10.7 m) |
|---|---|
| Length: | 23 ft 11½ in (7.3 m) |
| Height: | 9 ft 0¼ in (2.7 m) |
| Weight Empty: | 1,701 lb (773 kg) |
| Weight Loaded: | 2,493 lb (1,133 kg) |
| Engine: | One 160-hp Mercedes D.III six-cylinder, in-line, water-cooled |
| Maximum Speed: | 103 mph (165 km/h) |
| Service Ceiling: | 16,700 feet (5,100 m) |
| Endurance: | 3 hours |
| Armament: | Two fixed forward-firing Spandau machine guns |
| | One manually operated Parabellum machine gun in rear observer's cockpit |
| | Four 22 lb bombs |

## Halberstadt CL.IV

| | |
|---|---|
| Wing Span: | 35 ft 3 in (10.7 m) |
| Length: | 21 ft 5½ in (6.5 m) |
| Height: | 8 ft 9¼ in (2.6 m) |
| Weight Empty: | 1,602 lb (728 kg) |
| Weight Loaded: | 2,349 lb (1,068 kg) |
| Engine: | One 160-hp Mercedes D.III six-cylinder, in-line, water-cooled |
| Maximum Speed: | 103 mph (165 km/h) |
| Service Ceiling: | 16,400 feet (5,000 m) |
| Endurance: | 3 hours |
| Armament: | Two fixed forward-firing Spandau machine guns |
| | One manually operated Parabellum machine gun in rear observer's cockpit |
| | Four 22 lb bombs |

## Halberstadt CLS.I

| | |
|---|---|
| Wing Span: | 31 ft 10 in (9.7 m) |
| Length: | 22 ft 9½ in (6.9 m) |
| Height: | 10 ft 0¼ in (3.0 m) |
| Weight Empty: | 1,500 lb (682 kg) |
| Weight Loaded: | 2,424 lb (1,102 kg) |
| Engine: | One 160-hp Mercedes D.III six-cylinder, in-line, water-cooled |
| Maximum Speed: | 115 mph (185 km/h) |
| Service Ceiling: | 16,700 feet (5,100 m) |
| Endurance: | 3 hours |
| Armament: | One fixed forward-firing Spandau machine gun |
| | One manually operated Parabellum machine gun in rear observer's cockpit |
| | Four 22 lb bombs |

## Halberstadt D.I

| | |
|---|---|
| Wing Span: | 28 ft 10½ in (8.8 m) |
| Length: | 23 ft 11½ in (7.3 m) |
| Height: | 6 ft 9¼ in (2.6 m) |
| Weight Empty: | 1,234 lb (561 kg) |
| Weight Loaded: | 1,696 lb (771 kg) |
| Engine: | One 120-hp Mercedes D.II six-cylinder, in-line, water-cooled |
| Maximum Speed: | 90 mph (145 km/h) |
| Service Ceiling: | 19,600 feet (6,000 m) |
| Endurance: | 3 hours |
| Armament: | One fixed forward-firing Spandau machine gun |

## Halberstadt D.II

| | |
|---|---|
| Wing Span: | 28 ft 10½ in (8.8 m) |
| Length: | 23 ft 11½ in (7.3 m) |
| Height: | 6 ft 9¼ in (2.6 m) |

Weight Empty:     1,234 lb (561 kg)
Weight Loaded:    1,696 lb (771 kg)
Engine:           One 120-hp Argus As.II six-cylinder, in-line, water-cooled
Maximum Speed:    90 mph (145 km/h)
Service Ceiling:  19,600 feet (6,000 m)
Endurance:        3 hours
Armament:         One fixed forward-firing Spandau machine gun

## Halberstadt D.IV

Wing Span:        28 ft 10½ in (8.8 m)
Length:           23 ft 11½ in (7.3 m)
Height:           9 ft 0½ in (2.7 m)
Weight Empty:     1,155 lb (525 kg)
Weight Loaded:    1,621 lb (737 kg)
Engine:           One 150-hp Benz Bz.III
Maximum Speed:    90 mph (145 km/h)
Service Ceiling:  19,600 feet (6,000 m)
Endurance:        1½ hours
Armament:         One fixed forward-firing Spandau machine gun

## Halberstadt D.V

Wing Span:        28 ft 10½ in (8.8 m)
Length:           23 ft 11½ in (7.3 m)
Height:           9 ft 0½ in (2.7 m)
Weight Empty:     1,155 lb (525 kg)
Weight Loaded:    1,621 lb (737 kg)
Engine:           One 120-hp Mercedes D.II or 120-hp Argus As D.II
Maximum Speed:    90 mph (145 km/h)
Service Ceiling:  19,600 feet (6,000 m)
Endurance:        1½ hours
Armament:         One fixed forward-firing Spandau machine gun

## Halberstadt G.I

Wing Span:        50 ft 10½ in (15.5 m)
Length:           29 ft 6½ in (9.0 m)
Height:           10 ft 6 in (3.2 m)
Weight Empty:     2,684 lb (1,220 kg)
Weight Loaded:    4,169 lb (1,895 kg)
Engine:           One 160-hp Mercedes D.III
Maximum Speed:    95 mph (152 km/h)
Service Ceiling:  19,600 feet (6,000 m)
Endurance:        4 hours
Armament:         One fixed forward-firing Spandau machine gun
                  440 lb (200 kg) bombs

# Hannoversche Waggonfabrik AG

One of the major contributors to the German Air Service during the First World War was Hannoversche Waggonfabrik Company. Builders of some of the finest two-seater reconnaissance aircraft of the time, the company actually started life as a manufacturer of railway rolling stock. With the outbreak of the First World War, the German Government pressed all manufacturers of machinery into war service. In 1915, the Hannoversche Company were ordered to manufacture aircraft under licence from other aircraft manufacturers. A branch of the company was created under the name of Hannover-Linden, and some of the first aircraft produced by Hannover were the Rumpler C.Ia, Aviatik C.I and Halberstadt D.II.

As the company became more and more proficient at producing other manufacturer's aircraft, Hermann Dorner, Hannover's chief designer, decided it was about time that they produced one of their own. At the beginning of 1917, the Flugmeisterei (Air Ministry) called for a new type of two-seater aircraft that could be used both as a fighter and for reconnaissance. It was to be powered by a 160 – 180-hp engine and fit into the existing CL category of aircraft. The CL type of aircraft had been assigned to escort duties known as Schutzstaffeln (Escort Flights), but after a great deal of success they became flights in their own right and became known as Schlachtstaffeln (Battle Flights).

With this requirement in mind, Hermann Dorner produced the first of the Hannover aircraft, the Hannover CL.II. Because Hannover had built the Aviatik C.I, the designation given to the Hannover's aircraft was the CL.II. The prototype CL.II was powered with the Argus As.III engine, which gave the aircraft a top speed of 103 mph, an operating ceiling of 24,600 feet and an endurance of three hours. It had a wingspan of 38 ft 4 in, a fuselage length of 24 ft 10½ in and a height of 9 ft 2½ in.

The fuselage was of conventional construction and consisted of four main spruce longerons with plywood formers covered in thin plywood skinned with a doped fabric. The tail section, however, was unusual. The vertical fin of the tail was integral with the fuselage and constructed in the same manner. The lower tailplane was constructed and covered in a similar manner, but on top of the tail fin was another tailplane, this being constructed of steel tubing and covered in doped fabric, as were the elevators.

The aircraft was greatly respected by the Allies as it was capable of absorbing a great deal of punishment and more than capable of giving as good as it got. The Hannover CL.II was armed with one forward-firing, fixed Spandau machine gun and one manually operated rearward-firing Parabellum machine gun. A total of 439 of these aircraft were built.

The CL.III appeared later in 1917, and was almost identical save for the installation of a 160-hp Mercedes D.III engine. Within months this engine was replaced by the 180-hp Argus As.III engine, as it was decided that the Mercedes engine was desperately needed for single-seat fighters. The new aircraft with the Argus As.III engine were designated the CL.IIIa.

A total of 80 CL.IIIs and 587 CL.IIIbs were built, which brought the total of Hannover two-seat fighter/reconnaissance aircraft supplied to the German Army to over 1,000.

As with all the aircraft manufacturers at the time, variations were made and prototypes appeared. The Hannover CL.IIIb was almost identical to the CL.IIIa, but with longer wings. Only the one model was ever constructed.

At the beginning of 1918, Hannover produced the C.IV this was a high altitude reconnaissance aircraft powered by the 245-hp Maybach Mb.IV engine. This gave the aircraft a top speed of 100 mph, an operating ceiling of 29,520 feet with an endurance of three hours. The C.IV had a wingspan of 41 ft 2½ in and a fuselage length of 25 ft 7½ in, and was armed with one fixed, forward-firing Spandau machine gun and one manually operated rearward-firing Parabellum machine gun. The wings, because of their extended length, had a 'V' centre strut arrangement instead of the usual single 'I' interplane strut.

Unfortunately, when this prototype was tested by the military it showed no improvement on the existing Rumpler C.VII (Rubild) model, so only one was built.

Just before the Armistice, Hannover produced another model, the CL.V. There were in fact two variants of this model, one with the biplane tail configuration and one without. Both variants were powered by 185-hp BMW IIIa engines, that gave the aircraft a top speed of 115 mph and an operating ceiling of 29,520 feet with an endurance of three hours. The biplane tailed model had a wingspan of 34 ft 8 in; the monoplane tailed version had a wingspan 34 ft 5 in. The fuselage length was the same for both (23 ft 4 in), as was the height (9 ft 6½ in). Armament for both models was the same as for all the previous versions.

Fifty Hannover C.V aircraft were built, but none went into service as the Armistice was declared and the need was gone. The Hannover two-seat reconnaissance aircraft was one of the most respected of the two-seat aircraft in the war. Both sides in the conflict recognised its qualities and gave it the respect it deserved.


## SPECIFICATIONS


### Hannover CL.II, CL.III and CL.IIIa

| | |
|---|---|
| Wing Span: | 38 ft 4½ in (11.7 m) |
| Length: | 24 ft 10½ in (7.6 m) |
| Height: | 9 ft 2¼ in (2.8 m) |
| Weight Empty: | 1,577 lb (717 kg) |
| Weight Loaded: | 2,378 lb (1,081 kg) |
| Engine: | One 180-hp Argus As.III six-cylinder, in-line, water-cooled with high compression cylinders |
| Maximum Speed: | 103 mph (165 km/h) |
| Service Ceiling: | 24,700 feet (7,500 m) |
| Endurance: | 3 hours |
| Armament: | One fixed forward-firing Spandau machine gun |
| | One manually operated Parabellum machine gun in rear observer's cockpit |

## Hannover CL.IIIb

| | |
|---|---|
| Wing Span: | 44 ft 6 in (13.5 m) |
| Length: | 24 ft 10½ in (7.6 m) |
| Height: | 9 ft 2¼ in (2.8 m) |
| Weight Empty: | 1,577 lb (717 kg) |
| Weight Loaded: | 2,378 lb (1,081 kg) |
| Engine: | One 180-hp Argus As.III six-cylinder, in-line, water-cooled with high compression cylinders |
| Maximum Speed: | 103 mph (165 km/h) |
| Service Ceiling: | 24,700 feet (7,500 m) |
| Endurance: | 3 hours |
| Armament: | One fixed forward-firing Spandau machine gun
One manually operated Parabellum machine gun in rear observer's cockpit |

## Hannover CL.IV

| | |
|---|---|
| Wing Span: | 41 ft 2½ in (12.5 m) |
| Length: | 25 ft 7¼ in (7.8 m) |
| Height: | 9 ft. 2¼ in (2.8 m) |
| Weight Empty: | 2,112 lb (960 kg) |
| Weight Loaded: | 3,069 lb (1,395 kg) |
| Engine: | One 245-hp Maybach Mb.IV six-cylinder, in-line, water-cooled with high compression cylinders |
| Maximum Speed: | 100 mph (160 km/h) |
| Service Ceiling: | 29,520 feet (9,000 m) |
| Endurance: | 3 hours |
| Armament: | One fixed forward-firing Spandau machine gun
One manually operated Parabellum machine gun in rear observer's cockpit |

## Hannover CL.V

| | |
|---|---|
| Wing Span: | 34 ft 7½ in (10.5 m) |
| Length: | 23 ft 3½ in (7.1 m) |
| Height: | 9 ft 6¼ in (2.9 m) |
| Weight Empty: | 1,584 lb (720 kg) |
| Weight Loaded: | 2,376 lb (1,080 kg) |
| Engine: | One 185-hp BMW IIIa six-cylinder, in-line, water-cooled |
| Maximum Speed: | 115 mph (185 km/h) |
| Service Ceiling: | 29,520 feet (9,000 m) |
| Endurance: | 3 hours |
| Armament: | One fixed forward-firing Spandau machine gun
One manually operated Parabellum machine gun in rear observer's cockpit |

# Junkers Flugzeug-Werke AG

The Junkers Aircraft Company started life not as an aircraft manufacturer, but as a manufacturer of gas water heaters for bathtubs, industrial boilers and temperature gauges. Dr Hugo Junkers was one of the most innovative engineers of his time, and, during his lifetime, was awarded more than 1,000 patents covering an extremely wide variety of fields.

His first real introduction to the world of aviation was in 1909. He was a professor at Aachen Technical High School when a fellow professor invited him to collaborate on an aircraft project. Hugo Junkers had been studying aerodynamics while at the school and built a wind tunnel. He became more and more interested and finally decided to embark on a career in aviation at the age of fifty.

Hugo Junkers had for some years been looking at the concept of producing an all-metal monoplane aircraft, and at the beginning of December 1915 the Junkers J.1, also known as the E.I, appeared. The first test flight, carried out on 12 December by Leutnant Friedrich Mallinckrodt at Döberitz, was a resounding success. The thin sheet-metal covering the aircraft gave rise to the name 'Tin Donkey'. Powered by a 120-hp Mercedes D.II engine, the J.1 had a top speed of 100 mph, which was somewhat slower than the streamlined appearance indicated. It was this that probably gave the aircraft the additional name of 'Donkey'.

The J.1 had a wingspan of 42 ft 5½ in, a fuselage length of 24 ft 4½ in and a height of 10 ft 3 in. Only one of the aircraft was built, but it was enough to impress the Flugzeugmeisterei (Air Ministry) who asked Hugo Junkers to produce an armoured biplane.

In the meantime, a second all-metal monoplane was built in 1916, the Junkers J.2, also known as the E.I. Only six of these aircraft were built and they were powered by a 120-hp Mercedes D.II engine, which gave the aircraft a top speed of 90·mph. The sixth model was fitted with the more powerful 160-hp Mercedes D.III engine, but the performance differential was little. The J.2 had a wingspan of 36 ft 1 in, a fuselage length of 23 ft 11½ in and a height of 10 ft 3 in.

At the end of 1916, together with Professor Madelung, Hugo Junkers designed an armoured biplane that was to be covered in a corrugated metal sheet that was riveted to the duraluminium framework of the Junkers J.1. The factory designation of this aircraft was J.4, but the military designation has always been given as the J.1. This has given rise to confusion in the past when the J.1 has been discussed.

The first J.1 (J.4) models had a hexagonal-shaped fuselage. The nose section, which enclosed the engine and cockpits, was armoured and made of 5-mm chrome-nickel sheet. This section was then joined to the rear fabric-covered part of the fuselage; the tailplane and elevators were of standard construction. Later models of this aircraft had the corrugated metal skin covering the entire fuselage.

The J.1 (J.4) was powered by a six-cylinder, in-line, water-cooled 200-hp Benz Bz.IV engine with a rhino horn-type exhaust, that gave the aircraft a top speed of 96 mph and an endurance of two hours. It was armed with two synchronised forward-firing, fixed Spandau machine guns and one manually operated Parabellum machine gun mounted in the rear cockpit.

The Junkers J.1 (J.4) had an upper wingspan of 52 ft 6 in, a lower wingspan of 38 ft 9 in, a fuselage length of 29 ft 10½ in and a height of 11 ft 1½ in. In total, 227 Junkers J.1s (J.4) were built, the first of them arriving at Flieger-Abteilung (Inf) units at the end of 1917. The crews found the aircraft difficult and extremely cumbersome during landings and take-offs, because of the weight of the armour plating. This, however, was weighed against the extra protection that the armour plating offered, which more than compensated for the other problems. The J.1 (J.4) was used extensively for low-level reconnaissance missions and ammunition and ration supply drops to front-line troops.

Encouraged by the acceptance of his aircraft by aircrews, Hugo Junkers started on perhaps the most ambitious project of his First World War aeronautical career, the Junkers R.I. Powered by four 260-hp Mercedes D.IVa engines that turned two propellers of 16 ft 5 in diameter, the projected speed of the aircraft was 112 mph. Projected is the operative word, as although two models, the R.I and the R-plane project were ordered by Idflieg, none were ever actually constructed.

A great deal of experimentation using wind tunnels was carried out, but the project was so huge that even when the Fokker Company was ordered to merge with Junkers, progress was extremely slow. This was mainly due to the fact that Anthony Fokker was used to making wooden aircraft and in mass production, while Junkers made all-metal aircraft, which for obvious reasons took longer to construct. In addition, the two parties were not personally compatible. The Armistice put paid to any more progress and the parts that had been assembled were destroyed.

While the development work was being carried out on the R.I projects, work continued on producing the smaller J models. The J.3 was scheduled to be the first to be completely covered in the corrugated metal, but for some unknown reason the airframe was never completed. However, several experiments were carried out after a number of misgivings had been expressed regarding the safety of an all-metal cantilever wing. In order to dispel any fears, Junkers had forty-two of their workers stand on an unsupported J.3 wing. The experiment was a complete success and work continued on the production of the wing without any more concerns being expressed.

There was no J.4, J.5 or J.6, but the J.7 was built at the beginning of 1917. The J.7 was the prototype for the J.9 or D.I model that went into production at the beginning of 1918.

Still continuing with the monoplane theme, the J.7 was the subject of a number of variants, some with ailerons, and some without. Powered by a 160-hp Mercedes D.III engine with a car-type radiator at the nose, the J.7 had a top speed of 105 mph.

A matter of months later, the Junkers J.8 appeared. This all-metal aircraft was a two-seat prototype of what was to ultimately be the one of the mainstays of the Schlachtstaffeln, the J.10 (CL.I). It was powered by a 180-hp Mercedes D.IIIa engine, which gave it a top speed of 100 mph and a climb rate of almost 1,000 feet per minute. It had a wingspan of 39 ft 6 in, a fuselage length of 25 ft 11 in, and a height of 7 ft 8½ in. It was armed with twin synchronized fixed Spandau machine guns and one manually operated Parabellum machine gun mounted in the rear cockpit. In total, forty-seven Junkers J.10s were built and all were in action right up until the end of the war.

The German Navy, impressed with the J.10, requested a seaplane version. Three were converted and given the designation J.11 (CLS.I). It was almost identical to the J.10 with the exception of an additional fin fitted on the fuselage in front of the tailplane and, of course, the addition of floats instead of an undercarriage. It was powered by a 200-hp Benz engine, which gave the aircraft a top speed of 112 mph. It had a wingspan of 41 ft 10 in, a fuselage length of 29 ft 4½ in, and a height of 9 ft 8 in. Its armament was the same as that of the J.10.

Although Junkers' contribution to First World War aviation was not as great as some of the other aircraft manufacturers, they became one of the most prominent elements some years later when the two warring factions were once again at each other's throats.

## SPECIFICATIONS

### Junkers J.I

| | |
|---|---|
| Length: | 24 ft 4 in (7.43 m) |
| Height: | 10 ft 3¼ in (3.13 m) |
| Weight Empty: | 1,980 lb (900 kg) |
| Weight Loaded: | 2,222 lb (1,010 kg) |
| Engine: | One 120-hp Mercedes D.II six-cylinder, in-line, water-cooled |
| Maximum Speed: | 100 mph (160 km/h) |
| Service Ceiling: | 12,000 feet (3,657 m) |
| Endurance: | 1¼ hours |
| Armament: | None |

### Junkers J.I (J.4)

| | |
|---|---|
| Wing Span: | 52 ft 6 in (16.0 m) |
| Length: | 29 ft 10½ in (9.1 m) |
| Height: | 11 ft 1½ in (3.4 m) |
| Weight Empty: | 3,885 lb (1,766 kg) |
| Weight Loaded: | 4,787 lb (2,176 kg) |
| Engine: | One 200-hp Benz Bz.IV six-cylinder, in-line, water-cooled |
| Maximum Speed: | 97 mph (155 km/h) |
| Service Ceiling: | 26,520 feet (8,083 m) |
| Endurance: | 2 hours |
| Armament: | Two fixed forward-firing Spandau machine-guns One manually operated Parabellum machine-gun in rear observer's cockpit |

# Lohnerwerke GmbH

In 1909, the coach and automobile manufacturers Jakob Lohner & Co. decided to expand their business and enter the world of aviation. The manager of the company, Ludwig Lohner, son of the founder, called upon his friend Ferdinand Porsche to help him in the design and construction of the aircraft. Porsche had joined the company in 1899 and was instrumental in developing and constructing the first electric automobile built by Lohner. Over 300 of these vehicles were built, most of which were fire engines. In 1906, Porsche left Lohner to take up the position of Technical Director of the Oesterreichische Daimler Motoren AG (Austro-Daimler), but still retained his ties with Ludwig Lohner concerning the development of aircraft engines.

As was the trend in the early days of aviation, the only people who could afford to buy aircraft were the wealthy and they had the aircraft customised to their own requirements. The first of the Lohner aircraft to be produced was designed by an engineer and Army officer, Rittmeister Hans Umlauff von Frankwell. He took the company's shop floor manager, Karl Paulal, under his guidance and, despite him having no engineering background, made him chief aircraft designer at Lohner.

The biplane, designed and built by Umlauff and Paulal, was powered by a 65-hp Austro-Daimler engine – designed by Ferdinand Porsche – and took to the air in the summer of 1910. The first and second flight tests, flown by Umlauff, were so successful that an improved model, known as the Lohner-Daimler Pfeilflieger, was built. It had what was to become a Lohner trademark, swept-back wings, and had its first flight in October 1910. Piloted by Umlauff, the Pfeilflieger took part in a number of flying contests winning most of them, including the prestigious Vienna-Budapest-Vienna race on 24 June 1911.

Success with this aircraft brought about contracts to build more and over 200 were built in various forms. Other aircraft manufacturers started to take notice of the high standard of workmanship produced by the Lohner Company, and in July 1910 they were approached by Igor Etrich to build five of his designed Taube monoplanes. The following month, Igor Etrich sold the Taube design patents, together with the premises and airfield, to the Motor-Luftfahrzeug-Gesellschaft (MLG), one of the companies under the control of Camillo Castiglioni.

The Lohner Company continued to manufacture the Etrich Taube airframes, delivering them to MLG's facility at Wiener-Neustadt where the engines and instruments were installed. A total of fifty-eight of these airframes were built by Lohner, twenty-nine of which were delivered to the Austro-Hungarian Air Service on completion, and a further ten were sent to various countries for evaluation by them; sixteen were sold privately, the remaining three being retained by the MLG flying school.

A number of modifications were made to improve the Taube, but it soon became obvious that it was out of date and other designs were being considered. In September 1912, Camillo Castiglioni approached Ludwig Lohner with a proposition that would give his company, MLG, the world sales rights for any aircraft that Lohner built. In return, MLG would pay two-thirds of all the expenses that their design department incurred. Lohner took up the offer, even though he realised that there were going to be major differences between them because of their personalities.

The company rapidly made strides and quickly moved into second position behind French companies in the world rankings of manufacturers. This brought the company to the attention of the War Ministry, who were starting to take an interest in the use of the aeroplane for military purposes. In 1912, they ordered twenty-eight Type B Pfeilfliegers and were immediately criticised for not supporting smaller companies. The order in effect gave the Lohner Company a monopoly with regard to the supplying of military aircraft, which in turn also gave Camillo Castiglioni a firmer grasp of the Austro-Hungarian aviation industry.

The sale of these aircraft suffered a setback on 9 March 1914, when Leutnant Elsner, together with his observer, was killed when the wings of his Type C Pfeilflieger collapsed during an acceptance flight. Immediately, the War Ministry ordered that all the remaining aircraft be grounded, and that deliveries of the remaining order be halted until the cause was discovered. The Pfeilflieger's designer, Karl Paulal, was devastated when it was discovered that the wings had failed because they were well below the specified load factor. The company was accused by Oberstleutnant Emil Uzelac, Head of Luftschifferabteilung (LA), of complacency since acquiring the monopoly of providing aircraft to the military. He had been on inspection tours of both English and French aircraft manufacturing facilities and had seen the high degree of skill used on the production of their aircraft.

He ordered the firm to redesign and replace all the wings of all the remaining aircraft, and at their own cost. The load tests during the inquiry had been carried out by Professor Richard Knoller, who was immediately recruited by the Lohner Company to oversee the re-designing of the wing and its manufacture.

The first of the aircraft with the reinforced wing was the Type-B, but once again disaster struck when, during a test flight, the fuselage collapsed while the aircraft was in the air, killing the pilot. The fault was traced to the wood being used for the fuselage and once again Uzelac blamed the company for complacency and its failure to use flawless wood in the construction of its aircraft.

The Type B saw heavy action during the Balkans crisis and when, in December 1913, they were returned to the company for repairs, the top wing was replaced by a new type of cellule wing known as the 'Spanish Wing'. The two halves of the top wing were fixed at the centre line, which eliminated the need for a centre-section cabane; this was replaced by inverted-V struts. The rounded ailerons were replaced by rectangular ones and the tips of the wing could be folded down for ease of storing.

In June 1913, the Spanish Government placed an order for five Lohner B.Is, all of which were fitted with the 'Spanish Wing' and were delivered in October 1913 to Quatro Vientos by MLG's technical manager, Karl Illner.

With the advent of the First World War the Lohner Company sprang into production and the first of their operational aircraft, the military version of the Lohner Type B, the Lohner B.I, appeared. It was not the success hoped for, and after a brief sojourn at the front line they were returned to the factory to be converted into two-seater trainers with dual controls. The first tests revealed that the undercarriage needed strengthening and that the controls, which were said to be over-sensitive, were in fact extremely docile and ideal for training purposes.

The German Army had a total of thirty-nine aircraft available when they were mobilised on 25 July 1914, thirty of which were Lohner Type Bs. A further seven were Lohner Type Ds and two Type C prototypes. The majority of the aircraft were assigned to the Fifth Army and placed under the command of Oberleutnant Baar, who commanded Flik 2. The aircraft were not up to flying military missions and were literally kept in the air using bits of wire and cannibalised parts from other aircraft. Reports from the Fifth Army back to the factory condemned the aircraft out of hand, and as soon as aircraft started to arrive from other manufacturers, the Lohner B.Is were replaced.

In the meantime the company had been working on the Type C Gebirgsflieger (Mountain Flyer), which was a lighter version of the Type B (B.I) and was powered by an 85-hp Hiero four-cylinder engine. The prototype was sent to the Luftschifferabteilung (LA) in August 1913 for evaluation. A second prototype was delivered in January 1914 and after extensive tests the LA ordered twenty-four Type Cs (B.II). A third prototype was produced which had a longer fuselage and reinforced engine mounts in preparation for larger and more powerful engines to be fitted.

The first production model, given the designation C-1 (B.II), was delivered at the beginning of February 1914, quickly followed by a further five of the aircraft at the end of the month. Among the first pilots to test the aircraft were Lili Steinschneider, Hungary's first woman pilot, and Oberstleutnant Emil Uzelac. Uzelac almost always tried to fly any new aircraft that was sent to the LA for evaluation. He took the Lohner Type C (B.II) on a test flight, and on his return reported that there were severe vibration problems, that it was nose heavy and he was only able to land the aircraft safely after pulling the control wheel tight against his chest. Lohner blamed the Hiero engine, but Uzelac refuted this, saying that he had flown the Etrich Taube, which had been powered by a Hiero engine, and had had no problems with that aircraft at all.

Tragedy struck on 9 March 1914 when the second prototype Type C, flown by Oberleutnant Eugen Elsner with his observer Zugsführer Philipp Srna, crashed when the left wing collapsed while in level flight, killing both occupants. All the Lohner aircraft were immediately grounded and orders for additional aircraft suspended.

A new wing was designed by Professor Knoller and fitted to the B.II, which resolved the problem. All the existing B.IIs were fitted with the new wing, initially at the company's expense, but later funded by the LA. However, like the B.I, it was quickly replaced by better aircraft from other companies.

As new aircraft appeared from the Lohner factory, a new version was always on the drawing boards as in the case of the Type D (B.III). This aircraft, powered by a new 120-hp Daimler engine, made its appearance at the beginning of May 1913 and went into production the following month following its success at the Second International Flying Meeting. The LA ordered seven of the aircraft, all of which were delivered by the end of September 1913. Once again problems dogged the Lohner aircraft and after a series of emergency landings, the B.III was grounded until the problems had been resolved.

The escalation of the war prompted the LA and Lohner to accelerate the repair work and in July 1914, four of the B.IIIs were sent to the Russian Front. Two of the aircraft were shot down by Russian ground troops within days of arriving because they were unable to climb above 1,640 feet, making them vulnerable to ground fire. Another crashed after its wing collapsed, killing both crewmembers. The news reached the LA, who immediately grounded all the remaining aircraft and later scrapped most of them, although a number were used for training purposes. There were a couple of variations to the B.III; the Type E was one of them and this was fitted with strengthened wings.

Twenty-four Type Es were ordered, the bulk of which were delivered in April 1915. They were assigned to three Fliks, Nos 2, 12 and 16. Within weeks, a report from the commanding officer of Flik 12 complained that the Type E was virtually useless as a combat aircraft. The poor rate of climb and limited ceiling of the aircraft prohibited it from carrying machine guns or bombs; this, together with the mountainous terrain in which it was expected operate, made the aircraft almost useless. Once again, delivery of the Lohner B.III aircraft to combat groups was halted and the remaining aircraft re-directed to training units.

Concerned about the negative reports that were coming back from the various Fronts, Lohner, under the direction of Major von Umlauff, took one of the Type E aircraft and fitted newly designed wings, a simplified undercarriage and the latest 100-hp Mercedes engine. The Type G, as it was designated, was sent to the LA for evaluation, where it was given the designation Lohner B.IV. Only the one was built.

The Type H (Lohner B.V) was the next aircraft to appear, and this was fitted with the more powerful 140-hp Rapp engine. However, once again problems with the engine, carburettor fires and excessive oil consumption, coupled with structural problems with the aircraft itself caused it to be grounded. A total of twenty-four were ordered, but only six of the aircraft were built, none of which saw action. The Luftfahrtruppen (LFT) ordered that the remaining eighteen Type Hs be redesigned to meet the stringent requirements that were now being required for all combat aircraft.

The eighteen aircraft were modified by reducing the wingspan and replacing the plywood fuselage covering with traditional fabric. With the modifications completed on all the aircraft, they were assigned to Flugpark 1 and given the designation Lohner B.VI. Some of them were assigned to various Fliks, but only for training purposes.

The lessons learned from the problems with the previous Lohner aircraft finally came to fruition with the Lohner B.VII (Type J). The Rapp engine, the main cause of many of the problems, was replaced with the more powerful and reliable 150-hp Daimler engine. The plywood covering of the fuselage reverted back to fabric and a single machine gun was fitted on a pivot in the observer's cockpit. The LA placed an order for one prototype, which was quickly followed by a further twenty-four B.VIIs (Type J).

The first of the new aircraft were assigned to Fliks 6, 9 and 15, which were operating in the Balkans, and to Fliks 7, 16 and 19, which were operating on the Italian Front. The criticisms of the early Lohners disappeared with the B.VII. Reports coming back from the Fliks operating in the high mountains were extremely favourable and expressed their trust in the aircraft. During the next few months, the B.VII was involved in numerous long-range reconnaissance and bombing missions, but the reliability of the 150-hp Daimler was in doubt. The answer was to install the 160-hp Daimler engine into the next generation of Lohner B.VIIs, which increased the reliability and the range of the aircraft.

One of the first major raids carried out by the Austro-Hungarian Air Force was the attack against the Milan electro-generating plant on 14 February 1916. Twelve Lohner B.VIIs from Fliks 7, 17 and 16, based at Gardolo and Pergine, took off on the round trip of 260 miles, flying over mountainous terrain. Of the twelve aircraft that took off, only nine actually reached the target; of the remaining three, one bombed Monza by mistake and the other two had to make forced landings after engine trouble.

A third series of the Lohner B.VII appeared at the beginning of 1916. Having been fitted with a 160-hp Daimler engine, a modified fuselage and a machine gun mounted on a ring, the aircraft was assigned to Fliks 7, 8 and 17 based in the

Austrian Tyrol and Fliks 12 and 23 on the Italian Front. Within months they had been withdrawn and replaced by the Brandenburg C.I. The Lohner aircraft were returned to Flugpark 1, where they were assigned to training Fliks for advanced pilot instruction.

The appearance of the Lohner C.I (Type Jc) at the beginning of December 1915 was intended to herald a new era in aircraft manufacture for the Lohner Company, but things turned out differently. The prototype, powered by the 160-hp Daimler engine, was evaluated and described by the test pilots for the LA as an aircraft that was 'hopelessly inadequate' in every area. Because of the desperate situation, and the need for more and more aircraft, the flight specifications had been lowered, but even then the aircraft could not measure up to the standard required. Twenty-four of the aircraft had been ordered and when they finally did arrive, they were assigned to Fliks 1, 4, 9, 11 and 14 to be used as trainers.

An improved version, the Lohner C.I (Type Jcr), appeared in September 1916, again powered by the 160-hp Daimler engine but fitted with a new cellule wing. It was a slight improvement on the first version and just about scraped through the lowered specification requirements, but even then the Flik pilots were reluctant to fly the aircraft under combat conditions. Seventeen of the aircraft were produced and all assigned to Fliks as trainers, although a small number were armed with a machine gun and pressed into home-defence duties.

At the beginning of February 1916, with his order books virtually empty, Ludwig Lohner went to Berlin to try and persuade the Luft-Fahrzeug-Gesellschaft (LFG) to grant him a licence to build the Roland C.II. It was unsuccessful, but undaunted Lohner approached the Fliegerarsenal (Flars) with a design, which was at first rejected, but later, after some improvements, was accepted. Flars ordered four prototypes, the first being delivered on the 1 March 1917. Flars engineers examined the aircraft and immediately found fault with the forward visibility, which in their opinion was almost nil. They ordered that the fuselage be altered to improve the forward visibility, to increase the observer's area and to strengthen the gun mount.

The first test flight was carried out on 4 April 1917, and it was discovered that the wing struts were weak; it was later discovered that there had been a miscalculation in the design stage, and that the aircraft was tail-heavy. The aircraft was immediately grounded. Modifications were made, but did not improve the aircraft sufficiently for Flars to accept it and it was placed in storage. The remaining three prototypes were modified but Flars accepted none.

With nothing imminent on the Lohner drawing boards, the LA ordered the Lohner Company to assemble forty-eight Knoller C.II biplanes, the design for which had been inspired by the Fliegerarsenal (Flars). They were not the only company in this position; Aviatik and Wiener Karosserie und Flugzeugfabrik (WKF) were also contracted to assemble aircraft for other companies. The first of the Knoller C.II biplanes came off the Lohner production line in December 1916, the first being sent to the LA for flight-testing. Problems with the wing spars and the airframe were discovered, similar to the ones found in the Aviatik-built Knoller C.IIs. It wasn't until May 1917 that the first of the Lohner-built Knoller C.IIs was accepted, and only then after a number of modifications.

The first of the Knoller C.II aircraft were sent to Flars for evaluation; they, in turn, sent it to the Front, three of the Aviatik-built Knollers going to Flik 50. The response from the front-line pilots was not the one they wanted to hear. Reports coming back stated that the aircraft was useless as a combat aircraft because of its poor flight characteristics, the shoddy workmanship of the Lohner-built models and its fragility – it was withdrawn immediately. Some were scrapped, others ended up as trainers.

Despite the company's record for producing aircraft that were not up to standard, they were given another contract to build fifty Aviatik C.I biplanes. Construction began in April 1917, the first being delivered in August 1917. Twenty-four of the Aviatik C.I (Lo) aircraft were to be fitted with the 185-hp Daimler engine, while the remaining twenty-six were to be fitted with the 200-hp Daimler engine. Engine shortages were to reduce the number of aircraft delivered considerably.

Once again the workmanship of the Lohner Company was to let it down, and none of the Aviatik C.I aircraft built by Lohner were liked by the pilots and observers; they preferred the superior Aviatik-built models. The Lohner-built models were converted to single-seat reconnaissance aircraft by covering the observer's cockpit and placing a sack of sand equivalent to the weight of an observer inside.

In August 1916, Lohner put forward a proposal for a single-seater fighter – the Lohner D.I. Flars approved the initial design, by Leopold Bauer, and ordered four prototypes: three biplanes and one triplane. Once again the design of the aircraft did not match the end result. There were problems from the very start; during taxiing trials it was found that there was insufficient rudder area and despite an enlarged rudder being fitted, the problem was still not resolved. On the first short hop, several of the wing spars broke on landing. Numerous modifications were made to all the other prototypes, but Flars refused to accept them and the projects were abandoned.

In mid-1917, Lohner embarked on the production of the Aviatik D.I single-seater fighter. Ninety-three of these aircraft had been ordered initially, with a further ninety-six to follow, bringing the total to 189. In September 1918 this was reduced to 165. Two series, 115 and 315 were created; the first series aircraft were to be powered by the 200-hp Daimler engine, the second by the 225-hp Daimler engine. The first of the 115 series aircraft arrived at the Front in May 1918, and within days pilots were reporting the failure of the trailing edges of the wings. Lohner immediately sent a repair team to the front to carry out repairs, and with them an engineer. The engineer examined the trailing edge problem and found that Lohner had replaced the standard rib section with a much lighter one, and had fixed the fabric in such a way that it was contrary to the orders laid down by Aviatik.

Emil Uzelac was informed of the engineer's finding and ordered the series 115 aircraft to be returned to the factory for the wings to be replaced to the standard set down by Aviatik. Unfortunately, the order to send the aircraft back came too late for the Austro-Hungarian Air Force's top ace, Oberleutnant Frank Linke-Crawford. He was on patrol when he was attacked by British fighters; his aircraft was seen to pull out of a dive with fabric being torn from the wings and as he fought to regain control, he was shot down and killed. The majority of the 115 series of aircraft were never used in front-line combat except for photo-reconnaissance missions. Of the 315 series of aircraft built by Lohner, none ever saw front-line service.

Lohner's contribution to the part played by the Austro-Hungarian Air Force in the First World War was considerable and memorable, but not for the right reasons.

## SPECIFICATIONS

## Lohner B.I

Wingspan Upper:     43 ft 11 in (13.4 m)

| | |
|---|---|
| Wingspan Lower: | 31 ft 6 in (9.6 m) |
| Length: | 27 ft 10 in (8.5 m) |
| Height: | 9 ft 7 in (3.0 m) |
| Weight Empty: | 1,389 lb (630 kg) |
| Weight Loaded: | 2,139 lb (970 kg) |
| Maximum Speed: | 71 mph (115 km/h) |
| Engine: | One 90-hp Daimler |
| Armament: | None |

## Lohner B.II

| | |
|---|---|
| Wingspan Upper: | 42 ft 7 in (13.0 m) |
| Wingspan Lower: | 30 ft 2 in (9.2 m) |
| Length: | 27 ft 3 in (8.3 m) |
| Height: | 10 ft 6 in (3.2 m) |
| Weight Empty: | 1,235 lb (560 kg) |
| Weight Loaded: | 2,029 lb (920 kg) |
| Maximum Speed: | 78 mph (125 km/h) |
| Engine: | One 85-hp Hiero |
| Armament: | None |

## Lohner B.III

| | |
|---|---|
| Wingspan Lower: | 37 ft 5 in (11.4 m) |
| Length: | 31 ft 2 in (9.5 m) |
| Height: | 11 ft 6 in (3.5 m) |
| Weight Empty: | 1,665 lb (755 kg) |
| Weight Loaded: | 2,701 lb (1,225 kg) |
| Maximum Speed: | 81 mph (130 km/h) |
| Engine: | One 125-hp Daimler |
| Armament: | Machine gun in observer's cockpit |

## Lohner B.IV

| | |
|---|---|
| Wingspan Upper: | 44 ft 8 in (13.6 m) |
| Wingspan Lower: | 29 ft 10 in (9.1 m) |
| Length: | 27 ft 7 in (8.4 m) |
| Height: | 10 ft 9 in (3.3 m) |
| Weight Empty: | 1,599 lb (725 kg) |
| Weight Loaded: | 2,205 lb (1,000 kg) |
| Maximum Speed: | 71 mph (115 km/h) |
| Engine: | One 100-hp Mercedes |
| Armament: | None |

## Lohner B.VI

| | |
|---|---|
| Wingspan Upper: | 41 ft 11 in (12.8 m) |
| Wingspan Lower: | 37 ft 5 in (11.4 m) |
| Length: | 24 ft 11 in (7.6 m) |
| Height: | 9 ft 10 in (3.0 m) |
| Weight Empty: | 1,768 lb (802 kg) |
| Weight Loaded: | 2,657 lb (1,205 kg) |
| Maximum Speed: | 75 mph (123 km/h) |

Engine:               One 140-hp Rapp
Armament:             None

## Lohner B.VII

| | |
|---|---|
| Wingspan Upper: | 50 ft 6 in (15.4 m) |
| Wingspan Lower: | 36 ft 8 in (11.2 m) |
| Length: | 31 ft 11 in (9.5 m) |
| Height: | 12 ft 4 in (3.75 m) |
| Weight Empty: | 2,075 lb (941 kg) |
| Weight Loaded: | 3,069 lb (1,392 kg) |
| Maximum Speed: | 77 mph (124 km/h) |
| Engine: | One 160-hp Daimler |
| Armament: | None |

## Lohner C.I

| | |
|---|---|
| Wingspan Upper: | 41 ft 11 in (12.8 m) |
| Wingspan Lower: | 39 ft 8 in (12.1 m) |
| Length: | 30 ft 4 in (9.2 m) |
| Height: | 10 ft 9 in (3.3 m) |
| Weight Empty: | 1,916 lb (869 kg) |
| Weight Loaded: | 2,939 lb (1,333 kg) |
| Maximum Speed: | 82 mph (132 km/h) |
| Engine: | One 160-hp Daimler |
| Armament: | None |

## Knoller C.II (Lo)

| | |
|---|---|
| Wingspan Upper: | 32 ft 8 in (10.0 m) |
| Wingspan Lower: | 26 ft 4 in (8.0 m) |
| Length: | 27 ft 11 in (8.5 m) |
| Height: | 10 ft 6 in (3.2 m) |
| Weight Empty: | 1,656 lb (751 kg) |
| Weight Loaded: | 2,331 lb (1,057 kg) |
| Maximum Speed: | 100 mph (161 km/h) |
| Engine: | One 160-hp Daimler |
| Armament: | None |

## Aviatik C.I (Lo)

| | |
|---|---|
| Wingspan Upper: | 27 ft 6 in (8.4 m) |
| Wingspan Lower: | 27 ft 6 in (8.4 m) |
| Length: | 25 ft 3 in (7.6 m) |
| Height: | 9 ft 8 in (2.9 m) |
| Weight Empty: | 1,433 lb (650 kg) |
| Weight Loaded: | 2,183 lb (990 kg) |
| Maximum Speed: | 100 mph (161 km/h) |
| Engine: | One 185-hp Daimler |
| Armament: | None |

## Aviatik D.I (Lo)

Wingspan Lower:     25 ft 9 in (7.8 m)
Length:             22 ft 5 in (6.8 m)
Height:             8 ft 2 in (2.5 m)
Weight Empty:       1,407 lb (638 kg)
Weight Loaded:      2,011 lb (912 kg)
Maximum Speed:      115 mph (185 km/h)
Engine:             One 225-hp Daimler
Armament:           None

Gotha WD.2 seaplane.

Friedrichshafen FF.29 seaplane.

Gotha G.IV without camouflage paint.

Gotha G.IV of Flik 101G.

An engineer making his way to one of the upper gun stations of a Gotha bomber.

An Austro-Hungarian Hansa-Brandenburg B.I, after a landing accident.

Hansa-Brandenburg C.I (U) of Flik 26S.

Feldmarschalleutnant Zeidler in a Hansa-Brandenburg C.I (U).

Aircrew of Flik 16D posing in front of a Hansa-Brandenburg C.I (U) at Feltre airfield.

Junkers J.4.

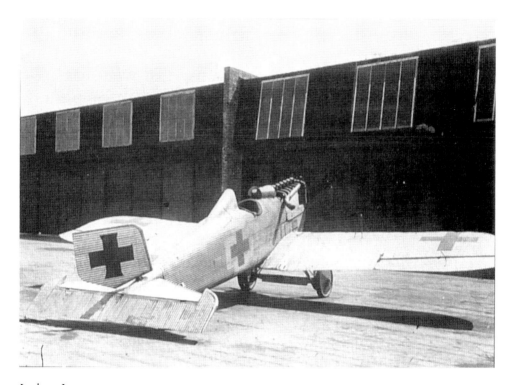

Junkers J.9.

Roland D.IIs of Jasta 25 in the Balkans.

Roland D.XVI.

Lohner B.II, showing the swept-back wing.

Lohner B.VII of Flik 16.

Lohner B.VII.

An Aviatik C.I built by Lohner, of Flik 49D.

Lohner C.II.

Aviatik D.I built by Lohner.

Lohner Dr.I triplane.

168

Lohner Type AA, third version.

Lohner Type AA, prototype.

Oberstleutnant Emil Uzelac talking to his pilots.

Ace pilot Max
Immelmann and
his observer,
Alfred von
Keller, in their
LVG C.I.

LVG C.V on patrol over the front in 1917.

LVG C.VI, flown by Leutnant Walter Igles and Deckoffizier Brandt, after a daylight raid over London.

Oeffag C.I fighter of Flik 25 on patrol over the Russian Front.

Oeffag C.II.

A new Oeffag C.II outside the factory.

An Oeffag-made Albatros D.III of Flik 17/D.

An Oeffag-made Albatros D.II taking off in Russia.

Oeffag-made Albatros D.II fighters of Jagdstaffel Essler.

Oeffag-made Albatros D.III taking off from Romagnano airfield.

Oeffag-made Albatros D.IIIs at Gardolo airfield.

The pilot of an Oeffag-made Albatros D.III waves his fist in triumph after shooting down a SPAD.

Mechanics of Flik 35/D with an Oeffag-made Albatros D.III.

Aircraft of Flik 91 lined up, including Phönix D.IIs and Oeffag-made Albatros D.IIIs.

The cockpit of an Oeffag-made Albatros D.III, showing the twin machine guns.

Otto pusher biplane.

Pfalz A.I.

Pfalz C.I.

Pfalz-Kampflugzeug
(Type: D. III)

Pfalz D.IIIa.

Pfalz D.XII.

Pfalz E.II.

Pfalz D.XV.

Leutnant Otto Kissenberth with his Pfalz E.I.

Pfalz E.IV, seen outside the factory.

Test pilot Eugen Wiencziers posing with a Pfalz E.V.

Mechanics servicing a Pfalz Dr.II.

A French Morane Parasol built under licence by Pfalz.

# Luftfahrzeug Gesellschaft (LFG)

The company LFG had its roots back in 1906, when a company by the name of Motorluftschiff Studiengesellschaft had been created at the instigation of Wilhelm II, to carry out the manufacture of airships. The company changed its name a few years later to LFG Bitterfeld, from which sprang another company by the name of Flugmaschine Wright GmbH. This company went into liquidation in 1912, but was revived by a number of top financiers, including among them Alfred Krupp. So as not to be confused with the aircraft company LVG, the name Roland was added to the chosen name for the company of LFG creating the company LFG Roland (Roland was the name of a legendary knight and symbolised strength and courage).

The first factory opened up at Aldershof, but was destroyed by a mysterious fire on 6 September 1916, said to have been caused by the British Secret Service. The company then moved to Charlottenburg, where it continued to manufacture aircraft.

One of the first military aircraft to be produced by LFG Roland was the C.II, a two-seat reconnaissance model. The C.I had been built by Albatros, so when LFG produced its own aircraft, its designation automatically started with C.II. The fuselage of the C.II was considered by some to possibly cause problems in control, because the top wing had been fitted directly to the top of the fuselage. In an attempt to re-create the problem, the airframe was mounted on top of a flat-top railway wagon and a series of fast runs made on a long stretch of fast, straight track. The results were encouraging but it wasn't the same as carrying out the tests under flying conditions because other aspects had to be considered.

The first prototype of the C.II appeared in October 1915, the brainchild of Dipl. Ing. Tantzen, but was lost on the second test flight due to engine failure. A second model was quickly produced, but problems were discovered in its directional stability; these were found to be due to the very thin wings that tended to distort after long periods of flight.

The first production models were supplied to various Flieger Abteilung (Fl.Abt.) units for reconnaissance missions. The only armament carried was a manually operated Parabellum machine gun mounted in the observer's rear cockpit. One of the Fl.Abt. units was Flieger Abteilung 4, commanded by Hauptmann Eduard Ritter von Schleich, holder of the *Pour le Mérite*, who was also known as the 'Black Knight' because of his all-black leather flying clothing. A number of Allied airmen who came in contact with these two-seat reconnaissance aircraft had tremendous respect for them. Some of the crews, however, said the aircraft resembled a whale and gave it the nickname of *Walfisch*.

The exact number of LFG Roland C.IIs that were built and supplied to the Army is not known, but it is believed to be several hundred. The Linke-Hoffman Company built a number of these aircraft under licence.

The design of the fuselage of the C.II was a departure from the traditional method. It was of a semi-monocoque construction and was built on a skeleton of spruce longerons and plywood formers. The fuselage was covered with a thin plywood strips which were spirally wound on to the frame then glued and pinned. This was then covered in fabric and doped. The unbalanced control surfaces were constructed of steel tube and covered in doped fabric, while the other control surfaces were made of wood and also covered in doped fabric.

The aircraft had a wingspan of 33 ft 9½ in, a fuselage length of 25 ft 3½ in and a height of 9 ft 6 in. Powered by a six-cylinder, in-line, water-cooled 160-hp Mercedes D.III engine, the C.II had a top speed of 103 mph, a relatively slow climb rate of 500 feet per minute and an endurance of 4-5 hours. Later models were armed with a fixed, forward-firing, Parabellum machine gun.

A number of Jastas were supplied with the aircraft including Jasta 27, which, at the time, was commanded by Oberleutnant Hermann Göring. There was one unit whose aircraft consisted entirely of LFG Roland C.IIs, and that was Marine Feldjagdstaffel 2. This unit's aircraft were entirely wiped out by a British bombardment a few months after receiving the aircraft. Their aircraft were replaced with Albatros D.IIIs.

An improved model of the C.II was produced early in 1916, powered by a 200-hp Benz Bz.IV engine. Only the one model was built and that was destroyed in the fire when the factory at Aldershof was burnt down.

Not to be deterred by the fire, the company, after moving to Charlottenburg, decided to produce a single-seat fighter, the LFG Roland D.I. The success of the C.II had given rise to the development of the new aircraft. Looking like a slimmer, more rakish model of the C.II, the D.I was powered by the 160-hp Mercedes D.III engine, which gave the aircraft a top speed of 105 mph. The appearance of the D.I gave rise to its name of *Haifisch* (Shark), which was in direct contrast to the C.II *Walfisch* (Whale) upon which it was based.

The D.I and D.II were powered by the same engine, although another engine was tried for the D.IIa: the 180-hp Argus As.III. This gave the aircraft a top speed of 105 mph and a climb rate of 800 feet per minute.

Both the D.I and D.II had minor differences in their construction, but in the main they were almost identical. Over three hundred of these aircraft were built, but surprisingly the vast majority of these were built by the Pfalz Flugzeug-Werke under licence. With a wingspan of 29 ft 4 in, a fuselage length of 22 ft 9 in, and a height of 10 ft, both aircraft were armed with two fixed, forward-firing Spandau machine guns.

In October 1916, the D.III appeared as a replacement for the D.IIa. Unfortunately, it appeared at the same time as the superior Albatros fighter and only a small number were ever built. Its specifications were the same as that of the D.IIa.

The C series continued to be built, but with no C.IV model, a prototype two-seater based on the D.II design was produced. The C.V model was powered by a 160-hp Mercedes engine and armed with one fixed, forward-firing Spandau machine gun and one manually operated Parabellum machine gun mounted in the observer's cockpit. Only one aircraft was built.

The first, and the last, of the LFG triplanes were built at the beginning of 1917: the single-seat LFG Roland D.IV. It had a number of unusual features, including a tailplane that could be adjusted for incidence prior to flight, and it had ailerons fitted to both upper and lower wings. It was powered by a 160-hp Mercedes D.III engine and was not one of the most elegant looking of all the triplanes built. During its second flight test, at the beginning of September 1917, the aircraft crashed on take-off. Fortunately the damage was repairable and within a week it had been rebuilt, but by the beginning of October the project had been dropped because it showed no advantages over the Roland D.III and D.V biplanes. It is not known how many were built.

The success of the D.I model prompted the Navy to request a single-seat seaplane. A converted D.I, the LFG WD, was produced and, powered by a 160-hp Mercedes engine, had its first flight on 29 June 1917. It was not the success hoped for and only the one prototype was built. There had been an earlier seaplane built by LFG, the LFG W, but it had been an Albatros C.Ia two-seat reconnaissance model that LFG had built under licence. Only one of this type had been built.

Continuing with the D series, the D.V model, a development of the D.III was produced. The fuselage, although based on the previous models, was considerably slimmer. It was powered by a 160-hp Mercedes engine. Only one prototype was built.

The last of the original design two-seaters, the C.VIII, was built at the end of 1917. Based on the design of the C.III, it was powered originally by a 260-hp Mercedes D.IVa engine, but then later by 245-hp Maybach Mb.IV engine. It carried one forward-firing Spandau machine gun and one manually operated Parabellum machine gun mounted in the rear cockpit.

One of the best fighter aircraft from the LFG stable was the LFG Roland D.VIa, the production models of which marked the 1,000th LFG Roland aircraft built. With its distinctive 'clinker-built' fuselage and droopy nose, it presented a sleek, racy look that was backed up with good performance.

The fuselage was constructed in the same manner as a small boat, with slightly tapered strips of spruce wood overlapping each other by two-thirds. It had a large horn-balanced rudder and overhung, balanced ailerons. It was powered by a six-cylinder, in-line, water-cooled Benz Bz.IIIa engine, which gave the D.VIa a top speed of 114 mph and a climb rate of about 1,000 feet per minute.

The LFG Roland D.VIa had a wingspan of 30 ft 10 in, a fuselage length of 20 ft 8½ in and a height of 9 ft 2½ in. A number of the aircraft were operational with Jagdstaffeln (Jasta 23); the remainder saw service with the German Navy, being used for seaplane defence duties.

Another prototype model – there were three in all – was a standard D.VIb, which was fitted with two-bay wings with 'I' interplane struts. Only one was built.

Two prototypes of the LFG Roland D.VII appeared at the beginning of 1918. The first, No. 224/18, was fitted with a 195-hp Benz IIIb direct-drive engine, which gave it a top speed of 108 mph. The second, No. 3910/18, which had differently shaped and balanced ailerons, was also fitted with a 195-hp Benz IIIb engine, although this model had reduction gears to decrease the airscrew speed. Only one of each model was built.

Three D.IX prototypes appeared just after the D.VIIs and were markedly different in every respect. The first version, No. 3001/18, was fitted with a 160-hp Siemens-Halske Sh.III geared rotary engine that turned a four-bladed airscrew. It was also fitted with overhung, balanced ailerons. This was the first time a rotary engine had been used by the LFG Company.

The second of the prototypes had much larger tail surfaces and had a 210-hp Siemens-Halske IIIa geared rotary engine installed. The third version was almost identical to the second, the only difference being the fitting of a large, horn-balanced rudder. All three versions were fitted with twin fixed, forward-firing Spandau machine guns.

The D.X series started with the D.XIII: there appears to have been no D.X, XI or XII. This in fact was no more than a re-engined D.VII with a 195-hp V-8 Korting engine with reduction gearing.

The arrival of the LFG Roland D.XIV, No. 300/18, coincided with the installation of a power plant, the 170-hp Goebel Goe.IIIa rotary engine. Four new versions of the LFG Roland D.XV, the first two using the D.VI airframe, were produced in May 1918. The first, No. 3004/18, incorporated the D.IV 'clinker-built' fuselage. The wings had a considerable stagger and were braced by twin-struts, but no bracing cables were used. It was powered by a 160-hp Mercedes D.III engine, had a wingspan of 28 ft 4½ in and a fuselage length of 20 ft 7 in.

The second D.XV version, No. 3006/18, used the D.VI airframe and was powered by a 180-hp Mercedes D.IIIa engine. The wings were braced by single 'I' struts and, like the first version, were without the use of cables. This was also the last of the LFG Roland fighters to use the 'clinker-built' fuselage.

The third version of the D.XV had slab-sided fuselage constructed of plywood. The wings were braced with 'N' struts made of tubular steel. The engine was a 185-hp BMW III, giving the aircraft a top speed of 105 mph. The fourth version, which was almost identical, was fitted with a 200-hp Benz Bz.IIIa engine that gave the aircraft a top speed of 108 mph.

Inspired by the success of the Fokker E.V fighter, LFG Roland produced the D.XVI. This was a parasol fighter with a plywood-covered fuselage and fabric covered wings. The D.XVI was powered by a 160-hp Siemens-Halske Sh.III rotary engine that drove a four-bladed airscrew. A second version was produced, which had slightly differently shaped vertical tail surfaces. The engine was also changed to the 170-hp Goebel Goe.III rotary.

Just before the Armistice the last in a long line of LFG Roland fighters appeared, the D.XVII. A parasol fighter, it incorporated the same fuselage and power plant as the D.XV prototype. It was armed, as all the previous fighters were, with twin, forward-firing, and synchronised Spandau machine guns.

There was one attempt at producing a bomber: the LFG Roland G.I. Although having two propellers, it was in fact a single-engine aircraft, turning both the propellers through a complicated system of gears and shafts. The aircraft was also fitted with heavy-duty tyres and had twin nose wheels. It was powered by a 245-hp Maybach Mb.IV engine, had a wingspan of 98 ft 9½ in, a fuselage length of 52 ft 2 in, and a top speed of 100 mph. It carried a crew of two and was armed with one manually operated Parabellum machine gun mounted in the rear cockpit.

The same year, LFG put forward a design for a single-seat scout plane. The LFG V.19, or Putbus, as it was called, was a long-wing monoplane built of aluminium and powered by a 110-hp Oberursel rotary engine. The V.19 was a very simply designed aircraft: the fuselage was just a tube of flat wrapped duraluminium. The wings held all the fuel and had automatic shut-off valves that enabled the wings to be removed without first draining the tanks.

Weighing 1,056 lb empty and with a wingspan of 31 ft, the Putbus could reach a speed of 112 mph. Although initially the V.19 Putbus appeared to be better than the W-20, this was proved not to be so. The main problem was that it took ten times longer to assemble and disassemble, and required five waterproof containers to house it. The German Navy's submarine arm was told that it was ready for trials, but then shortly afterwards came defeat for Germany and all such trials and experiments were shelved.

The Luftfahrzeug Gesellschaft Company contributed a great deal to the German war machine and left a lasting legacy in the world of aviation.


# SPECIFICATIONS

## LFG Roland C.II

Wingspan:            33 ft 9½ in (10.3 m)

| | |
|---|---|
| Length: | 25 ft 3½ in (7.7 m) |
| Height: | 9 ft 6 in (2.9 m) |
| Weight Empty: | 1,680 lb (764 kg) |
| Weight Loaded: | 2,824 lb (1,284 kg) |
| Maximum Speed: | 103 mph (165 km/h) |
| Ceiling: | 14,600 ft (4,450 m) |
| Endurance: | 4-5 hours |
| Armament: | One manually operated Parabellum machine-gun mounted in the observer's cockpit and one forward-firing synchronised Spandau machine gun |
| Engine: | One 160-hp Mercedes D.III six-cylinder, in-line, water-cooled |

## LFG Roland C.III

| | |
|---|---|
| Wingspan: | 33 ft 9½ in |
| Length: | 25 ft 3½ in |
| Height: | 9 ft 6 in |
| Weight Empty: | 1,680 lb |
| Weight Loaded: | 2,824 lb |
| Maximum Speed: | 103 mph |
| Ceiling: | 14,600 ft |
| Endurance: | 4-5 hours |
| Armament: | One manually operated Parabellum machine-gun mounted in the observer's cockpit and one forward-firing synchronised Spandau machine gun |
| Engine: | One 200-hp Benz Bz.IV six-cylinder, in-line, water-cooled |

## LFG Roland C.V

| | |
|---|---|
| Wingspan: | 29 ft 4 in (8.84 m) |
| Length: | 22 ft 9 in (6.93 m) |
| Height: | 10 ft 2½ in (3.11 m) |
| Weight Empty: | 1,573 lb (715 kg) |
| Weight Loaded: | 2,098 lb (954 kg) |
| Maximum Speed: | 105 mph (170 km/h) |
| Ceiling: | 14,600 ft (4,450 m) |
| Endurance: | 4-5 hours |
| Armament: | Two forward-firing synchronised Spandau machine-guns |
| Engine: | One 160-hp Mercedes D.III six-cylinder, in-line, water-cooled (D.II) |

## LFG Roland C.VIII

| | |
|---|---|
| Wingspan: | 33 ft 9½ in |
| Length: | 25 ft 3½ in |
| Height: | 9 ft 6 in |
| Weight Empty: | 1,680 lb |
| Weight Loaded: | 2,824 lb |
| Maximum Speed: | 103 mph |
| Ceiling: | 14,600 ft |
| Endurance: | 4-5 hours |
| Armament: | One manually operated Parabellum machine-gun mounted in the observer's cockpit and one forward-firing |

|                |                                                        |
|----------------|--------------------------------------------------------|
|                | synchronised Spandau machine gun                       |
| Engine:        | One 260-hp Mercedes D.IVa six-cylinder, in-line,       |
|                | water-cooled                                           |

## LFG Roland D.I

| | |
|----------------|--------------------------------------------------------|
| Wingspan:      | 29 ft 4 in (8.84 m)                                    |
| Length:        | 22 ft 9 in (6.93 m)                                    |
| Height:        | 10 ft 2½ in (3.11 m)                                   |
| Weight Empty:  | 1,573 lb (715 kg)                                      |
| Weight Loaded: | 2,098 lb (954 kg)                                      |
| Maximum Speed: | 105 mph (170 km/h)                                     |
| Ceiling:       | 14,600 ft (4,450m)                                     |
| Endurance:     | 4-5 hours                                              |
| Armament:      | Two forward-firing synchronised Spandau machine-guns   |
| Engine:        | One 100-hp Mercedes D.I six-cylinder, in-line, water-cooled |

## LFG Roland D.II & IIa

| | |
|----------------|--------------------------------------------------------|
| Wingspan:      | 29 ft 4 in (8.84 m) (D.II)                             |
|                | 29 ft 2½ in (8.9 m) (D.IIa)                            |
| Length:        | 22 ft 9 in (6.93 m) (D.II)                             |
|                | 22 ft 9½ in (6.95 m) (D.IIa)                           |
| Height:        | 10 ft 2½ in (3.11 m) (D.II)                            |
|                | 9 ft 8 in (2.95 m) (D.IIa)                             |
| Weight Empty:  | 1,573 lb (715 kg) (D.II)                               |
|                | 1,397 lb (635 kg) (D.IIa)                              |
| Weight Loaded: | 2,098 lb (954 kg) (D.II)                               |
|                | 1,749 lb (795 kg) (D.IIa)                              |
| Maximum Speed: | 105 mph (170 km/h)                                     |
| Ceiling:       | 14,600 ft (4,450 m)                                    |
| Endurance:     | 4-5 hours                                              |
| Armament:      | Two forward-firing synchronised Spandau machine guns   |
| Engine:        | One 160-hp Mercedes D.III six-cylinder, in-line,       |
|                | water-cooled (D.II)                                    |
|                | One 180-hp Argus As.III six-cylinder, in-line,         |
|                | water-cooled (D.IIa)                                   |

## LFG Roland D.III

| | |
|----------------|--------------------------------------------------------|
| Wingspan:      | 29 ft 4 in                                             |
| Length:        | 22 ft 9 in                                             |
| Height:        | 10 ft 2½ in                                            |
| Weight Empty:  | 1,577 lb (717 kg)                                      |
| Weight Loaded: | 2,114 lb (961 kg)                                      |
| Maximum Speed: | 105 mph                                                |
| Ceiling:       | 14,600 ft                                              |
| Endurance:     | 1 hour                                                 |
| Armament:      | Two forward-firing synchronised Spandau machine-guns   |
| Engine:        | One 180-hp Argus As.III six-cylinder, in-line, water-cooled |

## LFG Roland D.IV

| | |
|---|---|
| Wingspan: | 30 ft 10 in (9.4 m) |
| Length: | 20 ft 9 in (6.32 m) |
| Height: | 9 ft 2½ in (2.8 m) |
| Weight Empty: | 1,450 lb (650 kg) |
| Weight Loaded: | 1,892 lb (860 kg) |
| Maximum Speed: | 114 mph (182 km/h) |
| Ceiling: | 19,600 ft (5,974 m) |
| Endurance: | 2 hours |
| Armament: | Two forward-firing synchronised Spandau machine guns |
| Engine: | One 160-hp Mercedes D.III six-cylinder, in-line, water-cooled |

## LFG Roland D.V

| | |
|---|---|
| Wingspan: | 29 ft 4 in |
| Length: | 22 ft 9 in |
| Height: | 10 ft 2½ in |
| Weight Empty: | 1,577 lb (717 kg) |
| Weight Loaded: | 2,114 lb (961 kg) |
| Maximum Speed: | 105 mph |
| Ceiling: | 14,600 ft |
| Endurance: | 1 hour |
| Armament: | Two forward-firing synchronised Spandau machine guns |
| Engine: | One 160-hp Merecedes D.III. six-cylinder, in-line, water-cooled |

## LFG Roland D.VIa

| | |
|---|---|
| Wingspan: | 30 ft 10 in (9.4 m) |
| Length: | 20 ft 9 in (6.32 m) |
| Height: | 9 ft 2½ in (2.8 m) |
| Weight Empty: | 1,450 lb (650 kg) |
| Weight Loaded: | 1,892 lb (860 kg) |
| Maximum Speed: | 114 mph (182 km/h) |
| Ceiling: | 19,600 ft (5,974 m) |
| Endurance: | 2 hours |
| Armament: | Two forward-firing synchronised Spandau machine guns |
| Engine: | One 160-hp Mercedes D.III six-cylinder, in-line, water-cooled |

## LFG Roland D.VIb

| | |
|---|---|
| Wingspan: | 30 ft 10 in (9.4 m) |
| Length: | 20 ft 9 in (6.32 m) |
| Height: | 9 ft 2½ in (2.8 m) |
| Weight Empty: | 1,450 lb (650 kg) |
| Weight Loaded: | 1,892 lb (860 kg) |
| Maximum Speed: | 114 mph (182 km/h) |
| Ceiling: | 19,600 ft (5,974 m) |
| Endurance: | 2 hours |
| Armament: | Two forward-firing synchronised Spandau machine guns |
| Engine: | One 200-hp Benz Bz.IIIa six-cylinder, in-line, water-cooled |

## LFG Roland D.VII

| | |
|---|---|
| Wingspan: | 29 ft (8.8 m) |
| Length: | 20 ft 9 in (6.32 m) |
| Height: | 9 ft 2½ in (2.8 m) |
| Weight Empty: | 1,465 lb (666 kg) |
| Weight Loaded: | 1,947 lb (885 kg) |
| Maximum Speed: | 114 mph (182 km/h) |
| Ceiling: | 19,600 ft (5,974 m) |
| Endurance: | 2 hours |
| Armament: | Two forward-firing synchronised Spandau machine guns |
| Engine: | One 195-hp Benz Bz.IIIb six-cylinder, in-line, water-cooled |

## LFG Roland D.IX

| | |
|---|---|
| Wingspan: | 29 ft 3¼ in (8.9 m) |
| Length: | 20 ft 9 in (6.32 m) |
| Height: | 9 ft 2½ in (2.8 m) |
| Weight Empty: | 1,175 lb (534 kg) |
| Weight Loaded: | 1,658 lb (754 kg) |
| Maximum Speed: | 114 mph (182 km/h) |
| Ceiling: | 19,600 ft (5,974 m) |
| Endurance: | 2 hours |
| Armament: | Two forward-firing synchronised Spandau machine guns |
| Engine: | (First Version): One 160-hp Siemens-Halske Sh.III rotary |
| | (Second Version): One 210-hp Siemens-Halske IIIa |
| | (Third Version): One 210-hp Siemens-Halske IIIa |

## LFG Roland D.XIII

| | |
|---|---|
| Wingspan: | 29 ft 6½ in (9.0 m) |
| Length: | 20 ft 9 in (6.32 m) |
| Height: | 9 ft 2½ in (2.8 m) |
| Weight Empty: | 1,175 lb (534 kg) |
| Weight Loaded: | 1,658 lb (754 kg) |
| Maximum Speed: | 114 mph (182 km/h) |
| Ceiling: | 19,600 ft (5,974 m) |
| Endurance: | 2 hours |
| Armament: | Two forward-firing synchronised Spandau machine guns |
| Engine: | One 195-hp Korting V-8 |

## LFG Roland D.XIV

| | |
|---|---|
| Wingspan: | 29 ft 6½ in (9.0 m) |
| Length: | 20 ft 9 in (6.32 m) |
| Height: | 9 ft 2½ in (2.8 m) |
| Weight Empty: | 1,175 lb (534 kg) |
| Weight Loaded: | 1,658 lb (754 kg) |
| Maximum Speed: | 114 mph (182 km/h) |
| Ceiling: | 19,600 ft (5,974 m) |
| Endurance: | 2 hours |
| Armament: | Two forward-firing synchronised Spandau machine guns |
| Engine: | One 170-hp Goebel Goe.IIIa rotary |

## LFG Roland D.XV

| | |
|---|---|
| Wingspan: | 29 ft 4¼ in (8.6 m) |
| Length: | 20 ft 9 in (6.32 m) |
| Height: | 9 ft 2½ in (2.8 m) |
| Weight Empty: | 1,606 lb (730 kg) |
| Weight Loaded: | 2,002 lb (910 kg) |
| Maximum Speed: | 114 mph (182 km/h) |
| Ceiling: | 19,600 ft (5,974 m) |
| Endurance: | 2 hours |
| Armament: | Two forward-firing synchronised Spandau machine guns |
| Engine: | One 160-hp Mercedes D.III |

## LFG Roland D.XV (Second Version)

| | |
|---|---|
| Wingspan: | 29 ft 6½ in (9.0 m) |
| Length: | 20 ft 9 in (6.32 m) |
| Height: | 9 ft 2½ in (2.8 m) |
| Weight Empty: | 1,606 lb (730 kg) |
| Weight Loaded: | 2,002 lb (910 kg) |
| Maximum Speed: | 114 mph (182 km/h) |
| Ceiling: | 19,600 ft (5,974 m) |
| Endurance: | 2 hours |
| Armament: | Two forward-firing synchronised Spandau machine guns |
| Engine: | One 180-hp Mercedes D.IIIa |

## LFG Roland D.XV (Third Version)

| | |
|---|---|
| Wingspan: | 29 ft 6½ in (9.0 m) |
| Length: | 20 ft 9 in (6.32 m) |
| Height: | 9 ft 2½ in (2.8 m) |
| Weight Empty: | 1,606 lb (730 kg) |
| Weight Loaded: | 2,002 lb (910 kg) |
| Maximum Speed: | 114 mph (182 km/h) |
| Ceiling: | 19,600 ft (5,974 m) |
| Endurance: | 2 hours |
| Armament: | Two forward-firing synchronised Spandau machine guns |
| Engine: | One 185-hp BMW III |

## LFG Roland D.XV (Fourth Version)

| | |
|---|---|
| Wingspan: | 29 ft 6½ in (9.0 m) |
| Length: | 20 ft 9 in (6.32 m) |
| Height: | 9 ft 2½ in (2.8 m) |
| Weight Empty: | 1,606 lb (730 kg) |
| Weight Loaded: | 2,002 lb (910 kg) |
| Maximum Speed: | 114 mph (182 km/h) |
| Ceiling: | 19,600 ft (5,974 m) |
| Endurance: | 2 hours |
| Armament: | Two forward-firing synchronised Spandau machine guns |
| Engine: | One 200-hp Benz Bz.IIIa |

## LFG Roland D.XVI

| | |
|---|---|
| Wingspan: | 27 ft 6 in (8.3 m) |
| Length: | 19 ft 8 in (6.0 m) |
| Height: | 8 ft 7½ in (2.6 m) |
| Weight Empty: | Unknown |
| Weight Loaded: | Unknown |
| Maximum Speed: | 124 mph (200 km/h) |
| Ceiling: | 19,600 ft (5,974 m) |
| Endurance: | 1½ hours |
| Armament: | Two forward-firing synchronised Spandau machine guns |
| Engine: | One 160-hp Siemens-Halske Sh.III rotary |

## LFG Roland D.XVI (Second Version)

| | |
|---|---|
| Wingspan: | 27 ft 6 in (8.3 m) |
| Length: | 19 ft 8 in (6.0 m) |
| Height: | 8 ft 7½ in (2.6 m) |
| Weight Empty: | Unknown |
| Weight Loaded: | Unknown |
| Maximum Speed: | 124 mph (200 km/h) |
| Ceiling: | 19,600 ft (5,974 m) |
| Endurance: | 1½ hours |
| Armament: | Two forward-firing synchronised Spandau machine-guns |
| Engine: | One 170-hp Siemens-Halske Sh.III rotary |

## LFG Roland D.XVII

| | |
|---|---|
| Wingspan: | 27 ft 6 in (8.3 m) |
| Length: | 19 ft 8 in (6.0 m) |
| Height: | 8 ft 7½ in (2.6 m) |
| Weight Empty: | Unknown |
| Weight Loaded: | Unknown |
| Maximum Speed: | 124 mph (200 km/h) |
| Ceiling: | 19,600 ft (5,974 m) |
| Endurance: | 1½ hours |
| Armament: | Two forward-firing synchronised Spandau machine guns |
| Engine: | One 185-hp BMW III |

## LFG Roland G.I

| | |
|---|---|
| Wingspan: | 98 ft 9¼ in (30.1 m) |
| Length: | 52 ft 2½ in (15.9 m) |
| Height: | 12 ft 2½ in (3.7 m) |
| Weight Empty: | 6,050 lb (2,750 kg) |
| Weight Loaded: | 9,460 lb (4,300 kg) |
| Maximum Speed: | 100 mph (160 km/h) |
| Ceiling: | 16,600 ft (5,050 m) |
| Endurance: | 4 hours |
| Armament: | One manually operated Parabellum machine gun |
| Engine: | Two 245-hp Maybach Mb.IV six-cylinder, in-line, water-cooled |

## LFG Roland W

| | |
|---|---|
| Wingspan: | 42 ft 4 in (12.9 m) |
| Length: | 25 ft 9 in (7.8 m) |
| Height: | 10 ft 3½ in (3.1 m) |
| Weight Empty: | 1,925 lb (875 kg) |
| Weight Loaded: | 2,618 lb (1,190 kg) |
| Maximum Speed: | 82 mph (160 km/h) |
| Ceiling: | 16,600 ft (5,050 m) |
| Endurance: | 2 hours |
| Armament: | One manually operated Parabellum machine gun |
| Engine: | One 150-hp Benz Bz.III |

## LFG Roland WD

| | |
|---|---|
| Wingspan: | 29 ft 4 in (8.84 m) |
| Length: | 22 ft 9 in (6.93 m) |
| Height: | 10 ft 2½ in (3.11 m) |
| Weight Empty: | 1,573 lb (715 kg) |
| Weight Loaded: | 2,098 lb (954 kg) |
| Maximum Speed: | 105 mph (170 km/h) |
| Ceiling: | 14,600 ft (4,450 m) |
| Endurance: | 4-5 hours |
| Armament: | Two forward-firing synchronised Spandau machine guns |
| Engine: | One 160-hp Mercedes D.III six-cylinder, in-line, water-cooled |

## LFG Stralsund V.19

| | |
|---|---|
| Wingspan: | 32 ft 9 in (9.9 m) |
| Length: | 21 ft 8 in (6.6 m) |
| Height: | 6 ft 6 in (1.9 m) |
| Weight Empty: | 1,623 lb (736 kg) |
| Weight Loaded: | 2,098 lb (951 kg) |
| Maximum Speed: | 112 mph (180 km/h) |
| Ceiling: | 14,600 ft (4,450 m) |
| Endurance: | 4-5 hours |
| Armament: | None |
| Engine: | One 110-hp Oberursel U.I |

# Luft-Verkehrs Gesellschaft GmbH (LVG)

The company was started in 1909 by Arthur Mueller as a small aircraft manufacturer; in 1911, he purchased three Albatros aircraft for 100,000 marks, and by doing so prevented the Albatros Company from collapsing. When LVG approached the Inspectorate of Military Aviation with regard to building aircraft for the military, they discovered that a Colonel Messing from the inspectorate had been persuaded by Otto Weiner, a director of the Albatros Company that Mueller had saved, not to deal with LVG, claiming that the company was merely an agent for Albatros. The head of LVG's research section, Kapitän de la Roi, formerly of the Research Unit, complained to Colonel Schmiedecke of the War Ministry who upheld his appeal, saying that LVG had shown itself to have considerable financial resources and a potential for expanding its aircraft manufacturing business at a time when there was a dire need for aircraft.

Things came to a head in July 1911 when a pilot from LVG, flying one of the Albatros aircraft purchased by LVG, won the Circuit of German Flight. The prize for the contest was an order from the Army for one of the aircraft. Albatros refused to sell one of its airframes, but Schmeidecke maintained that the aircraft had to come from the winning company and if the Ministry could not get an Albatros type of aircraft from LVG, then the contract would be void. A compromise was reached between the Ministry and LVG when Colonel Schmeidecke stated that the Ministry would accept any aircraft that LVG offered, as long as it met the standard required by the Army. The precedent had been set and the LVG Company was established with the military.

Located at Johannisthal, Berlin, Luft-Verkehrs Gesellschaft was one of the largest German aircraft manufacturers of the First World War. The use of the old Parseval airship hangar at the base gave the company all the room they needed to produce some of Germany's finest two-seater aircraft. The first aircraft produced in 1912 were of the standard Farman type. Then in 1912 a Swiss aeronautical engineer by the name of Franz Schneider joined LVG from the French Nieuport company and started building aircraft that had been designed by LVG's own designers. The first of these aircraft, the LVG B.I, an unarmed, two-seat reconnaissance/trainer, was built in 1913. It was a conventional two-bay aircraft, the fuselage being of a simple box-girder construction with wire bracing, made of spruce longerons and plywood cross members covered in doped fabric.

Franz Schneider came up with an invention for firing a machine gun through the blades of the propeller. This was not his first idea; he originally came up with a system whereby the propellers were driven by a gearbox outside the crankcase so that a machine gun could fire through a hollow propeller shaft. On 11 January 1913, the idea was patented by Daimler Motoren-Gesellschaft and given patent

No. 290120. Daimler built a four-cylinder engine with an external gearbox. From the onset it became obvious that it wasn't going to work; the lubrication problems alone were enough to convince the engineers that it wasn't going to be practical to put the engine into production, and so it was shelved.

It was then that Schneider's second invention came to the fore. The patent description described the design simply:

> The basis of the invention is a mechanism which permits a gun to fire between the propeller blades without damaging them. To this end the gun is mounted immediately in front of the pilot and behind the propeller. In order to avoid damage to the propeller, a blocking mechanism is fitted to the trigger. This mechanism is rotated constantly by the propeller shaft and blocks the gun's trigger at the moment when the propeller blade is located in front of the muzzle of the machine gun. In consequence the weapon can only be fired between the propeller blades.

When, two years later, Anthony Fokker patented his invention for an interruptor gear mechanism, Schneider was quick to claim that Fokker had stolen his idea, but Fokker stated that his idea was nowhere near the design of Schneider's and the patent office agreed.

In June 1914, six B.Is took part in the Ostmarkenflug, taking the first four places. With the onset of war the existing B.Is were immediately pressed into service and production lines started. To meet the immediate demand, the Otto-Werke, Münich were licensed to build the B.I. As with all the early aircraft, the pilot sat in the rear cockpit. Powered by a 100-hp Mercedes D.I engine, the B.I had a top speed of 63 mph. It had a wingspan of 47 ft 8½ in, a fuselage length of 25 ft 7½ in and a height of 10 ft 6 in.

The arrival of the improved version of the B.I, the B.II, some months later, showed only minor improvements. A semi-circular cutout in the upper wing intended to improve the pilot's upward visibility and a small reduction in the wingspan were the only noticeable differences. An improved engine, the 120-hp six-cylinder, in-line, water-cooled Mercedes D.II, gave the aircraft a top speed of 67 mph. The B.II was the main production model and a considerable number were built at the beginning of 1915. They were used mainly for scouting/reconnaissance and training purposes.

As the war intensified the casualty rate of the unarmed reconnaissance and scouting aircraft rose alarmingly, so it was decided to introduce a purpose-built armed reconnaissance aircraft. With the additional weight of guns and ammunition, it became necessary to install more powerful engines. With this in mind Franz Schneider produced a C series of aircraft, the first being the LVG C.I.

In reality, the C.I was no more than a strengthened B.I airframe fitted with a 150-hp Benz Bz.III engine and a ring-mounted manually operated Parabellum machine gun in the observer's cockpit. Later models were fitted with twin forward-firing fixed Spandau machine guns. A small number of the aircraft were built and shipped to the Front, where they were employed on bombing duties with the Kampfgeschwadern, and scouting and photo-reconnaissance duties with a number of Flieger Abteilung units. In appearance the C.I was almost identical to the B.II, except for a number of minor physical changes and was easily mistaken for that model.

A single-seat derivative of the C.I was built for the German Navy as a torpedo bomber. Experiments were carried out with a mock torpedo mounted beneath the fuselage and in the middle of the undercarriage. No further details are available and no official designation was given to the aircraft.

Early in 1915, Franz Schneider came up with a quite revolutionary two-seat, monoplane fighter. Given the designation of LVG E.I, the aircraft was fitted with both a fixed, forward-firing Spandau machine gun and a manually operated Parabellum machine gun mounted on a ring. Powered by a 120-hp Mercedes D.II engine, the prototype was being flown to the front for operational evaluation by a Leutnant Wentsch when, during the flight, the wings collapsed. The pilot was killed and it was discovered later that the lower wing struts had not been fixed properly. Only one aircraft of that type was built.

There was also an attempt to produce a bomber during 1915: the LVG G.I. Placed in the G series of aircraft, it was powered by two 150-hp Benz Bz.III engines. Greatly underpowered for a bomber, the G.I was not a success and was scrapped.

The C.II, which appeared a few months later, was again almost identical to the C. I, the main difference being the engine, a 160-hp six-cylinder, in-line, water-cooled Mercedes D.III.

The ongoing problem of having the pilot flying the aircraft from the rear cockpit was resolved with an experimental model, the LVG C.III. The aircraft was in effect a C.II with the cockpits changed around and only the one model was built.

Derived from this was the LVG C.IV, which was a slightly enlarged model, powered by a straight eight 220-hp Mercedes D.IV engine. The reduction gearing in the engine turned one of the largest propellers fitted to a single-engine aircraft. It was one of these aircraft that made the first daylight raid on London in November 1916. With a wingspan of 44 ft 7 in, a fuselage length of 27 ft 10½ in and a height of 10 ft 2 in, the C.IV was one of the best two-seat aircraft in the German Army.

One experimental single-seat aircraft, the LVG D.10 was also one of the most unusual. Given the name *Walfisch* (Whale), it had a wrapped plywood strip fuselage, which was not much longer than the aircraft's wingspan. This bulbous looking aircraft was powered by a 120-hp Mercedes D.II. Details of its performance are not known and only the one was built.

Probably one of the most successful, and one of the biggest, of the German two-seat reconnaissance/scout aircraft of the First World War, was the LVG C.V. Although overshadowed by the Rumpler C.IV, the LVG C.V came a very close second. The C.V was not as fast as the Rumpler, but what it lacked in speed and power it more than made up for by being a total 'all-round' aircraft, sturdy, stable and capable of absorbing punishment. It had a wingspan of 44 ft 8 in, a fuselage length of 26 ft 5½ in, and a height of 10 ft 6 in. Powered by a six-cylinder in-line, water-cooled 200-hp Benz Bz.IV engine, the C.IV had a top speed of 103 mph and an endurance of 3½ hours. It was armed with one fixed, forward-firing Spandau machine gun, and one manually operated Parabellum machine gun in the rear observer's cockpit.

A second single-seat fighter was built at the end of 1916, the LVG D.II (D 12). It had a monocoque-type fuselage with a headrest behind the pilot and was the second in a series of experimental D types. The D.II was powered by a 160-hp six-cylinder, in-line, water-cooled Mercedes D.III engine. The wings were braced by means of 'V' interplane struts.

At the beginning of 1917 an experimental single-seat fighter, the LVG D.III, was produced with semi-rigid bracing in the form of struts. Although the landing wires were removed, the flying wires remained. It retained the monocoque-type fuselage covered in plywood, but the wings were more suited to that of a two-seater reconnaissance than a fighter. The wingspan was 32 ft 10 in, the fuselage 24 ft 8½ in and the height 9 ft 7 in. Powered by a 190-hp NAG III engine, the D.III had a top speed of 109 mph and an endurance of two hours. Only one type was built.

Another fighter appeared out of the LVG stable at the end of 1917, the LVG D.IV. A much smaller model than the D.III, the D.IV had a single-spar lower wing braced with 'V' interplane struts. It had a wingspan of 27 ft 11 in, a fuselage length of 20 ft 7½ in, and a height of 8 ft 10½ in. The nose of the aircraft was considerably blunter than previous models and housed the V-8, direct drive, 195-hp Benz Bz.IIIb engine which gave the aircraft a top speed of 110 mph.

After participating in the second of the D-type competitions at Aldershof in June 1918, a small number were built and supplied to the Army. The Armistice arrived before any more could be manufactured.

One of the finest two-seater aircraft to come out of the LVG factory was the LVG C.VI. Over 1,000 examples of this aircraft were built and although physically there was hardly any difference between the C.V and the C.VI, the latter was much lighter and far more compact. The aesthetic look was put aside in favour of serviceability and practicability. The need for this type of aircraft at this stage of the war was desperate and the C.VI fulfilled this role.

Powered by a 200-hp six-cylinder, in-line, water-cooled Benz Bz.IV engine, the aircraft had a top speed of 106 mph, an operating ceiling of 21,350 feet and an endurance of 3½ hours. It was armed with a single fixed, forward-firing Spandau machine gun and a single manually operated Parabellum machine gun mounted in the rear observer's cockpit.

Among the observers that flew in the LVG C.VI was Hauptmann Paul Freiherr von Pechmann, who flew somewhere between 400 and 500 observation flights as an observer (the exact figure is not known, but some historians have placed it as high as 700). For these exploits he was awarded, among numerous other awards and medals, the *Pour le Mérite*, one of only two observers to be awarded the highest of all Prussia's aviation awards.

Toward the end of 1917, the Idflieg had been watching the load-carrying capacity of the Caproni bombers with great interest. With this in mind they instigated a programme of building similar aircraft. The only completed model at this time was the twin-engine LVG G.III triplane designed by Dipl.Ing. Wilhelm Hillmann. Constructed of wood and covered in plywood, it was the largest aircraft ever built by the LVG Company and had a wingspan of 80 ft 4½ in, a fuselage length of 33 ft 7½ in, and a height of 12 ft 9½ in. Powered by two 245-hp Maybach Mb IV engines, it gave the aircraft a top speed of 81 mph and a flight endurance of 5½ hours. Its armament consisted of manually operated Parabellum machine guns mounted in the nose and dorsal positions. It also carried a limited bomb load. The aircraft was given the designation G.III by the factory, but official records list the aircraft as the G.I. Only one was completed.

The final fighter to come from the LVG factory was the LVG D.VI. This was a short fuselage stubby-looking aircraft with a swept lower wing and a chin-type radiator air intake. It was powered by a 195-hp Benz Bz.IIIb engine and had a top speed of 121 mph (195 km/h).

The Luft-Verkehrs Gesellschaft Company made more than a passing contribution to Germany's war machine and was a major contributor to the world of aviation.


## SPECIFICATIONS

### LVG B.I

| | |
|---|---|
| Wingspan: | 47 ft 8½ in (14.5 m) |
| Length: | 25 ft 7½ in (7.8 m) |
| Height: | 10 ft 6 in (3.2 m) |
| Weight Empty: | 1,683 lb (765 kg) |
| Weight Loaded: | 2,490 lb (1,132 kg) |
| Maximum Speed: | 62 mph (100 km/h) |

| | |
|---|---|
| Endurance: | 2 hours |
| Armament: | None |
| Engine: | One 100-hp Mercedes D.I six-cylinder, in-line, water-cooled |

## LVG B.II

| | |
|---|---|
| Wingspan: | 39 ft 9¼ in (12.1 m) |
| Length: | 27 ft 3½ in (8.3 m) |
| Height: | 9 ft 8 in (2.9 m) |
| Weight Empty: | 1,597 lb (726 kg) |
| Weight Loaded: | 2,362 lb (1,074 kg) |
| Maximum Speed: | 65 mph (105 km/h) |
| Endurance: | 4 hours |
| Armament: | None |
| Engine: | One 100-hp Mercedes D.I six-cylinder, in-line, water-cooled |

## LVG B.III

| | |
|---|---|
| Wingspan: | 42 ft 0¼ in (12.5 m) |
| Length: | 25 ft 11 in (7.8 m) |
| Height: | 9 ft 6 in (2.9 m) |
| Weight Empty: | 1,785 lb (738 kg) |
| Weight Loaded: | 2,292 lb (1,042 kg) |
| Maximum Speed: | 75 mph (120 km/h) |
| Endurance: | 2½ hours |
| Armament: | None |
| Engine: | One 120-hp Mercedes D.II six-cylinder, in-line, water-cooled |

## LVG C.I

| | |
|---|---|
| Wingspan: | 47 ft 7 in (14.5 m) |
| Length: | 28 ft 3 in (8.6 m) |
| Height: | 10 ft 9 in (3.2 m) |
| Weight Empty: | 1,837 lb (835 kg) |
| Weight Loaded: | 3,021 lb (1,373 kg) |
| Maximum Speed: | 62 mph (100 km/h) |
| Endurance: | 4 hours |
| Armament: | One manually operated Parabellum machine gun mounted in the rear cockpit |
| Engine: | One 150-hp Benz Bz.III |

## LVG C.II

| | |
|---|---|
| Wingspan: | 42 ft 2 in (12.8 m) |
| Length: | 26 ft 7 in (8.1 m) |
| Height: | 9 ft 7¼ in (2.9 m) |
| Weight Empty: | 1,859 lb (845 kg) |
| Weight Loaded: | 3,091 lb (1,405 kg) |
| Maximum Speed: | 81 mph (130 km/h) |
| Endurance: | 4 hours |
| Armament: | One manually operated Parabellum machine gun mounted in the rear cockpit |
| Engine: | One 160-hp Mercedes D.III six-cylinder, in-line, water-cooled |

## LVG C.III

| | |
|---|---|
| Wingspan: | 41 ft 8 in (12.7 m) |
| Length: | 26 ft 3 in (8.0 m) |
| Height: | 10 ft 6 in (3.2 m) |
| Weight Empty: | 1,859 lb (845 kg) |
| Weight Loaded: | 3,091 lb (1,405 kg) |
| Maximum Speed: | 81 mph (130 km/h) |
| Endurance: | 4 hours |
| Armament: | One manually operated Parabellum machine gun mounted in the rear cockpit |
| Engine: | One 160-hp Mercedes D.III six-cylinder, in-line, water-cooled |

## LVG C.IV

| | |
|---|---|
| Wingspan: | 44 ft 7½ in (13.6 m) |
| Length: | 27 ft 11 in (8.5 m) |
| Height: | 10 ft 2¼ in (3.1 m) |
| Weight Empty: | 2,310 lb (1,050 kg) |
| Weight Loaded: | 3,520 lb (1,600 kg) |
| Maximum Speed: | 81 mph (130 km/h) |
| Endurance: | 4 hours |
| Armament: | One manually operated Parabellum machine gun mounted in the rear cockpit |
| Engine: | One 220-hp Mercedes D.IV six-cylinder, in-line, water-cooled |

## LVG C.V

| | |
|---|---|
| Wingspan: | 44 ft 8½ in (13.6 m) |
| Length: | 26 ft 6 in (8.0 m) |
| Height: | 10 ft 6 in (3.2 m) |
| Weight Empty: | 2,188 lb (1,013 kg) |
| Weight Loaded: | 5,372 lb (1,533 kg) |
| Maximum Speed: | 103 mph (164 km/h) |
| Endurance: | 3½ hours |
| Armament: | One manually operated Parabellum machine gun mounted in the rear cockpit. One fixed forward-firing Spandau machine gun |
| Engine: | One 200-hp Benz Bz.IV six-cylinder, in-line, water-cooled |

## LVG C.VI

| | |
|---|---|
| Wingspan: | 42 ft 8 in (13.0 m) |
| Length: | 24 ft 5¼ in (7.4 m) |
| Height: | 9 ft 2¼ in (2.8 m) |
| Weight Empty: | 2,046 lb (930 kg) |
| Weight Loaded: | 3,058 lb (1,309 kg) |
| Maximum Speed: | 106 mph (170 kmh) |
| Endurance: | 3½ hours |
| Service Ceiling: | 21,350 ft (6,500 m) |

| | |
|---|---|
| Armament: | One manually operated Parabellum machine gun mounted in the rear cockpit. One fixed forward-firing Spandau machine gun |
| Engine: | One 200-hp Benz Bz.IV six-cylinder, in-line, water-cooled |

## LVG C.VIII

| | |
|---|---|
| Wingspan: | 42 ft 8 in (13.0 m) |
| Length: | 22 ft 11½ in (7.0 m) |
| Height: | 9 ft 2¼ in (2.8 m) |
| Weight Empty: | 2,146 lb (9,976 kg) |
| Weight Loaded: | 3,038 lb (1,381 kg) |
| Maximum Speed: | 103 mph (165 km/h) |
| Endurance: | 4 hours |
| Service Ceiling: | 21,350 ft (6,500 m) |
| Armament: | One manually operated Parabellum machine gun mounted in the rear cockpit. One fixed forward-firing Spandau machine gun |
| Engine: | One 200-hp Benz Bz.IV six-cylinder, in-line, water-cooled |

## LVG 1915 (Experimental)

| | |
|---|---|
| Wingspan: | 47 ft 7 in (14.5 m) |
| Length: | 28 ft 3 in (8.6 m) |
| Height: | 10 ft 9 in (3.2 m) |
| Weight Empty: | 1,837 lb (835 kg) |
| Weight Loaded: | 3,021 lb (1,373 kg) |
| Maximum Speed: | 62 mph (100 km/h) |
| Endurance: | 4 hours |
| Armament: | One manually operated Parabellum machine gun mounted in the rear cockpit |
| Engine: | One 200-hp Benz Bz.IV |

## LVG D.10

No specification details available

## LVG D.II

No specification details available

## LVG D.III

| | |
|---|---|
| Wingspan: | 32 ft 9½ in (10.0 m) |
| Length: | 24 ft 8½ in (7.5 m) |
| Height: | 9 ft 7 in (2.9 m) |
| Weight Empty: | 1,795 lb (816 kg) |
| Weight Loaded: | 2,356 lb (1,071 kg) |
| Maximum Speed: | 109 mph (175 km/h) |
| Service Ceiling: | 16,400 ft (5,000 m) |
| Endurance: | 2 hours |
| Armament: | Two fixed forward-firing Spandau machine guns |
| Engine: | One 190-hp NAG III |

## LVG D.IV

| | |
|---|---|
| Wingspan: | 27 ft 10½ in (8.5 m) |
| Length: | 20 ft 7¼ in (6.3 m) |
| Height: | 8 ft 10¼ in (2.7 m) |
| Weight Empty: | 1,496 lb (680 kg) |
| Weight Loaded: | 2,057 lb (935 kg) |
| Maximum Speed: | 109 mph (175 km/h) |
| Service Ceiling: | 16,400 ft (5,000 m) |
| Endurance: | 2 hours |
| Armament: | Two fixed forward-firing Spandau machine guns |
| Engine: | One 195-hp Benz Bz.IIIb |

## LVG D.V

No specification details available

## LVG D.VI

No specification details available

## LVG E.I

| | |
|---|---|
| Wingspan: | 31 ft 2½ in (9.5 m) |
| Length: | 24 ft 9½ in (7.5 m) |
| Height: | 7 ft 10¼ in (2.3 m) |
| Weight Empty: | 870 lb (395 kg) |
| Weight Loaded: | 1,230 lb (550 kg) |
| Maximum Speed: | 80 mph (130 km/h) |
| Service Ceiling: | 11,400 ft (3,440 m) |
| Endurance: | 1 hours |
| Armament: | One fixed forward-firing Spandau machine gun |
| | One manually operated Parabellum in the observer's cockpit |
| Engine: | One 120-hp Mercedes D.II |

## LVG G.I

No specification details available

## LVG G.III

| | |
|---|---|
| Wingspan: | 80 ft 5 in (24.6 m) |
| Length: | 33 ft 7½ in (10.2 m) |
| Height: | 12 ft 9½ in (3.9 m) |
| Weight Empty: | 5,920 lb (2,960 kg) |
| Weight Loaded: | 9,020 lb (4,100 kg) |
| Maximum Speed: | 81 mph (130 km/h) |
| Endurance: | 5½ hours |
| Armament: | One manually operated Parabellum machine gun in the nose and one in the dorsal position |
| Engine: | Two 245-hp Maybach Mb.IV six-cylinder, in-line, water-cooled |

# Oesterreichische Flugzeugfabrik AG (Oeffag)

At the end of 1913, with the winds of war starting to blow through Europe, the Daimler Motoren AG Company, who were a subsidiary of Skodawerke AG, applied to the council in Wiener-Neustadt to build an aircraft factory. Daimler's interest in aviation went back some years to when their technical director, Ferdinand Porsche, had designed a lightweight engine for the Etrich Taube aircraft in 1909. Permission was granted and construction of the buildings began at the beginning of 1915. The main investors of the company, Dr Karl Freiherr von Skoda, Ferdinand Porsche and the Austrian Creditbank, with backing from the Government, took control of the company on 3 March 1915. The company was known as the Oesterreichische Flugzeugfabrik AG (Oeffag).

Brought in to manage the new works was Ingenieur Leo Portsch from the Skoda Works; the technical director was Ingenieur Karl Ockermüller, who had been involved in the designs of the early Luft-Fahrzeug-Gesellschaft (Roland) aircraft. The first of the aircraft from the new company, the Oeffag C.I, appeared in March 1915. The designs for the aircraft had been completed in January 1915 and included experimental triple 'I' struts with the staggered, sweptback wings in place of the conventional ones. There were problems with this strut design right from the start and so the wing struts reverted back to the conventional design.

The prototype of the production models was delivered on 15 June 1915, powered by a 160-hp Daimler engine. The three-bay biplane was evaluated by LFT and on 17 July 1915, a total of twenty-four were ordered. The first of the production aircraft were assigned to Fliks 25 and 27, the remainder to Fliks 9, 11 and 18. At the end of 1916, the C.I was replaced and twenty-two of the surviving aircraft were turned into trainers.

At the beginning of 1916, the prototype for the Oeffag C.II appeared. This was slightly smaller than the C.I and had a two-bay, shortened wingspan that had no sweepback or stagger. The LFT evaluated the aircraft and informed Oeffag that it failed to meet the performance requirements laid down. Despite this, Oeffag signed a production contract for thirty-two C.II reconnaissance biplanes, but it wasn't until October 1916 that the first nine of the aircraft were accepted and assigned to the Fliks operating on the Russian Front.

Reports coming back from the various Fliks complained that the observer's cockpit was far too small to take the kind of equipment required by the observers when they went on a mission, including ammunition, bombs, cameras, map cases, machine guns and flare pistols. The controls were sluggish, visibility was limited, manoeuvrability was not good and the speed too slow. A second order was received at the beginning of December 1916 for a further thirty-two of the second series of Oeffag C.II biplanes, and these too were sent to Fliks on the Russian

Front. Within weeks the reports coming back were almost identical to those on the first series of aircraft.

The success of the Oeffag-designed and -constructed aircraft was not the success that had been hoped for, and, in the autumn of 1916, the company obtained the rights to build the German Albatros D.III fighter. There were a number of reasons why Oeffag were able to obtain the rights: the war was by now well under way and the demand for good fighter aircraft was at a premium. The Albatros Company was unable to keep up with demand, so other companies were sought that could build Albatros aircraft under licence. One of these, the Albatros Company (Phönix), belonged to Camilio Castaglioni's Brandenburg-Phönix-UFAG cartel that was starting to monopolise the aviation market. The War Ministry wanted to put a stop to this and awarded the contract to Oeffag.

This decision turned out to be the saving grace for the Oeffag Company because the Albatros D.III (Oef) that they produced turned out to be the Austro-Hungarian Air Force's most successful fighter.

The original Albatros D.II appeared at a time when the Brandenburg D.I fighter, which it was to replace, was giving serious cause for concern regarding its stability and manoeuvrability. A contract signed by Oeffag on 4 December 1916 called for fifty aircraft to be built: twenty Albatros D.IIs (only sixteen of which were actually built) and thirty D.IIIs.

The Oeffag-built Albatros D.II was fitted with a 185-hp Daimler engine and the wing chord increased. There were some other minor alterations to the fuselage, and they were fitted with two Bernatzik synchronised machine guns. The completed D.IIs were assigned to Fliks on both the Russian and Italian Fronts. There were very few criticisms to come back from the Fronts, which was a pleasant surprise for Oeffag, who by this time had become used to scathing reports about their aircraft. Because of the relative inactivity on both the Fronts at the time, the Albatros D.II (Oef) was relegated to training duties as it was slowly replaced by the D.III (Oef)

The Albatros D.III (Oef) shared the same fuselage, undercarriage and tail section as the D.II (Oef). Because of reports coming back from the Western Front of wing failure on the Albatros D.II, the wings and airframe were strengthened considerably from the original German design, making it capable of taking increasingly bigger and more powerful engines. The result was the appearance of one of the toughest fighter aircraft of the First World War. The first reports coming back from the LFT vindicated the Oeffag engineers, who had been criticised for not adhering to the original design. The reports stated that Oeffag engineers and designers had made significant improvements, culminating in one of the best fighters of the time.

Production of the aircraft increased rapidly, but once again the problem of obtaining parts not manufactured by Oeffag, like the synchronisation machine gun mechanisms, slowed deliveries down. In an attempt to solve the problem, the company decided to manufacture some of the more precision parts themselves. The first of the Albatros D.III (Oef) arrived at the Russian Front at the beginning of June 1917. The pilots were delighted; they now had an aircraft that could be flown comfortably by any competent pilot and was superior in every way to the Brandenburg D.Is they were currently flying. A number of minor problems were found: poor quality cowling fasteners and a weak tailskid, both of which were quickly resolved without affecting the Fliks' operational status.

The reputation of the Oeffag Company was further enhanced when the Austro-Hungarian Navy requested that they build the Hansa-Brandenburg W.13 flying boat. Designed by Ernst Heinkel, this single-engine flying boat carried a crew of two and was used for reconnaissance and bombing missions. It was also built under licence by Ufag, but it was the Oeffag-built model that was preferred by the crews. The fuselage was of a simple wooden and fabric construction with a single-step hull. Powered by a 350-hp Daimler pusher engine, cut-outs in the trailing edges of the upper wing provided the clearance for the tips of the propeller. The two-crew positions were in a side-by-side configuration. It is not know how many were built.

The production of the first series of Albatros D.III (Oef) ended in July 1917 and immediately production of the next series, which was powered by a 200-hp Daimler engine, began. This new, more powerful model was fitted without a spinner, because German wind tunnel tests had shown that the spinner was liable to fly off and could damage the airframe. The report from Flars praised the new model, stating that the 200-hp D.III was the first of the fighter aircraft capable of engaging the French Hanriot and the British Sopwith Camel as an equal. A total of 201 Albatros D.III (Oef) of the second series were produced, all of which were assigned to various Fliks on both the Russian and Italian Fronts.

The next series of D.IIIs to appear came from a contract for 230 of the aircraft on 18 May 1918. These were to be powered by the latest 225-hp Daimler engine, all to be delivered by the end of December 1918. The first units to receive the new aircraft were Fliks 61/J and 63/J, whose pilots rated the aircraft the finest they had ever flown. There was virtually nothing to complain about: the aircraft did everything asked of it and never caused them a moment of problem. In July 1918, two of the Albatros D.III (Oef) aircraft from the second series took part in the Fighter Evaluation Trials at Aspern. Of the twenty-four participants in the competition, only three were production models: the two Albatros D.IIIs (Oef) and the Aviatik D.I. The performance of the two Albatros aircraft delighted the War Ministry as the aircraft out-flew all the other participants in every category.

The production lines turned the aircraft out, and by the end of October all but twenty-nine of those ordered had been delivered. The end of the war saw the end of production, but not the sales of the aircraft already built. Poland bought thirty-eight of the aircraft and extolled their virtues in a letter of commendation to the company the following year.

There was even talk of the company building the Friedrichshafen G.IIIa bomber under licence but this came to nothing. The Oeffag Company, from such a relatively disastrous start, produced some of the finest fighter aircraft of the First World War, but was unable to survive the post-war depression that followed.

## SPECIFICATIONS

### Oeffag C.I

| | |
|---|---|
| Wingspan Upper: | 47 ft 9 in (14.5 m) |
| Wingspan Lower: | 45 ft 7 in (13.9 m) |
| Length: | 27 ft 6 in (8.4 m) |
| Height: | 10 ft 8 in (3.2m) |
| Weight Empty: | 2,094 lb (950 kg) |
| Weight Loaded: | 2,977 lb (1,350 kg) |
| Maximum Speed: | 78 mph (125 km/h) |
| Engine: | One 160-hp Daimler |
| Armament: | None |

## Oeffag C.II

| | |
|---|---|
| Wingspan Upper: | 41 ft 8 in (12.7 m) |
| Wingspan Lower: | 38 ft 7 in (11.8 m) |
| Length: | 27 ft 6 in (8.4 m) |
| Height: | 10 ft 8 in (3.2 m) |
| Weight Empty: | 2,094 lb (950 kg) |
| Weight Loaded: | 2,657 lb (1,205 kg) |
| Maximum Speed: | 87 mph (140 km/h) |
| Engine: | One 160-hp Daimler |
| Armament: | None |

## Albatros D.II (Oef)

| | |
|---|---|
| Wingspan Upper: | 27 ft 10 in (8.5 m) |
| Wingspan Lower: | 26 ft 3 in (8.0 m) |
| Length: | 24 ft 2 in (7.3 m) |
| Height: | 8 ft 10 in (2.7 m) |
| Weight Empty: | 1,521 lb (690 kg) |
| Weight Loaded: | 1,980 lb (898 kg) |
| Maximum Speed: | 106 mph (170 km/h) |
| Engine: | One 185-hp Daimler |
| Armament: | One forward-firing machine gun |

## Albatros D.III (Oef)

| | |
|---|---|
| Wingspan Upper: | 29 ft 6 in (9.0 m) |
| Wingspan Lower: | 28 ft 7 in (8.7 m) |
| Length: | 24 ft 2 in (7.3 m) |
| Height: | 9 ft 2 in (2.8 m) |
| Weight Empty: | 1,521 lb (690 kg) |
| Weight Loaded: | 1,980 lb (898 kg) |
| Maximum Speed: | 112 mph (180 km/h) |
| Engine: | One 185-hp Daimler |
| Armament: | Twin forward-firing machine guns |

## Hansa-Brandenburg W.13 (Oef)

| | |
|---|---|
| Wingspan Upper: | 66 ft 9 in (20.4 m) |
| Wingspan Lower: | 58 ft 6 in (17.8 m) |
| Length: | 44 ft 11 in (13.7 m) |
| Height: | 13 ft 10½ in (4.2 m) |
| Weight Empty: | 3,410 lb (1,550 kg) |
| Weight Loaded: | 6,270 lb (2,850 kg) |
| Maximum Speed: | 93 mph (150 km/h) |
| Engine: | One 350-hp Austro-Daimler |
| Armament: | One Schwarzlöse machine gun |

# Otto-Werke GmbH (AGO)

As Prussia started to develop its own aircraft manufacturing empire, so Bavaria looked to achieve the same. The rivalry and friction between the two states in the formative years hampered any form of co-operation within the German empire.

The Bavarian Army Inspectorate of Engineering embarked on training their pilots using private flying schools, whereas the Prussian Army's pilots were taught to fly by the aircraft manufacturers as part of the purchasing agreement. The problems started when the Bavarian Army needed to expand their aviation section, which inevitably led to the need for more pilots. The Bavarian liaison officer at the Prussian Army's Research Unit passed on information on flying training and the Prussians' experience using manufacturers to train pilots. The Albatros Werke offered to train the Bavarian pilots and to supply the Bavarian Army with aircraft. The offer was declined.

At this point General von Brug, the Engineering Corps Inspector, decided that all flying training was to be carried out using a private school run by aircraft manufacturer August Euler. When asked about his choice of training establishments, von Brug remarked that 'Frankfurt was closer than Berlin-Johannisthal and at least August Euler, if not a Bavarian, was not a Prussian.' The Bavarian Army bought seven aircraft from the Euler Company and they trained the pilots as part of the agreement.

At the beginning of 1911, financier Gustav Otto founded the Bavarian state's first aircraft manufacturing plant – Otto-Werke GmbH, Munich. This was not the first aircraft-manufacturing venture that Otto was involved with, as he had recently acquired a financial interest in the Pfalz Werke. By the end of the summer, the Otto-Werke plant employed forty people, much to the delight of General von Brug who was the Bavarian Inspector of Aviation and Motor Vehicles. Von Brug had recently negotiated the purchase of the flying school and renamed it the Bavarian Military Flying School. Von Brug almost immediately coerced Gustav Otto into supplying him with one of his mechanics to train the Army ground personnel.

The friction between the two states raised its head when Gustav Otto asked the Prussian Army to consider a proposal from him for supplying aircraft and pilot training. This was in addition to asking for entry into an aircraft competition that the Prussians had planned for September 1912. Initially, the application was turned down out of hand because the competition was only open to Prussian aircraft manufacturers, but it was decided to admit Otto-built aircraft on the condition that in the event that his aircraft was placed in the competition, the Bavarian Army would award him 60,000 marks and accept two of the award-winning Prussian-built aircraft. This was, in the eyes of the Bavarian Army, a bonus, because not only would they have a Bavarian aircraft participating in a Prussian competition, they would be able to obtain two of the best of Prussian aircraft manufacturers.

As it turned out none of this was needed, because Gustav Otto, being the entrepreneur that he was, founded the Ago Flugzeugwerke in Johannisthal and contracted to handle all the repairs, pilot training and other contracts with the Prussian Army. The Prussian Army also put the date of the competition back until the following year and eventually cancelled it altogether.

The Ago works, a subsidiary of the Otto Werke, Munich, started building Henry Farman aircraft under licence. The Farman was a tried and trusted aircraft, at least as far as any of the very early models could be, and gave them a good foothold into the aircraft-manufacturing world. The first of these aircraft, the Ago C.I, appeared in the summer of 1915. It had a twin-boomed fuselage powered by a 150-hp Benz III engine and was used purely as a reconnaissance aircraft. It was armed with a manually operated machine gun mounted in the nose, but this was just for defensive purposes.

At the beginning of 1913, the Prussian Army had asked for tenders from the German Bristol Works, Rumpler, Albatros, Aviatik, Euler, AEG and Fokker to build an aircraft that was capable of being dismantled and transported on a purpose-built vehicle. The manufacturer selected would win an order for twelve of these aircraft and the vehicles to go with them. On hearing of this competition, General von Brug contacted Gustav Otto and suggested that he put forward a tender, which he duly did. However, the powers that be informed the Bavarian War Ministry that the General Inspectorate of the Prussian Army were only considering aircraft manufacturers that had already built successful aircraft and because the Ago Works and the AEG Werke had not even built any aircraft of their own, they were removed from the list of participants.

The second of the Ago C-models, the C.II, appeared at the end of 1915 and still retained the twin-boomed fuselage configuration, but was fitted with a more powerful 220-hp Benz IV pusher engine. The C.III, however, was a smaller twin-boomed fuselage version and was powered by a 160-hp Mercedes D.III engine. At the beginning of 1916 came the first of the single-fuselage models, the C.IV. The C.IV was the result of a great deal of experimentation with the wing design, which was one of the more unusual features of the aircraft. The wings tapered not only in shape but also in thickness and although extremely efficient, took so long to make that it limited the number of aircraft built. In order to give the observer a forward field of fire, the inner front interplane strut was removed and the outer struts placed closer together to compensate. A total of 260 of these aircraft were ordered, but it is not known exactly how many were delivered, although over seventy were known to be flying between 1917 and 1918.

Meanwhile the company produced a floatplane for the Navy at the end of 1915, the Ago C.I W. It was in reality a C.I fitted with floats and only the one was built, and that was handed over to the Navy for trials. The results from the trials produced two Ago C.II Ws, Nos. 539 and 586. The latter was fitted with a four-bladed propeller and produced excellent results. It is not known how many were built resulting from the trials.

Also in 1915 there appeared a small single-seat aircraft, the Ago DV.3. It was an unarmed reconnaissance model powered by a 100-hp Oberursel U.I rotary engine, but trials of the aircraft were unsatisfactory and only the one was built. Towards the end of the war another version, this time a single-seat fighter, the Ago S.I, was built, but the war ended before it could be tested.

Gustav Otto realised that the Prussians had the monopoly on all the non-Bavarian aircraft manufacturers and that the friction between the two major states was not going away. It was obvious that in the event of a war, and signs of this were becoming more imminent, the Bavarian War Ministry would lay claim to the entire production of his aircraft. He made General von Brug aware of his concerns, and von Brug in turn went to the Bavarian War Ministry to also voice his concerns. He realised that the Bavarian manufacturers should become an integral part of the German aircraft industry and set aside any prejudices that the individual states may have to ensure that a strict level of manufacture was maintained.

The Bavarian War Ministry agreed that there should be some form of uniformity, but would not accept any of Gustav Otto's aircraft because they considered them to be substandard. The fact that one of his biplane aircraft had crashed on a number of occasions during the Prince Heinrich Flight demonstrations did nothing to encourage confidence in the aircraft. The Prussian Inspectorate of Flying Troops in fact accused the factory of being incapable of building any reliable military aircraft. Strangely enough, Gustav Otto's Ago factory became one of Germany's leading manufacturers of seaplanes and supplied large numbers of the aircraft to the German Navy, but was never able to build an aircraft that was accepted by the Prussian Army.

## SPECIFICATIONS

### Ago C.I

| | |
|---|---|
| Wingspan: | 47 ft 7 in (14·5 m) |
| Length: | 32 ft 3½ in (9.8 m) |
| Height: | 11 ft 1½ ins (3.4 m) |
| Weight Empty: | 1,760 lb (800 kg) |
| Weight Loaded: | 2,904 lb (1,320 kg) |
| Maximum speed: | 90 mph (145 km/h) |
| Endurance: | 4 hours |
| Armament: | One manually operated machine gun in the nose |
| Engine: | 150-hp Benz Bz.III |

### Ago C.II

| | |
|---|---|
| Wingspan: | 47 ft 7 in (14.5 m) |
| Length: | 32 ft 3½ in (9.8 m) |
| Height: | 11ft. 1½ ins (3·4 m) |
| Weight Empty: | 2,992 lb (1,360 kg) |
| Weight Loaded: | 4,281 lb (1,946 kg) |
| Maximum speed: | 85 mph (136 km/h) |
| Endurance: | 4 hour |
| Armament: | One manually operated machine gun in the nose |
| Engine: | 220-hp Benz Bz.IV six-cylinder, in-line, water-cooled |

### Ago C.III

| | |
|---|---|
| Wingspan: | 36 ft 1¼ in (11 m) |
| Length; | 22 ft 11½ in (7 m) |
| Height: | 11 ft 1½ in (3.4 m) |
| Weight Empty: | 2,992 lb (1,360 kg). |
| Weight Loaded: | 4,281 lb (1,946 kg). |
| Maximum speed: | 85 mph (136 km/h) |
| Endurance: | 4 hour |
| Armament: | One manually operated machine gun in the nose |
| Engine: | 160-hp Mercedes D.III six-cylinder, in-line, water-cooled |

## Ago C.IV

| | |
|---|---|
| Wingspan: | 39 ft 0½ in (11.9 m) |
| Length: | 26 ft 4½ in (8.3 m) |
| Height: | 11 ft 1½ in (3.4 m) |
| Weight Empty: | 1,980 lb (900 kg) |
| Weight Loaded: | 2,970 lb (1,350 kg) |
| Maximum speed: | 118 mph (190 km/h) |
| Endurance: | 4 hour |
| Ceiling: | 18,040 ft (5,500 m) |
| Armament: | One fixed forward-firing Spandau machine gun for pilot |
| | One manually operated machine gun for observer |
| Engine: | 220-hp Benz Bz.IV six-cylinder, in-line, water-cooled |

## Ago C.VII

No specification details available

## Ago C.VIII

No specification details available

## Ago C.I W

| | |
|---|---|
| Wingspan: | 47 ft 7 in (14·5 m) |
| Length: | 32 ft 3½ ins (9.8 m) |
| Height: | 11 ft 1½ in (3.4 m) |
| Weight Empty: | 1,760 lb (800 kg) |
| Weight Loaded: | 2,904 lb (1,320 kg) |
| Maximum speed: | 90 mph (145 km/h) |
| Endurance: | 4 hour |
| Armament: | One manually operated machine gun in the nose |
| Engine: | 150-hp Benz Bz.III |

## Ago C.II W

| | |
|---|---|
| Wingspan: | 60 ft 0½ in (18.3 m) |
| Length: | 36 ft 10½ in (11.3 m) |
| Height: | 14 ft 2 in (4.32 m) |
| Weight Empty: | 2,992 lb (1,360 kg) |
| Weight Loaded: | 4,281 lb (1,946 kg) |
| Maximum speed: | 85 mph (136 km/h) |
| Endurance: | 4 hour |
| Armament: | One manually operated machine gun in the nose |
| Engine: | 220-hp Benz Bz.IV six-cylinder, in-line, water-cooled |

## Ago DV.3

No details available

## Ago S.I

No details available

Phönix D.I of Flik 14/1.

Phönix Prototype 18.20, the basis of the D.II.

Josef Kiss leaning against his D.IIa.

Phönix D.IIa of Flik 55.

Phönix D.IIIa.

Phönix 20.01 (Albatros B.I).

Phönix 20.09.

Phönix 20.14.

Phönix 20.15.

Phönix 20.16 – second version.

Phönix 20.24.

Phönix D.II.

Phönix-built Albatros B.I of Flik 20.

Phönix fighters of Flik 55J.

Phönix 20.10 battleplane prototype.

Phönix C.I with crew.

Phönix-built Brandenburg C.I of Flik 32.

Crew of Phönix-built Brandenburg C.I, wearing parachute harnesses.

Rumpler Taube at Berlin-Doebertiz military airfield with its pilot and ground crew.

Rumpler Taube taking off from Cologne-Longerich airfield, 1913.

Rumpler C.I trainer.

Rumpler C.I.

Rumpler C.I.

Leutnant Adolf Sehringer (left), with fellow crew members beside his Rumpler C.VI.

Rumpler VIb-1
seaplane fighter.

Sablatnig SF.5.

Sablatnig SF.7.

Sablatnig SF.5.

Siemens-Schuckert R-Type.

Lloyd C.I.

Zeppelin-Staaken R.IV in flight.

Pilot and ground crew in front of their Zeppelin-Staaken R.IV.

Zeppelin-Staaken R.IV No. 29/16.

Dornier Rs.II.

Wreckage of Zeppelin VGO II after a landing accident.

Dornier Rs.I flying boat.

The wreckage of Zeppelin VGO I after a crash in which both crew members were killed.

# Pfalz Flugzeug-Werke GmbH

Germany, prior to the First World War, was a country made up of a number of minor kingdoms and principalities. Among them was the Kingdom of Bavaria, which, after Prussia, was the second most powerful state in the German Reich. Bavaria enjoyed considerable autonomy and military privileges, and at the onset of the First World War had its own air service, War Ministry and General Staff. There was a bitter underlying rivalry between some of the states, as became apparent when bravery awards were given. There were even Jastas made up of only Bavarians or Prussians in the early stages of the war. Unlike the other states, Bavaria's armed forces were only under the command of the Emperor Kaiser Wilhelm in time of war.

With the threat of the First World War looming, three brothers, Alfred, Walter and Ernst Eversbusch established an aircraft manufacturing plant with the financial aid of the Bavarian Government. The Government were concerned that unless they contributed to the manufacture of the aircraft they would have no say in the equipment that would be used by the Bavarian pilots. Initially, the intention was to approach the Albatros Company and to acquire the rights to build their aircraft in Bavaria, but negotiations fell through. Then the Bavarian Flying Service stepped in, and at their instigation the Pfalz Company approached Gustav Otto, a financier who helped finance the new company and assisted in the development of the business. They also acquired the rights to build the Otto biplane. The Pfalz Flugzeug-Werke was built at Speyer am Rhein in July 1913. The first aircraft to be produced there was not one of their own designs, but an Otto pusher biplane that was powered by a 100-hp Rapp engine.

Later, Alfred Eversbusch managed to obtain a licence from the French Morane-Saulnier Company to manufacture the 'L' type parasol monoplane. The first parasol was built at the end of 1914 and only a few of these were built. It is interesting to note that the cockpit had transparent sides, which, with hindsight, was totally unnecessary because the downward view was excellent without them. The next model was later given the military designation of Pfalz A.I and powered with an 80-hp, seven-cylinder Oberursel U.O rotary engine. Their role was for photo-reconnaissance and scouting missions. There was a Pfalz A.II, which was no more than an A.I with a 100-hp nine-cylinder Oberursel U.I rotary engine fitted.

At the same time as acquiring a licence to build the Morane-Saulnier 'L' type, Pfalz also obtained permission to build the 'H' type, which was re-designated the Pfalz E.I and fitted with the 80-hp Oberursel U.O seven-cylinder engine. Walter Eversbusch, the youngest of the three brothers, enrolled in the Morane-Saulnier flying school near Paris in the spring of 1914, from where he graduated with his flying licence. He became the company's test pilot, but was killed on 1 June 1916 when he crashed testing one of the company's aircraft.

When the war began in August 1914, the company had produced only three Otto biplane pushers, which were immediately dispatched to the Bavarian squadrons. It soon became obvious that the Otto was seriously underpowered, taking fifteen minutes to reach a height of 2,500 ft, and considering they only had an operating ceiling of 3,600 ft, they were not really that suitable for reconnaissance missions. There was also another problem: the Otto bore a strong resemblance to the French pusher aircraft and was often shot at by German infantrymen. It has to be remembered that German soldiers, and Allied soldiers, had rarely, if ever, seen an aircraft, let alone recognised it as one of their own. Fortunately for the pilots of these aircraft, by December, Albatros B and LVG models had replaced the Otto.

As the war progressed, large numbers of the Pfalz E.I were built but very few saw service on the front line as they were assigned to Bavarian flying schools as unarmed trainers. A small number of E.Is saw action in Macedonia, Syria and Palestine.

The Pfalz parasol was in action in Italy before the war between Germany and Italy had actually started. On 31 July 1915 a German aircraft, with simulated Austro-Hungarian markings covering the German crosses and flown by Leutnant Otto Kissenberth of Feldflieger-Abteilung 9b, attacked Italian Alpine positions. He dropped five 10 kg Carbonit bombs on the positions, causing a number of casualties. Because of the high-altitude position of the Italian troops, they were able to subject aircraft to a heavy rate of fire, but fortunately the Pfalz had a good rate of climb and Otto Kissenberth was able to climb his aircraft away and out of danger.

The first ten Pfalz E.Is were unarmed scouts, but with the development of synchronisation gear, the remaining fifty were fitted with a fixed, forward-firing Spandau machine gun. In total, sixty of these aircraft were built and sent to the Front. The Pfalz E.II was produced some months later, but this was just an E.I with the 100-hp Oberursel U.I nine-cylinder rotary engine fitted and with the synchronised Spandau machine gun. The E.II had a wingspan of 33 ft 5 in, which was slightly longer than that of the E.I. Such was the need for aircraft at this time that the E.II was already in service with a number of the Bavarian squadrons before the Idflieg (Inspektion der Fliegentruppen) had finished the Typen-Prufung (Acceptance Test), which wasn't completed until July 1916.

This was followed by the debut of the Pfalz E.III, which was in fact an armed version of the A.II parasol monoplane. Only six were built, four of which managed to make the front line and see service. It was powered by a 100-hp Oberursel U.I rotary engine, had a wingspan of 36 ft 9 in and a fuselage length of 22 ft 5½ in.

The next in the 'E' series of fighters was the Pfalz E.IV. Almost identical to the other E-series fighters, the E.IV was fitted with the 160-hp two-row Oberursel U.III rotary engine. It had a wingspan of 33 ft 5½ in, a fuselage length of 21 ft 8 in, a top speed of 100 mph and a climb rate of 1,300 feet per minute. It carried twin, synchronised forward-firing Spandau machine guns. This feisty little fighter was built, surprisingly, in small numbers as no more than twenty-five were known to have been manufactured.

The last of the E-series fighters was the Pfalz E.V. Constructed on the standard E-type airframe, the E.V was powered by a 100-hp Mercedes D.I engine, giving the aircraft a top speed of 103 mph. This was a deviation from the rotary engines that powered the previous E-series of aircraft. It was armed with a synchronised forward-firing Spandau machine gun and was only slightly different from the other Pfalz monoplanes by means of an enlarged and different shaped rudder.

The more rugged and manoeuvrable biplane fighter was rapidly replacing the monoplane fighter, so in an effort to stay in contention, Pfalz produced the Pfalz D.4. The fuselage of an E.V was taken and broadened, while the rudder assembly came from another of the E-series. The first version produced was an unmitigated disaster and was virtually uncontrollable. The second version had some modifications but couldn't resolve the main problems. Only one of each was built.

At the end of 1916, with the E-series of monoplane aircraft completed, the Pfalz Company was instructed to build the LFG (Luft-Fahrzeug-Gesellschaft) Roland D.I under licence. Up to this point a total of 300 of the A and E-types had been constructed by Pfalz. The reason that Pfalz had been asked to build the Roland was because the Roland factory had been destroyed by fire and Pfalz had just completed building the last of their E-series of fighter/reconnaissance aircraft.

During the period of constructing the LFG, the Pfalz design office was working on their own design for biplane fighters. Then, at the beginning of 1917, the first of the D-series of Pfalz aircraft appeared. This was a biplane version of the E.V monoplane and was given the name of *Walfisch* (Whale). This short, tubby little aircraft, thought to have been powered by a 100-hp Mercedes D.I engine with a car-type radiator at the nose, was unusual in that it had almost an enclosed cockpit. From information gathered, it appears that it was never designed as a fighter, but was to be used for reconnaissance missions. It is not known exactly how many were built, but it is thought that there were only two.

Another aircraft appeared at the beginning of 1917, and was designated the Pfalz C.I. It was, in reality, a Rumpler C.IV, built under licence by the Pfalz Company. It had additional bracing struts from the tailplane to the fin and ailerons on all four wingtips. Powered by a 260-hp Mercedes D.IVa engine, this two-seat reconnaissance aircraft was armed with one forward-firing Spandau machine gun and one manually operated Parabellum machine gun mounted in the observer's cockpit. The designation of the Rumpler C.IV as the Pfalz C.I was a perfect example of the rivalry that existed between the various states and principalities. The Bavarian leaders insisted on purchasing only Bavarian-built aircraft, so when Bavarian companies built aircraft from other states, which were given designations pertaining to Bavarian companies, the leaders felt justified in purchasing them. It was this petty-minded thinking that hampered the flow of materials and aircraft to the front.

By the summer of 1917 the first of the Pfalz fighters had appeared, the Pfalz D.III. The fuselage was of a wooden semi-monocoque construction made up of spruce longerons and oval plywood formers. The fuselage was then wrapped with two layers of plywood strip in a spiral fashion in opposing directions, and then covered in fabric that was then painted with dope. The vertical tail fin was part of the main fuselage and made of fabric covered wood. The rounded rudder, however, was made of welded steel tubes covered in fabric. The aircraft was powered by a six-cylinder, in-line, water-cooled Mercedes D.III engine, which gave the D.III a top speed of 102 mph, a climb rate of almost 1,000 feet per minute and an operating ceiling of 17,000 ft with an endurance of 2½ hours. It was armed with two synchronised, forward-firing Spandau machine guns.

The Pfalz D.VI was the next in the series and was one of the most elegant of Pfalz aircraft. The fuselage was constructed with the now-familiar wrapped strip plywood, which was then covered in fabric and painted with dope. The D.VI was powered by a 110-hp Oberursel U.II rotary engine that was completely enclosed in a metal cowl. It had a wingspan of 23 ft 3 in and a top speed of 110 mph. No actual figures are available as to the number built, but it is believed to have been around twenty.

Shortly after the D.VI model was dispatched to the front, the Pfalz D.VII appeared. There were two versions of this aircraft: one with the 160-hp Siemens-Halske Sh.III geared rotary engine, and the other with a 160-hp Oberursel UR.III rotary engine. A third engine was also tried in the D.VII, the 160-hp Goebel Goe.III. There were some slight differences in the dimension of each aircraft: the wingspan on the first version was 24 ft 8 in and 26 ft 7 in on the second. The fuselage length on the first version was 18 ft 6½ in, and on the second was 18 ft 2½ in. Top speed for both aircraft was 118 mph and both were equipped with twin synchronised forward-firing Spandau machine guns.

At the same time as the D.VII was being constructed, a triplane was being developed. The Pfalz experimental triplane was a D.III conversion and fitted with a six-cylinder, in-line, water-cooled 160-hp Mercedes D.III engine. For some unknown reason it never flew and was scrapped. The information gained, however, was not lost and some months later came another triplane, the Pfalz Dr.I.

The Pfalz Dr.I was a stocky, powerful, little aircraft with a wingspan of 28 ft 1 in and a fuselage length of 18 ft. It was powered with the 160-hp Siemens-Halske Sh.III rotary engine that gave it a top speed of 112 mph and a climb rate of almost 1,500 feet per minute. Despite the powerful engine, its performance rating was not as good as the Fokker Dr.Is and because of this less than ten were manufactured. In an attempt to find an improved version of the Pfalz Dr.I, the Dr.II and Dr.IIa were developed. These two aircraft were powered by the 110-hp Oberursel UR.II and 110-hp Siemens Sh.I respectively. Neither was successful and they were not put into production.

At the beginning of 1918, another single-seat fighter appeared, the Pfalz D.VIII. Three versions of this aircraft existed, each powered by a different engine: a 160-hp Siemens-Halske Sh.III, a 160-hp Oberursel U.III and a Goebel Goe.III. Of the three variants only the Siemens-Halske-engined model was manufactured in any number, forty being built. The aircraft had a wingspan of 24 ft 8 in, a fuselage length of 118 ft 6½ in and a height of 9 ft. The Siemens-Halske-powered model had a top speed of 112 mph and a climb rate of 1,200 feet per minute. Almost identical to the D.VII, the aircraft was sent to the front line for evaluation with Jagdstaffeln 5, 14 and 29. Reports came back saying that, although the aircraft was excellent to fly, its undercarriage had a tendency to collapse on landing. However, nineteen of the aircraft were still in operational service by the end of the year, although it never went into full production. Two modified versions were produced with different engines, but the confidence in the aircraft had gone and neither went into production.

One interesting experiment was carried out with the Pfalz D.VIII, using a Rhemag R.II engine that drove two counter-rotating propellers. On its first flight the aircraft crashed because it was excessively nose-heavy. The engine was then removed and repaired and shipped to Aldershof, Berlin, to be fitted into a Siemens-Schuckert D.IV, but before the tests could begin the war came to an end and the project was scrapped.

Although the Pfalz company had produced a number of excellent aircraft, with the exception of the Pfalz D.III, none of them had been particularly successful. The only other model that came anywhere near the D.III was the Pfalz D.XII. Looking similar to the Fokker D.VII, the D.XII was of a semi-monocoque design, constructed of spruce longerons with plywood formers. The fuselage was then wrapped with two layers of thin plywood strip, applied in opposite directions, then covered in fabric and painted with dope. Powered by a 160-hp six-cylinder, in-line, water-cooled Mercedes D.IIIa engine with a 'car-type' radiator mounted on the front, the D.XII had a top speed of 106 mph, a climb rate of almost 1,000 feet per minute and an operating ceiling of 18,500 feet.

The Pfalz D.XII had a wingspan of 29 ft 6½ in, a fuselage length of 20 ft 10 in and a height of 8 ft 10½ in. It was armed with two forward-firing, synchronised Spandau machine guns.

When the first production models were sent to the front to replace the worn out Albatros D.Vas and Pfalz D.IIIs, some of Germany's top pilots, including Oberleutnant Ernst Udet and Oberleutnant Hans Weiss, flew the aircraft and declared it as good as, if not better in some regards, as the already established Fokker D.VII. The Bavarian Jagdgeschwader IV, commanded by Oberleutnant Eduard Ritter von Schleich, reported that although initially his pilots did not look too favourably on the replacement aircraft, their opinion changed rapidly after they had flown them in combat.

Whether or not their recommendation carried any real weight, more than 300 Pfalz D XIIs were supplied to Jastas 23, 32, 34, 35, 64, 65, 66, 77, 78 and 81. By the end of 1918, over 180 of the aircraft were still in operation on the Western Front.

Later in 1918 an improved model, the Pfalz D.IIIa, appeared. It had an improved engine, the 180-hp Mercedes D.IIIa, the tailplane area had been increased and a modification was made to the wingtips of the lower wing. In all other areas it was the same as the D.III model. In all, over 800 of the Pfalz D.III and D.IIIa were built and according to the Inter-Allied Control Commission's figures, at least 350 were still operational on the front line at the end of the war. It was, without question, the most successful fighter produced by the Pfalz factory.

While still continuing to upgrade their existing aircraft, Pfalz produced an experimental model, the Pfalz D.XIV. Slightly larger than the D.XII, it had a larger vertical fin and was powered by a 200-hp Benz Bz.IVü engine. This gave the aircraft a top speed of 112.5 mph and a climb rate of just over 1,000 feet per minute. Only the one was built.

The results gained from this aircraft resulted in the production of the last of the single-seat fighters, the Pfalz D.XV. Its first official test flight was on 4 November 1918 and 180 were ordered. It is not known how many were actually built, but it is unlikely to have been the full complement, bearing in mind the Armistice came a week later. The D.XV was powered by a 180-hp Mercedes D.IIIa engine, but there were a number of models that were fitted with the 185-hp BMW IIIa engine that gave the aircraft a top speed of 125 mph. The aircraft had a wingspan of 28 ft 2½ in, a fuselage length of 21 ft 4 in and a height of 8 ft 10 in.

Like a number of German aircraft, the Pfalz became one of the most respected fighter aircraft of the First World War by both its pilots and its opponents.

## SPECIFICATIONS

### Pfalz A.I & A.II

| | |
|---|---|
| Wingspan: | 36 ft 6½ in (11.2 m) |
| Length: | 22 ft 6 in (6.9 m) |
| Height: | 11 ft 1½ in (3.4 m) |
| Weight Empty: | 804 lb (365 kg) |
| Weight Loaded: | 1,309 lb (595 kg) |
| Maximum speed: | 83 mph (135 km/h) |
| Endurance: | 4 hour – A.I; 2 hour – A.II |
| Armament: | None |
| Engine: | 80-hp Oberursel U.o (A.I) |
| | 100-hp Oberursel U.I (A.II) |

## Pfalz E.I

| | |
|---|---|
| Wingspan: | 30 ft 6½ in (9.2 m) |
| Length: | 20 ft 6 in (6.3 m) |
| Height: | 11 ft 1½ in (3.4 m) |
| Weight Empty: | 760 lb (345 kg) |
| Weight Loaded: | 1,179 lb (535 kg) |
| Maximum speed: | 93 mph (145 km/h) |
| Endurance: | 1½ hours |
| Armament: | None. The last fifty were fitted with a single synchronised, forward-firing, Spandau machine-gun |
| Engine: | 80-hp Oberursel U.o |

## Pfalz E.II

| | |
|---|---|
| Wingspan: | 330 ft 4 in (10.2 m) |
| Length: | 21 ft 2 in (6.45 m) |
| Height: | 8 ft 3 in (2·55 m) |
| Weight Empty: | 904 lb (410 kg) |
| Weight Loaded: | 1,261 lb (572 kg) |
| Maximum speed: | 93 mph (150 km/h) |
| Endurance: | 1½ hours |
| Armament: | One synchronised, forward-firing, Spandau machine-gun |
| Engine: | 100-hp Oberursel U.I |

## Pfalz E.III

| | |
|---|---|
| Wingspan: | 36 ft 6½ in (11.2 m) |
| Length: | 22 ft 4 in (6.85 m) |
| Height: | 11 ft 1½ in (3.4 m) |
| Weight Empty: | 981 lb (445 kg) |
| Weight Loaded: | 1,554 lb (705 kg) |
| Maximum speed: | 93 mph |
| Endurance: | 2 hours |
| Armament: | None |
| Engine: | 100-hp Oberursel U.I |

## Pfalz E.IV

| | |
|---|---|
| Wingspan: | 33 ft 4½ in (10.2 m) |
| Length: | 21 ft 6 in (6.6 m) |
| Height: | 8 ft 2 in (2.55 m) |
| Weight Empty: | 1,038 lb (471 kg) |
| Weight Loaded: | 1,554 lb (705 kg) |
| Maximum speed: | 99 mph |
| Endurance: | 1 hour |
| Armament: | Two synchronised, forward-firing, Spandau machine guns |
| Engine: | 160-hp Oberursel U.III |

## Pfalz E.V

| | |
|---|---|
| Wingspan: | 33 ft 4½ in (10.2 m) |
| Length: | 21 ft 6 in (6.6 m) |

| | |
|---|---|
| Height: | 8 ft 2 in (2.55 m) |
| Weight Empty: | 1,124 lb (510 kg) |
| Weight Loaded: | 1,477 lb (670 kg) |
| Maximum speed: | 99 mph (159 km/h) |
| Endurance: | 1 hour |
| Armament: | Two synchronised, forward-firing, Spandau machine guns |
| Engine: | 100-hp Mercedes D.I |

## Pfalz D.II

| | |
|---|---|
| Wingspan Upper: | 29 ft 2 in (8.9 m) |
| Wingspan Lower: | 27 ft 9 in (8.5 m) |
| Length: | 22 ft 8 in (6.95 m) |
| Height: | 10 ft 1 in (3.11 m) |
| Weight Empty: | 1,400 lb (635 kg) |
| Weight Loaded: | 1,797 lb (815 kg) |
| Maximum speed: | 112 mph (180 km/h) |
| Endurance: | 2 hours |
| Armament: | Two synchronised, forward-firing, Spandau machine guns |
| Engine: | 160-hp Mercedes D.III |

## Pfalz D.III

| | |
|---|---|
| Wingspan: | 30 ft 9 in (9.4 m) |
| Length: | 22 ft 8 in (6.95 m) |
| Height: | 8 ft 7 in (2.67 m) |
| Weight Empty: | 1,519 lb (689 kg) |
| Weight Loaded: | 2,033 lb (922 kg) |
| Maximum speed: | 102 mph (164 km/h) |
| Endurance: | 2 hours |
| Armament: | Two synchronised, forward-firing, Spandau machine guns |
| Engine: | 160-hp Mercedes D.III |

## Pfalz D.IIIa

| | |
|---|---|
| Wingspan: | 36 ft 6½ in (11.2 m) |
| Length: | 23 ft 2 in (7.06 m) |
| Height: | 8 ft 7½ in (2.68 m) |
| Weight Empty: | 1,532 lb (695 kg) |
| Weight Loaded: | 2,017 lb (915 kg) |
| Maximum speed: | 93 mph (149 km/h) |
| Endurance: | 2 hours |
| Armament: | Two synchronised, forward-firing, Spandau machine guns |
| Engine: | 100-hp Oberursel U.I |

## Pfalz D.VI

| | |
|---|---|
| Wingspan Upper: | 23 ft 1 in (7.0 m) |
| Wingspan Lower: | 20 ft 7 in (6.3 m) |
| Length: | 23 ft 2 in (7 m) |
| Height: | 8 ft 7½ in (2.68 m) |
| Weight Empty: | 917 lb (416 kg) |
| Weight Loaded: | 1,336 lb (606 kg) |

| | |
|---|---|
| Maximum speed: | 93 mph (149 km/h) |
| Endurance: | 2 hours |
| Armament: | Two synchronised, forward-firing, Spandau machine guns |
| Engine: | 110-hp Oberursel UR.II |

## Pfalz D.VII

| | |
|---|---|
| Wingspan Upper: | 24 ft 7 in (7.5 m) |
| Wingspan Lower: | 22 ft 7 in (6.9 m) |
| Length: | 18 ft 4 in (5.6 m) |
| Height: | 9 ft 1 in (2.8 m) |
| Weight Empty: | 1,146 lb (520 kg) |
| Weight Loaded: | 1,576 lb (715 kg) |
| Maximum speed: | 93 mph (149 km/h) |
| Endurance: | 2 hours |
| Armament: | Two synchronised, forward-firing, Spandau machine guns |
| Engine: | 160-hp Siemens-Halske Sh.III |

## Pfalz D.VIII

| | |
|---|---|
| Wingspan Upper: | 24 ft 7 in (7.5 m) |
| Wingspan Lower: | 22 ft 7 in (6.9 m) |
| Length: | 18 ft 4 in (5.6 m) |
| Height: | 9 ft 1 in (2.8 m) |
| Weight Empty: | 1,195 lb (542 kg) |
| Weight Loaded: | 1,691 lb (767 kg) |
| Maximum speed: | 93 mph (149 km/h) |
| Endurance: | 2 hours |
| Armament: | Two synchronised, forward-firing, Spandau machine guns |
| Engine: | 160-hp Siemens-Halske Sh.III |
| | 145-hp Oberursel Ur.II |
| | 200-hp Goebel Goe.III |

## Pfalz Dr.I

| | |
|---|---|
| Wingspan Upper: | 27 ft 9½ in (8.5 m) |
| Wingspan Middle: | 26 ft 6 in (8.10 m) |
| Wingspan Lower: | 25 ft 7 in (7.82 m) |
| Length: | 18 ft 1 in (5.50 m) |
| Height: | 8 ft 8½ in (2.7 m) |
| Weight Empty: | 1,124 lb (510 kg) |
| Weight Loaded: | 1,554 lb (705 kg) |
| Maximum speed: | 93 mph (149 km/h) |
| Endurance: | 2 hours |
| Armament: | Two synchronised, forward-firing, Spandau machine guns |
| Engine: | 160-hp Siemens & Halske Sh.III |

## Pfalz Dr.II & IIIa

| | |
|---|---|
| Wingspan Upper: | 23 ft 7 in (7.2 m) |
| Wingspan Middle: | 23 ft 7 in (7.2 m) |
| Wingspan Lower: | 23 ft 7 in (7.2 m) |
| Length: | 18 ft 1 in (5.50 m) |

| | |
|---|---|
| Height: | 8 ft 8½ in (2.7 m) |
| Weight Empty: | 1,124 lb (510 kg) |
| Weight Loaded: | 1,554 lb (705 kg) |
| Maximum speed: | 93 mph (149 km/h) |
| Endurance: | 2 hours |
| Armament: | Two synchronised, forward-firing, Spandau machine guns |
| Engine: | 160-hp Siemens & Halske Sh.III |

## Pfalz D.IX, D.X and D.XI

Almost no information on these three types exists.

## Pfalz D.XII

| | |
|---|---|
| Wingspan: | 29 ft 5 in (9.0 m) |
| Length: | 20 ft 8 in (6.35 m) |
| Height: | 8 ft 7½ in (2.70 m) |
| Weight Empty: | 1,569 lb (712 kg) |
| Weight Loaded: | 1,966 lb (892 kg) |
| Maximum speed: | 111 mph |
| Endurance: | 1½ hours |
| Armament: | Two synchronised, forward-firing, Spandau machine guns |
| Engine: | 170-hp Mercedes D.IIIa |
| | 180-hp Mercedes D.IIIaü / 185-hp BMW IIa |

## Pfalz D.XIV

| | |
|---|---|
| Wingspan Upper: | 32 ft 10 in (10.0 m) |
| Wingspan Lower: | 30 ft 1 in (9.1 m) |
| Length: | 20 ft 8 in (6.3 m) |
| Height: | 8 ft 7½ in (2.7 m) |
| Weight Empty: | 1,960 lb (889 kg) |
| Weight Loaded: | 2,275 lb (1,032 kg) |
| Maximum speed: | 111 mph (178 km/h) |
| Endurance: | 1½ hours |
| Armament: | Two synchronised, forward-firing, Spandau machine guns |
| Engine: | 200-hp Benz Bz.IVü |

## Pfalz D.XV

| | |
|---|---|
| Wingspan Upper: | 28 ft 3 in (8.6 m) |
| Wingspan Lower: | 23 ft 8 in (7.2 m) |
| Length: | 20 ft 9 in (6.5 m) |
| Height: | 8 ft 7½ in (2.7 m) |
| Weight Empty: | 1,627 lb (738 kg) |
| Weight Loaded: | 2,046 lb (928 kg) |
| Maximum speed: | 111 mph (178 km/h) |
| Endurance: | 1½ hours |
| Armament: | Two synchronised, forward-firing, Spandau machine guns |
| Engine: | 185-hp BMW IIIa |

# Phönix Flugzeugwerke AG

The Phönix Flugzeugwerke was initially created as a 'backdoor' means of purchasing the Oesterreichisch-Ungarische Albatros-Flugzeugwerke (Oest-Ung), a subsidiary of the Albatros Company in Berlin. This was just another one of the companies that Camillo Castiglioni was intent on obtaining to expand his already exceptionally large share of the aircraft manufacturing market in Austria.

The Oest-Ung Company, as it was known, had been founded on 28 April 1914 and was managed by Rudolf Weiner and Michael Gabriel, both of whom had worked for Albatros in Berlin. Rudolf was the brother of one of the founders of the Albatros Company, while Michael had been the company's chief engineer. Within a year Michael Gabriel had taken control of the company by purchasing the outstanding shares and becoming the sole owner. It was at this point that Camillo Castiglioni appeared on the scene, and it was suspected that it was he who had financially supported Michael Gabriel in order to gain a foothold in the company.

Castiglioni already owned Hansa-Brandenburg and Ungarische Luftschiff und Flugmaschinen AG (UFAG) and had investments in Lohner and Aviatik. Speculation about his ever-increasing control over the Austrian aviation industry was causing a great deal of concern among the senior officers of the Luftfahrtruppen or LFT (Flying Troops), so much so, that in order to obtain the Oest-Ung Albatros Company, Castiglioni, together with Prinz August Lobkowitz, created the Phönix Flugzeugwerke AG. The company then, very quietly, acquired the majority of the shares, taking control of Oest-Ung and all their contracts. In order not to lose the name of the company, it was given responsibility for the design and testing of all prototype aircraft and made part of a subsidiary company to Phönix. It came as no surprise to anyone when Michael Gabriel was appointed general manager of the new Phönix Flugzeugwerke.

The new company searched for the best designers and engineers and among them was Dipl.Ing. Leo Kirste, who had worked for the French Breguet Company in London after earning his degree in aeronautical engineering in Paris. He then joined the Rumpler Company in Berlin before being 'headhunted' by Phönix and all before he was twenty-five years old. On joining the Phönix Company he was made head of the design department. In May 1916, he was joined in the department by Dipl.Ing. Edmund Sparmann, who had been assigned to the company by the military to oversee the aircraft that were built. Sparmann had been a pilot before the war and had built, and flown, his own monoplane. When the war started he was a reserve officer and saw action on the Russian Front with Flik 5 before being assigned as a test pilot. He was to make a major contribution by designing the 'Sparmann Wing', which was successfully used on a number of Phönix built aircraft.

Another designer/engineer, who joined the company in 1918, was Ingenieur Eduard Zaparka, a graduate aeronautical engineer from Berlin University. Zaparka had one of the most inventive minds in the aviation industry, and among other things designed and developed a machine gun synchronisation system which was widely used on most of the Phönix aircraft. He had designed a rotary-engined parasol fighter, but it was too late to make any impact on the war.

The first of the Oest-Ung aircraft appeared on 1 October 1914 and was used a test bed for the first of the Phönix models, which appeared in July 1916. The aircraft, later known as the Phönix 20.01, was assigned to Flik 12 in an unarmed reconnaissance role and later to Flek 8 as a trainer. In 1917, information was received that the aircraft was in storage after being extensively damaged, so the Phönix Company bought the aircraft back from the LFT for 500 crowns. The aircraft was repaired and given to the Heeresgeschichtliches Museum in Vienna, where it stands proudly to this day.

With the information gathered from the 20.01 model, the first of the Phönix-built aircraft, the 20.02, appeared. Powered by an inverted V-8 200-hp Hiero engine, the aircraft was also fitted with a rear gun turret capable of taking a 7 cm cannon. Although the Phönix Company built the aircraft, the designation was, in the case of the 20.02, the Albatros B.I (Ph). This was because it belonged to the contracts that had been obtained by the Albatros Company prior to the take-over. The 20.02 was used purely as an experimental model and later a 300-hp Daimler V-12 engine was fitted but proved to be unsatisfactory.

There followed a series of two-seat armed reconnaissance 20.03 – 20.07, all variations of the Albatros B.I (Ph) with a variety of different Hiero engines. The development of the Hiero 200-hp engine resulted in it being installed into two Brandenburg C.I (Ph)s, 20.08 and 20.09. Both these aircraft, after intensive trials, were allocated to Flik 19 and saw active service.

On 18 August 1914, a request from the Austrian War Ministry for a twin-engined *Kampflugzeug* (Battleplane) was submitted to a number of the top aviation manufacturers, among them the Albatros company. With the company now under the control of the Phönix Company, a proposal was submitted to Fliegerarsenal or Flars (Aviation Arsenal), who, after requesting a number of modifications, accepted it. Designated the 20.10, the completed aircraft, with a crew of three, pilot and two gunners, and powered by two 200-hp Hiero engines carried out a series of ground and flight tests. There apparently was no provision for bombs and maybe it was this, and the fact that it was considered to be underpowered and had a weak undercarriage, that persuaded Flars to cancel the order for twenty-four of the aircraft.

A second series of the Albatros B.I, known as the 24 Series, was being worked on. The weight was reduced considerably and, together with an improved sweepback adjusting mechanism and a newly designed radiator, a total of fifty-three of these aircraft were built. An additional twenty-nine B.I (Ph) Series 23 and 24 airframes were converted to 24 Series, bringing a total of eighty-two of the aircraft delivered to the Army. Later twelve of these aircraft were modified, fitted with dual controls and assigned to various Fliks as trainers.

The first contracts awarded to the Phönix Company for the manufacture of an aircraft in its own right came on 3 March 1916 when they received a contract to design and build two triplane bombers. Given the designation 20.11 and 20.12, the two aircraft were designed by Leo Kirste, who placed the fuselage between the lower two wings. Flars rejected the initial design, as they felt the position of the fuselage placed a restriction on the field of fire. However, after examining a similar design by Ungarische Lloyd Flugzeug und Motorenfabrik with the fuselage in an alternative position, they changed their mind and accepted the original design. Despite this encouragement, construction of the prototypes went slowly, so slowly in fact that Flars expressed concern about them ever being finished and so cancelled the contract.

The company was becoming involved in the installation and testing of various engines into aircraft from other companies and in March 1917 they began work installing the new 220-hp Benz engine in the Brandenburg C.I (Ph). Each time this kind of work was carried out, the aircraft involved was given a numerical designation and this was no exception. Given the number 20.13 by Phönix it nevertheless, but unusually, retained its original number of 29.90 given to it by Brandenburg. Phönix had started constructing Brandenburg aircraft under licence at the end of 1916, the first of these being the Leo Kirste-designed 20.14, which was a sesquiplane. Based on the Nieuport configuration, Kirste raised the D.I fuselage to the level of the upper wings, whose area had been increased, thus eliminating the need for centre-section struts. The support was provided by an angled fuselage brace and a single V-strut. Powered by a 185-hp Daimler engine, the first flight took place on 16 January 1917 and was flown by Hauptmann Karl Nikitsch. During the flight a vibration problem arose and the aircraft crashed on returning to the airfield. Although extensively damaged, the airframe was rebuilt and the fuselage extended. A pair of additional wing struts solved the vibration problem, but again, while on loan to the Navy and flown by Linienschiffsleutnant Wenzel Wosecek, the aircraft crashed during a night landing. This time the fault was that of the pilot and not the aircraft.

The results from the testing of the prototype gave rise to the production of the first Phönix D.I fighter (20.16) built for both the Army and the Navy. An improved version appeared in October 1917 (20.18). There had been a 20.17, which was a D.I with a different engine, and was put into production as the D.II and IIa fitted with 200-hp and 230-hp Hiero engines respectively. The 20.18, with a 230-hp Hiero engine installed, was given to the Navy with the designation D.III.

The arrival of Eduard Zaparka at the company saw the development of the 20.19 and 20.21 aircraft fitted with the unique Zaparka wing structure and both powered by a 230-hp Hiero engine. The Phönix 20.20 was a modified C.I, which widened the fuselage but made it shallower in order to accommodate an aerial camera.

In July 1918, in preparation for the Fighter Evaluation trials, Phönix developed five prototypes, the 20.22, 20.23, 20.24, 20.25 and 422.23. The 20.23, 20.24 and 422.23 were developed from modified Phönix D.II/IIa airframes. During the evaluation trials Stabsfeldwebel Karl Urban, an experienced pilot from Flik 14/J, was carrying out a series of manoeuvres when, while carrying out a sharp loop, the wingtips of the 20.22 folded back. The aircraft spun out of control and crashed, killing the pilot instantly. This wasn't the first time that this type of incident had occurred and Flars ordered that all Phönix D.II fighters be grounded until their wings had been reinforced.

There were no such problems with 20.23, which was powered by a 225-hp Daimler engine. Oberleutnants Benno Fiala Ritter von Fernbrugg and Frank Linke-Crawford, both of whom extolled the virtues of the aircraft, flew the aircraft during the trials. The two pilots also carried out tests on the Phönix 20.24 and 20.25, both of which had been designed by Leo Kirste. The aircraft had a much narrower lower wing, which gave the pilot an excellent field of view, and a fireproof fuel tank that was mounted between the engine and the pilot.

There were a number of other projects started by the company: the Phönix 350-hp biplane, Phönix Monoplane, the rotary-engined fighter, rotary-engined parasol fighter and the Reconnaissance Type 13 Biplane, none of which came to fruition.

Using the results from the Fighter Evaluation Trials, Flars ordered Phönix to construct two experimental fighters, implementing all the improvements that had been evaluated during the trials. These included the fitting of four ailerons, which increased the aircraft's manoeuvrability, the modifying of the elevator and rudder controls to increase sensitivity and the re-positioning of the machine guns so that they were within easy reach of the pilot. The two experimental aircraft were the Phönix 20.28 and 20.29.

The development of the Series 23 had started in 1915 and was based on the design of the Albatros B.II, but with slightly larger overall dimensions. The aircraft were used for reconnaissance sorties throughout 1915; then in 1916, twenty of the aircraft were returned to the factory, ten of which were to be converted to Series 24 trainers, the remaining ten becoming the Albatros B.I (Ph) Series 21 models. Earlier, in 1914, Phönix engineers and designers had been endeavouring to improve the Albatros B.I (Ph); the results came late in 1915, when the Series 24 appeared. The Series 24 aircraft was readily accepted by the Austro-Hungarian Fliks, although they soon discovered problems climbing over mountains that were in excess of 7,218 ft (2,200 m). The problem was that most of the areas in which the aircraft served were in mountainous regions. It was decided that if the span and area of the aircraft's wings were increased then this might solve the problem. Professor Richard Knoller was approached by Flars to design a new wing and twelve of the Series 24 aircraft were fitted with the KNV (Knoller-Verspannung) wing and were successful, but there were long delays in producing the remainder, and the remaining Series 24 aircraft were replaced by the Brandenburg C.I (Ph) the following year.

The success of the Knoller wing prompted the LFT and Flars to place an order with the Phönix Company for forty-eight Knoller C.I (Ph) Series 25 biplanes, all to be fitted with the 200-hp Hiero engine. With production under way and the first of the aircraft ready to come off the production line, albeit months behind schedule, there was no Hiero engine available, so a 160-hp Daimler was fitted. During tests a number of problems were discovered, two being that the controls were far too heavy and the aircraft was tail-heavy.

Flars were not happy with the delays in production, which were linked to problems being discovered in the aircraft, and reduced the number ordered to sixteen. The first of the aircraft, 25.01, had been returned to the factory five times for modifications to be carried out, and during one taxiing trial the frame of the fuselage broke. After one particularly scathing report on the aircraft from an experienced military pilot, Hauptmann Heinrich Kostrba, Flars cancelled the contract, ordering Phönix to concentrate on building the Brandenburg C.I (Ph).

The contract for building the Brandenburg C.I (Ph) under licence had been given to Phönix by LFT. This was to be the Series 26 model and they were to be powered by the 160-hp Daimler engine. The initial contract was for thirty aircraft. Then, in May 1916, a second contract was issued for a further forty to be built, and these were to be fitted with the improved 185-hp Daimler engine. One of the aircraft, 26.17, was fitted with a gun turret and assigned to Flik 7 for evaluation. The report was scathing: the observer's view was almost non-existent, there was no communication possible between the pilot and the observer and it was extremely difficult to train the gun forward. The idea was scrapped.

The Brandenburg C.I (Ph) Series 27 had a newly developed fuselage, which had been designed to allow the installation of various engines, and also to enable the aircraft to be adapted to carry photographic equipment, wireless equipment and bombs. The first contract for fifty-six of the aircraft to be built was awarded in June 1916, followed by a contract for a further thirty-two in the September. All the aircraft were to be powered by the 160-hp Daimler engine. The first of the aircraft came off the production line in September 1916 and were assigned to various Fliks. By mid-1917, it was realised that although the aircraft was highly regarded by all who flew it, it was seriously underpowered and it was relegated to training duties.

The replacement for Series 27 was the Series 29, and this was powered by the 200-hp Hiero engine. The design was almost identical to that of the Series 27 and proved to be one of the most robust and reliable of all the reconnaissance and observation aircraft produced.

In an effort to improve the performance, Phönix engineers designed an airfoil radiator and re-designed the undercarriage, but they were not the success hoped for. These were known as the Series 129 and 229 aircraft. The difference was that 129.01 to 129.72 were powered by the 200-hp Hiero engine, while the Series 229.01 to 229.32 were powered by the original Hiero engine. Both models were constructed alongside each other.

At the beginning of March 1917, Flars placed a blanket order for 264 aircraft, fifty-six of which were to be Brandenburg C.I (Ph) Series 329 models powered by a 230-hp Hiero engine. The specifications were almost identical to the earlier models, the only difference being the weights. Initially, the aircraft suffered from nose-heaviness and some of the Fliks that took delivery of the aircraft, installed either a 70 cm camera or a fuselage-mounted gun behind the observer to counteract the problem.

The breakthrough, as far as the Phönix Company were concerned, came in July 1917, when Flars accepted the Phönix C.I Series 121 model. The aircraft had started life earlier in the year as the basis of the Brandenburg C.II, but had been cancelled by Flars for a variety of reasons. The designers re-designed the fuselage, fitted a Sparmann wing and installed the 230-hp Hiero engine. All the flight tests were carried out satisfactorily and an order for twenty-four of the aircraft was placed. In October 1917, a second contract for a further twenty-four was received, but by now the Phönix factory was becoming seriously over-worked and was struggling to keep up with orders. The situation at the front was becoming desperate and more and more new aircraft were required to replace the losses. Emil Uzelac, who was in a position to order aircraft to be dispatched to the Front, dispatched a number of the Phönix C.Is to the Front for evaluation, despite protests from the Army High Command not to.

Uzelac's confidence in the aircraft was found to be fully justified when favourable reports came back from the various Fliks who had been evaluating the aircraft. In the meantime, Emil Uzelac had ordered a further sixty of the machines to be built. Because of its size, the Allies often mistook the Phönix C.I as a fighter, and many an Allied pilot was given a nasty shock when attacking it from the rear to discover a machine gun open up on him. One in particular was Maggiore Francesco Barraca, Italy's top ace, who was shot down by observer Oberleutnant Arnold Barwig and Zugsführer Max Kauer of Flik 28/D, flying a Phönix C.I.

By the beginning of 1918, Emil Uzelac realised that the development and production of the Phönix C.I was not going as well as expected. In an effort to boost production while the problems with the Phönix C.I were being solved, the Phönix Company were ordered to build forty Ungarische Flugzeug Werke (UFAG) C.I (Ph) aircraft. Within weeks the production lines were going flat out, but the problems with the Phönix C.I had been solved and the production of the UFAG aircraft was, if anything, slowing things up. In fact, over half of the completed UFAG aircraft were still in storage when the war ended.

One of the aircraft produced by the Phönix Company, the Brandenburg D.I (Ph) Series 28, was one of the aircraft most preferred by experienced Austro-Hungarian pilots. Three of the pilots, Offizierstellvertreter Josef Kiss, Oberleutnant Godwin

Brumowski and Oberleutnant Frank Linke-Crawford, scored the majority of their victories in this aircraft. The aircraft was powered by a 185-hp Daimler engine, with a raised centre section that allowed the pilot to aim his machine gun without leaning out of the cockpit. It had a much lighter airframe than many of its counterparts and, although not for the novice, in the hands of the experienced pilot it outclassed many of its opponents.

With the war now becoming increasingly desperate for the German and Austro-Hungarian armies, the LFT started to award 'open' contracts to the various aircraft manufacturers; the idea was that they would take aircraft from these companies as and when they needed them. The Phönix Company was ordered to produce 120 Phönix D.I fighters. There was a condition, and this was that their 20.15 and 20.16 prototype testing programme was successfully completed. In August 1917, the first of the D.I fighters was built and was almost identical to the 20.16 prototype, the exception being it had a longer, stronger fuselage to accommodate the 200-hp Hiero engine and the twin machine guns mounted alongside the engine.

Problems arose when Emil Uzelac discovered that fifty of the completed aircraft were in storage, awaiting the installation of the synchronised machine guns. He ordered that they be flown to the front, where LFT armourers would install the machine guns and get the aircraft into the war. There were minor differences between the Series 128, 226 and 328 models.

In March 1918, the Series 122, 222 and 322 Phönix D.II fighters appeared. The only real difference between the D.I and D.II was that the weight of the airframe had been reduced by 110 lb (50 kg), a new tailplane was fitted and it had balanced ailerons. There were a number of accidents attributed to the engine bearers, causing the aircraft to be grounded while modifications were carried out, but when the wings folded during a familiarisation flight, killing the pilot, the aircraft was finally grounded.

The Phönix D.IIa appeared at the same time as the D.II, but was powered by a 230-hp Hiero engine. The specifications were identical to that of the D.II and it was hoped that the extra power would enable the fighter to outclass its opponents but, because of manufacturing problems, over 20 per cent of the aircraft were powered by a 200-hp Hiero engine. Those that were powered by the 230-hp model were highly regarded by the pilots who flew them.

In July 1918, a modified D.IIa, given the designation of D.III, was put forward in the Fighter Evaluation Trials. After extensive testing by LFT test pilots, it was strongly recommended that after minor modifications to the re-positioning of the guns, the aircraft be put into immediate production. A contract for 100 of the fighters was awarded to the company on 18 September 1918, and by October sixty-one of the aircraft had been sent to the front in a desperate effort to help stem the Allied advance. One month later it was all over and Germany capitulated, leaving production lines at a standstill.

The Phönix Company had proved itself to be one of the top aircraft manufacturers and left its own legacy to the world of aviation.

## SPECIFICATIONS

### Albatros B.I (Ph) Series 20

Wingspan Upper:   43 ft 4 in (13.2 m)
Wingspan Lower:   37 ft 2 in (11.37 m)
Length:           27 ft 2 in (8.3 m)

Height:              10 ft 11 in (3.3 m)
Weight Empty:        1,896 lb (860 kg)
Weight Loaded:       2,723 lb (1,235 kg)
Maximum Speed:       68 mph (110 km/h)
Ceiling:             9,840 ft (3,000 m)
Endurance:           3 hours
Engine:              One 145-hp Hiero
Armament:            None

## Phönix Series 20 and 21

Wingspan Upper:      34 ft 3 in (10.6 m)
Wingspan Lower:      29 ft 2 in (8.8 m)
Length:              27 ft 2 in (8.3 m)
Height:              10 ft 11 in (3.3 m)
Weight Empty:        1,610 lb (730 kg)
Weight Loaded:       2,315 lb (1,050 kg)
Maximum Speed:       68 mph (110 km/h)
Ceiling:             16,400 ft (5,000 m)
Endurance:           3 hours
Engine:              One 230-hp Hiero
Armament:            None

## Phönix 20

Wingspan Upper:      27 ft 10 in (8.6 m)
Wingspan Lower:      24 ft 5 in (7.5 m)
Length:              21 ft 6 in (6.6 m)
Height:              8 ft 9 in (2.7m)
Weight Empty:        1,466 lb (665 kg)
Weight Loaded:       2,095 lb (950 kg)
Maximum Speed:       115 mph (190 km/h)
Ceiling:             16,450 ft (5,000 m)
Endurance:           3 hours
Engine:              One 230-hp Hiero
Armament:            Not known

## Albatros B.I (Ph) Series 24

Wingspan Upper:      45 ft 6 in (13.9 m)
Wingspan Lower:      38 ft 7 in (11.8 m)
Length:              27 ft 2 in (8.3 m)
Height:              11 ft 6 in (3.5 m)
Weight Empty:        1,797 lb (815 kg)
Weight Loaded:       2,761 lb (1,252 kg)
Maximum Speed:       75 mph (121 km/h)
Ceiling:             9,840 ft (3,000 m)
Endurance:           3 hours
Engine:              One 145-hp Hiero
Armament:            None

## Albatros B.II (Ph) Series 23

| | |
|---|---|
| Wingspan Upper: | 43 ft 4 in (13.2 m) |
| Wingspan Lower: | 37 ft 2 in (11.7 m) |
| Length: | 27 ft 2 in (8.3 m) |
| Height: | 10 ft 11 in (3.3 m) |
| Weight Empty: | 1,896 lb (860 kg) |
| Weight Loaded: | 2,723 lb (1,235 kg) |
| Maximum Speed: | 68 mph (110 km/h) |
| Ceiling: | 9,840 ft (3,000 m) |
| Endurance: | 3 hours |
| Engine: | One 145-hp Hiero |
| Armament: | None |

## Albatros B.II (Ph) Series 24

| | |
|---|---|
| Wingspan Upper: | 43 ft 8 in (13.4 m) |
| Wingspan Lower: | 37 ft 5 in (11.7 m) |
| Length: | 27 ft 2 in (8.3 m) |
| Height: | 10 ft 11 in (3.3 m) |
| Weight Empty: | 1,839 lb (834 kg) |
| Weight Loaded: | 2,814 lb (1,276 kg) |
| Maximum Speed: | 68 mph (110 km/h) |
| Ceiling: | 9,840 ft (3,000 m) |
| Endurance: | 3 hours |
| Engine: | One 145-hp Hiero |
| Armament: | None |

## Albatros B.I (Ph) Series 25 (Knoller Wing)

| | |
|---|---|
| Wingspan Upper: | 45 ft 6 in (13.9 m) |
| Wingspan Lower: | 38 ft 8 in (11.8 m) |
| Length: | 27 ft 2 in (8.3 m) |
| Height: | 11 ft 6 in (3.5 m) |
| Weight Empty: | 1,797 lb (815 kg) |
| Weight Loaded: | 2,761 lb (1,252 kg) |
| Maximum Speed: | 75 mph (121 km/h) |
| Ceiling: | 9,840 ft (3,000 m) |
| Endurance: | 3 hours |
| Engine: | One 145-hp Hiero |
| Armament: | None |

## Knoller C.I (Ph) Series 25

| | |
|---|---|
| Wingspan Upper: | 41 ft 6 in (12.7 m) |
| Wingspan Lower: | 41 ft 6 in (12.7 m) |
| Length: | 27 ft 9 in (8.5 m) |
| Height: | 10 ft 7 in (3.3 m) |
| Weight Empty: | 1,720 lb (780 kg) |
| Weight Loaded: | 2,683 lb (1,217 kg) |
| Maximum Speed: | 100 mph (160 km/h) |
| Ceiling: | 9,840 ft (3,000 m) |
| Endurance: | 3 hours |

Engine:              One 160-hp Daimler
Armament:            None

## Brandenburg C.I (Ph) Series 26

Wingspan Upper:      40 ft 4 in (12.3 m)
Wingspan Lower:      38 ft 2 in (11.7 m)
Length:              27 ft 9 in (8.5 m)
Height:              9 ft 5 in (2.9 m)
Weight Empty:        1,757 lb (797 kg)
Weight Loaded:       2,730 lb (1,238 kg)
Maximum Speed:       90 mph (145 km/h)
Ceiling:             9,840 ft (3,000 m)
Endurance:           3 hours
Engine:              One 160-hp Daimler
Armament:            Not known

## Brandenburg C.I (Ph) Series 28

Wingspan Upper:      27 ft 9 in (8.5 m)
Wingspan Lower:      27 ft 9 in (8.5 m)
Length:              20 ft 7 in (6.3 m)
Height:              9 ft 1 in (2.7 m)
Weight Empty:        1,574 lb (714 kg)
Weight Loaded:       2,309 lb (1,047 kg)
Maximum Speed:       115 mph (185 km/h)
Ceiling:             9,840 ft (3,000 m)
Endurance:           3 hours
Engine:              One 185-hp Daimler
Armament:            One Parabellum machine gun in the observer's cockpit

## Phönix D.I (Ph) Series 128, 228 and 328

Wingspan Upper:      32 ft 3 in (9.8 m)
Wingspan Lower:      29 ft 6 in (9.0 m)
Length:              22 ft 1 in (6.7 m)
Height:              8 ft 7 in (2.6 m)
Weight Empty:        1,579 lb (716 kg)
Weight Loaded:       2,097 lb (951 kg)
Maximum Speed:       110 mph (178 km/h)
Ceiling:             16,405 ft (3,000 m)
Endurance:           3 hours
Engine:              One 200-hp Hiero
Armament:            Two synchronised machine guns mounted either side of
                     the engine

# Rumpler Flugzeug-Werke GmbH

The Rumpler aircraft manufacturing company started building aircraft well before the First World War started. The first aircraft to come from their factory was the Rumpler Eindecker, which was based on the Taube design. A flimsy-looking machine, as indeed most of the early aircraft were, the Eindecker was powered by a 100-hp Mercedes D.I engine and saw a great deal of service in the initial stages of the war on reconnaissance missions.

As the need for aircraft intensified, the first of the Rumpler biplanes appeared in 1914: the Rumpler B.I. A small number were built and supplied to the German Army for training purposes and reconnaissance duties. The B.I was powered by a 100-hp Mercedes D.I engine that gave the aircraft a top speed of over 90 mph. It had a wingspan of 42 ft 8 in, a fuselage length of 27 ft 7 in and a height of 10 ft 2 in.

Within a few months an improved version of the B.I appeared, the Rumpler 4A 13. Basically the same design as the B.I, the 4A 13 was also powered by a 100-hp Mercedes D.I engine; however, the radiators were fitted either side of the fuselage beneath the pilot's cockpit. It also had a 'comma-type' balanced rudder fitted. The 4A 13 had a wingspan of 47 ft 7 in, otherwise all the remaining specification were the same. There was a Rumpler 4A 14 built the following month which was identical to the 4A 13 with the exception of the engine, which was a 150-hp Benz Bz.III.

The German Navy expressed an interest in the 4A 13 and ordered nine to be converted to seaplanes. Given the designation of Rumpler 4B 11, they were powered with a 100-hp Benz Bz.I engine, which gave the aircraft a top speed of 81 mph and it was used for reconnaissance missions. Pleased with the success of the 4B 11 seaplanes, the German Navy ordered another eighteen. These were converted 4A 14s powered by a 150-hp Benz Bz.III engine and were given the designation 4B 12. Ten further models were ordered but these were powered by a 160-hp Gnome engine and given the designation of 4B 13.

Another flying boat was built in 1914 by Rumpler, the Rumpler 4E. This was a purpose built model, unlike the others, which were conversions of landplanes. Powered by a 120-hp Austro-Daimler engine, the 4E had a wingspan of 51 ft 5 in, a fuselage length of 29 ft and a height of 11 ft. Only the one was built.

One of the most famous and successful of all the two-seater reconnaissance aircraft built during the First World War was the Rumpler C.I model. The first model appeared during 1915, and by October 1916, over 250 C.Is and C.Ias were in service on all fronts. The C.Ia was only a C.I fitted with a 180-hp Argus engine. The C.I was powered by a six-cylinder, in-line, water-cooled 160-hp Mercedes D.III engine, with its back-sloping 'chimney' exhaust that protruded over the top wing. This was fitted into the nose of a slab-sided fuselage, constructed in a box-girder design with a rounded top section. The fuselage was constructed of four longerons that were made of pine facing toward the rear of the aircraft and four that were made of ash facing toward the nose. They were spliced together in the cockpit region. Ash was also used for the lateral and vertical spacers at the rear of the cockpit, while steel tubing was used for the front section. All the tail and fin surfaces were constructed of welded steel tube and covered in dope-painted fabric.

The Rumpler C.I was used widely for photo-reconnaissance missions and its exploits are a matter of record. One problem did arise with these flights while in Damascus in 1917 when, because of the heat, many of the missions were a waste of time. This was because the high temperatures affected the gelatine emulsion on the photographic plates.

There was no C.II. The C.III was produced in limited numbers. It was powered a 220-hp Benz Bz.IV engine and had a distinctive 'comma'-shaped rudder and large angular balances on the ailerons. The top of the fuselage behind the observer's cockpit was shaped as if to be part of a streamlined headrest; this was to be removed on the next model.

The next version, the C.IV, was another of the major production versions like the C.I. This was one of the most successful of all the two-seat reconnaissance aircraft built by Rumpler. At altitudes exceeding 15,000 feet there were very few Allied fighters capable of even getting near it, let alone catching it. Almost identical to the C.I in appearance, the C.IV differed in that the wings had a slight sweep and a stagger. The lower wing was considered to have an unusual profile inasmuch as it resembled the lower wing of the *Liebellen-Form* (dragonfly).

The fuselage spacers were of steel tube, while the front section of the longerons, from the cockpit on, were made of ash; these were spliced to the rear longeron section that was made of spruce. A trap door was placed in the floor of the observer's cockpit for the photo-reconnaissance missions. The tail surfaces were constructed of steel tube and covered with doped fabric.

The Rumpler C.IV was powered by a six-cylinder, in-line, water-cooled 260-hp Mercedes D.IVa engine, which gave the aircraft a top speed of 106 mph, a climb rate of almost 1,000 feet per minute, and an operating ceiling of 21,000 feet with an endurance of between 3 and 4 hours depending on bomb load carried. It had a wingspan of 41 ft 6½ in, a fuselage length of 27 ft 7 in, and a height of 10 ft 8 in. The C.IV was armed with a single fixed, forward-firing synchronised Spandau machine gun, a manually operated Parabellum machine gun and four bombs totalling 220 lb carried in external racks.

The Rumpler C.V that followed was no more than a C.III airframe fitted with the 260-hp six-cylinder, in-line, water-cooled Mercedes D.IVa engine and constructed identically to the C.IV. The success of the C.IV prompted the manufacturers to produce an improved model and this they did at the end of 1917 in the shape of the C.VII. It was almost identical in construction and design to the C.IV, the only difference being in overall dimension. The only visible difference was that the engine exhaust was shaped to exhaust sideways instead of upwards and over the top. It was powered by a super-compressed, six-cylinder, in-line, water-cooled 240-hp Maybach Mb.IV engine, which gave the aircraft a top speed of 109 mph, an operating ceiling of 23,944 feet and an endurance of 4 hours.

The British ace Major James B. McCudden, VC, gives an account of his encounter with a German reconnaissance aircraft that turned out to be a Rumpler C.VII. Flying an S.E.5, McCudden attacked the Rumpler at 18,200 feet, but then the German aircraft started to climb until it reached 20,000 feet. Struggling to keep up with it, McCudden realised that he was flying over enemy territory and the German aircraft was still climbing and flying away from him. Discretion being the better part of valour, McCudden turned away and headed back to his own lines. His report on the performance of this new German reconnaissance two-seater gave rise to concern and a wary eye was kept out for this type of aircraft. A large number of these aircraft were built.

A specialised version of the C.VII was built at the same time: the Rubild. This specially equipped photo-reconnaissance aircraft was fitted with highly specialised camera equipment and was capable of flying at heights in excess of 24,000 feet.

The German Army's plans for a major offensive at the beginning of 1918 included the extensive use of reconnaissance aircraft. The continued success of the Rumpler C series prompted Idflieg to request that the company produce a trainer with the emphasis on the training of observers. This meant it had to have the facilities for gunnery, photographic, radio and observation training. The aircraft had to be up to operational standard while still being economical. This was achieved by fitting a six-cylinder, in-line, water-cooled 180-hp Argus As.III engine, which gave the aircraft a speed of 87 mph and an operational endurance of four hours.

Rumpler produced the C.VIII, which was supplied to the Flieger Ersatz Abteilungen or FEA (Flying Training Units). Based on the C-series design, the construction was almost identical to that of the C.IV and C.VII. The wing surfaces, however, reverted back to the C.I model, both wings having angular, raked tips.

The C.VIII had a wingspan of 39 ft 11½ in, a fuselage length of 26 ft 4 in and a height of 10 ft 6 in. It was armed with one synchronised, fixed, forward-firing, Spandau machine gun and one manually operated Parabellum machine gun. It had a flight endurance of 4 hours, which was ideal for training purposes.

At the end of 1917 an experimental model appeared, the Rumpler C.IX. Intended as a two-seater fighter, the C.IX presented a startling design with single 'I'-type interplane struts, a smooth, oval multi-stringered fuselage and was powered by a 160-hp Mercedes D.III engine. It was fitted with an 'all-moving' rudder that proved to be unsatisfactory. After a series of flight tests, which proved to be unsuccessful, the aircraft was scrapped. A second version that had a totally revised rudder also proved to be unsatisfactory and that version, too, was scrapped.

The company turned back to the existing C-series design, but with single-bay 'X' interplane struts. The Rumpler C.X was powered by a 240-hp Maybach Mb.IV engine which gave it a top speed of 121 mph. The aircraft had a wingspan of 34 ft 5½ in, a fuselage length of 22 ft 8 in and a height of 10 ft 3 in. On returning from its first test flight it was damaged in a collision while on the ground and was damaged beyond repair. It was decided not to continue with this model.

Another model, the Rumpler Experimental C Type, had a 350-hp Austro-Daimler V-12 engine fitted into a C.IV airframe. Only one was built.

The design of the Rumpler C.IX surfaced again at the beginning of 1918, with the Rumpler 7D 1. This model was the first in a series of six experimental single-seater fighters that was to culminate in the production of the D.I some months later. The first, the Rumpler 7D 1, had the wrap-around streamlined fuselage which was plywood-skinned and then covered in a dope-painted fabric. It also incorporated the six-cylinder, in-line, water-cooled 160-hp Mercedes D.III engine and radiator. One of the other features was the wide-chord 'I'-section interplane struts between the wings.

The second of the six models, the Rumpler 7D 2, had the fuselage plywood skin only covering the fore and aft sections, while the middle section was just covered in doped fabric. The streamlined interplane 'I'-section struts were replaced with the conventional twin struts. This too was powered by the 160-hp Mercedes D.III engine. In an effort to reduce drag, the interplane struts of the next model, the

7D 4, (there was no 7D 3) were replaced with single struts of C-section and this was also powered by the 160-hp Mercedes D.III engine. There was a 7D 5, but it appeared to be exactly the same as the 7D 4 and any modifications were very minor.

The next model to appear in this experimental series was the 7D 6. This was a revolutionary quadruplane project, for which there is no information available. The Rumpler 7D 7, which was based on the design of the 7D 4, had the bracing cables encased in streamlined casings. This was to be the last of the series and the one that was to be the prototype for the highly successful Rumpler D.I.

Two of the D.Is were entered into the 1918 mid-summer D-type Competition and excelled themselves. Powered by a 180-hp Mercedes D.IIIa engine, the D.I had a top speed of 112 mph and a climb rate of nearly 1,000 feet per minute. It had a wingspan of 27 ft 7½ in, a fuselage length of 18 ft 10½ in and a height of 8 ft 5 in. A number were produced, but the end of the war interrupted the production of any more of the aircraft. In the autumn of 1918, another version fitted with a 185-hp BMW high-compression engine emerged, but it never reached the production stage.

Information obtained in 1970 from the papers in the A. R. Weyl collection indicated that the Rubild was in fact a Rumpler C.VI, but then as both the C.VI and C.VII were almost identical it really does not matter.


## SPECIFICATIONS

### Rumpler B.I

| | |
|---|---|
| Wing Span: | 42 ft 8 in (13.0 m) |
| Length: | 27 ft 6½ in (8.4 m) |
| Height: | 10 ft 2½ in (3.1 m) |
| Weight Empty: | 1,650 lb (750 kg) |
| Weight Loaded: | 2,134 lb (970 kg) |
| Engine: | One 100-hp Mercedes D.I six-cylinder, in-line, water-cooled |
| Maximum Speed: | 90 mph (145 km/h) |
| Service Ceiling: | 16,520 feet |
| Endurance: | 1½ hours |
| Armament: | None |

### Rumpler 4A 13

| | |
|---|---|
| Wing Span: | 47 ft 7 in (14.5 m) |
| Length: | 27 ft 6½ in (8.4 m) |
| Height: | 10 ft 6 in (3.1 m) |
| Weight Empty: | 1,716 lb (780 kg) |
| Weight Loaded: | 2,341 lb (1,064 kg) |
| Engine: | One 100-hp Mercedes D.I six-cylinder, in-line, water-cooled |
| Maximum Speed: | 90 mph (145 km/h) |
| Service Ceiling: | 16,520 feet |
| Endurance: | 1½ hours |
| Armament: | None |

## Rumpler 4B 11

| | |
|---|---|
| Wing Span: | 42 ft 8 in (13.0 m) |
| Length: | 32 ft 2 in (9.8 m) |
| Height: | 11 ft 6½ in (3.5 m) |
| Weight Empty: | 1,782 lb (810 kg) |
| Weight Loaded: | 2,266 lb (1,030 kg) |
| Engine: | One 100-hp Benz Bz.I six-cylinder, in-line, water-cooled |
| Maximum Speed: | 81 mph (130 km/h) |
| Service Ceiling: | 16,520 feet |
| Endurance: | 1½ hours |
| Armament: | None |

## Rumpler 4B 12

| | |
|---|---|
| Wing Span: | 47 ft 7 in (14.5 m) |
| Length: | 31 ft 6 in (9.6 m) |
| Height: | 11 ft 10 in (3.6 m) |
| Weight Empty: | 2,112 lb (960 kg) |
| Weight Loaded: | 2,816 lb (1,280 kg) |
| Engine: | One 150-hp Benz Bz.III six-cylinder, in-line, water-cooled |
| Maximum Speed: | 81 mph (130 km/h) |
| Service Ceiling: | 16,520 feet |
| Endurance: | 1½ hours |
| Armament: | None |

## Rumpler C.I

| | |
|---|---|
| Wing Span: | 39 ft 10½ in |
| Length: | 25 ft 9 in |
| Height: | 10 ft 0½ in |
| Weight Empty: | 1,744 lb |
| Weight Loaded: | 2,866 lb |
| Engine: | One 150-hp Benz Bz.III six-cylinder, in-line, water-cooled |
| Maximum Speed: | 95 mph |
| Service Ceiling: | 16,660 feet |
| Endurance: | 4 hours |
| Armament: | One fixed forward-firing Spandau machine gun<br>One manually operated Parabellum machine gun mounted in the rear observer's cockpit |

## Rumpler 5A 4

| | |
|---|---|
| Wing Span: | 39 ft 10½ in (12.15 m) |
| Length: | 25 ft 9 in (7.85 m) |
| Height: | 10 ft 0½ in (3.0 m) |
| Weight Empty: | 1,408 lb (640 kg) |
| Weight Loaded: | 2,464 lb (1,120 kg) |
| Engine: | One 160-hp Mercedes D.III six-cylinder, in-line, water-cooled |
| Maximum Speed: | 95 mph |
| Service Ceiling: | 16,660 feet |
| Endurance: | 4 hours |

Armament:                One fixed forward-firing Spandau machine gun
                         One manually operated Parabellum machine gun mounted
                         in the rear observer's cockpit

## Rumpler 4E

Wing Span:               51 ft 4½ in (15.6 m)
Length:                  29 ft (8.9 m)
Height:                  11 ft (3.4 m)
Weight Empty:            1,408 lb (640 kg)
Weight Loaded:           2,464 lb (1,120 kg)
Engine:                  One 120-hp Austro-Daimler
Maximum Speed:           Not known
Service Ceiling:         Not known
Endurance:               2 hours
Armament:                None

## Rumpler C.III

Wing Span:               41 ft 6½ in (12.6 m)
Length:                  27 ft 7 in (8.4 m)
Height:                  10 ft 8 in (3.2 m)
Weight Empty:            2,097 lb (953 kg)
Weight Loaded:           3,234 lb (1,470 kg)
Engine:                  One 220-hp Benz Bz.IV six-cylinder, in-line, water-cooled
Maximum Speed:           106 mph (171 km/h)
Service Ceiling:         21,000 feet (6,400 m)
Endurance:               4 hours
Armament:                One fixed forward-firing Spandau machine gun
                         One manually operated Parabellum machine gun mounted
                         in the rear observer's cockpit
                         Four 55 lb bombs

## Rumpler C.IV

Wing Span:               41 ft 6½ in (12.6 m)
Length:                  27 ft 7 in (8.4 m)
Height:                  10 ft 8 in (3.2 m)
Weight Empty:            2,376 lb (1,080 kg)
Weight Loaded:           3,366 lb (1,530 kg)
Engine:                  One 260-hp Mercedes D.IVa six-cylinder, in-line,
                         water-cooled
Maximum Speed:           106 mph (170 km/h)
Service Ceiling:         21,000 feet (6,400 m)
Endurance:               4 hours
Armament:                One fixed forward-firing Spandau machine gun
                         One manually operated Parabellum machine gun mounted
                         in the rear observer's cockpit
                         Four 55 lb bombs

## Rumpler C.V

Identical specifications to the C.IV with just minor modifications.

## Rumpler C.IX

This was an experimental two-version model with staggered wings. No specifications available.

## Rumpler C.X

| | |
|---|---|
| Wing Span: | 34 ft 5½ in (10.5 m) |
| Length: | 22 ft 8 in (6.9 m) |
| Height: | 10 ft 3¼ in (3.1 m) |
| Weight Empty: | 2,090 lb (950 kg) |
| Weight Loaded: | 3,047 lb (1,385 kg) |
| Engine: | One 240-hp Maybach Mb.IV six-cylinder, in-line, water-cooled |
| Maximum Speed: | 122 mph (195 km/h) |
| Service Ceiling: | 21,000 feet (6,400 m) |
| Endurance: | 4 hours |
| Armament: | One fixed forward-firing Spandau machine gun |
| | One manually operated Parabellum machine gun mounted in the rear observer's cockpit |

## Rumpler C (Experimental)

| | |
|---|---|
| Wing Span: | 41 ft 6½ in (12.6 m) |
| Length: | 27 ft 7 in (8.4 m) |
| Height: | 10 ft 8 in (3.2 m) |
| Weight Empty: | 2,376 lb (1,080 kg) |
| Weight Loaded: | 3,366 lb (1,530 kg) |
| Engine: | One 350-hp Austro-Daimler V-12 |
| Maximum Speed: | Not known |
| Service Ceiling: | Not known |
| Endurance: | Not known |
| Armament: | None |

## Rumpler 6A 2 (Experimental Two-Seat)

| | |
|---|---|
| Wing Span: | 33 ft 4½ in (10.2 m) |
| Length: | 27 ft 6 in (8.3 m) |
| Height: | 11 ft 6 in (3.5 m) |
| Weight Empty: | 1,738 lb (790 kg) |
| Weight Loaded: | 2,772 lb (1,260 kg) |
| Engine: | One 160-hp Mercedes D.III six-cylinder, in-line, water-cooled |
| Maximum Speed: | 122 mph (195 km/h) |
| Service Ceiling: | Not known |
| Endurance: | 4 hours |
| Armament: | None |

## Rumpler 6B 1 & 2

| | |
|---|---|
| Wing Span: | 40 ft 1 in (12.2 m) |
| Length: | 29 ft 9 in (9.0 m) |
| Height: | 11 ft 6 in (3.5 m) |

Weight Empty:           1,738 lb (790 kg)
Weight Loaded:          2,508 lb (1,140 kg)
Engine:                 One 160-hp Mercedes D.III six-cylinder, in-line,
                        water-cooled
Maximum Speed:          122 mph (195 km/h)
Service Ceiling:        21,000 feet (6,400 m)
Endurance:              4 hours
Armament:               One fixed forward-firing Spandau machine gun

## Rumpler D.I

Wing Span:              27 ft 7½ in (8.4 m)
Length:                 18 ft 11 in (5.7 m)
Height:                 8 ft 5 in (2.5 m)
Weight Empty:           1,353 lb (615 kg)
Weight Loaded:          1,771 lb (805 kg)
Engine:                 One 180-hp Mercedes D.IIIa six-cylinder, in-line,
                        water-cooled
Maximum Speed:          112 mph (180 km/h)
Service Ceiling:        17,000 feet (5,186 m)
Endurance:              2 hours
Armament:               Two fixed forward-firing Spandau machine guns

## Rumpler G.I & II

Wing Span:              63 ft 3¼ in (19.2 m)
Length:                 38 ft 8½ in (11.8 m)
Height:                 13 ft 1½ in (4.0 m)
Weight Empty:           4,396 lb (1,998 kg)
Weight Loaded:          6,574 lb (2,938 kg)
Engine:                 One 160-hp Mercedes D.III six-cylinder, in-line,
                        water-cooled
Maximum Speed:          91 mph (145 km/h)
Service Ceiling:        21,000 feet (6,400 m)
Endurance:              4 hours
Armament:               One Parabellum machine gun

## Rumpler G.III

Wing Span:              63 ft 4 in (19.3 m)
Length:                 39 ft 4½ in (12.0 m)
Height:                 14 ft 9¼ in (4.5 m)
Weight Empty:           5,049 lb (2,295 kg)
Weight Loaded:          7,964 lb (3,620 kg)
Engine:                 Two 260-hp Mercedes D.IV six-cylinder, in-line,
                        water-cooled
Maximum Speed:          91 mph (145 km/h)
Service Ceiling:        21,000 feet (6,400 m)
Endurance:              4 hours
Armament:               One Parabellum machine gun mounted in the nose

# Sablatnig Flugzeugbau GmbH

Dr Josef Sablatnig was born in Klagenfurt, Austria, and regarded as one of Germany's 'Old Eagles'. In 1903, he built his first aircraft, possibly a glider (there is no record of it ever having been flown), and deciding that there was more of a future for aviation in Germany, Josef Sablatnig moved to Berlin in 1910. That same year, he and six other aviators learned to fly on a Wright Biplane at Johannisthal, Berlin. In 1912 he entered the 'Austrian Circuit' race and won.

In 1913, Josef Sablatnig became a director of the Union Aircraft works at Tetlow, where he was responsible for developing the Bombhardt's Arrow Biplane into the Union Arrow Biplane – an outstanding aircraft. During the next few years Josef Sablatnig, together with another pilot by the name of Walter Höhndorf, who later became a German fighter pilot and holder of the Order *Pour le Mérite*, flew the aircraft in a number of aerobatic competitions.

The exploits of these two intrepid aviators did not escape the attention of the Kaiser's brother, Prince Heinrich, who invited Josef Sablatnig to accept German nationality. The Union Aircraft Firm ran into trouble early in 1915 and went into liquidation. Josef Sablatnig, now a nationalised German living in Berlin-Koepenick, decided to found his own company: Sablatnig Flugzeugbau GmbH.

The first aircraft to come out of the new factory was the Sablatnig SF.1. Powered by a 160-hp Mercedes D.III engine, the SF.1 was an unarmed, two-seat reconnaissance floatplane and was accepted by the Navy. Only the one was built. The long, sleek fuselage of the SF.1 was to become a characteristic of the Sablatnig aircraft that were to follow.

The SF.1 was quickly replaced by the SF.2, again unarmed, but this time fitted with a radio transmitter. The first six were delivered to the Navy between June and September 1916, and such were performance results that LFG and LVG began to produce the aircraft under licence. Seeing the potential of the seaplane, Josef Sablatnig started to explore the use of a heavy seaplane for escort duties. The result was the SF.3. Powered by a 220-hp Benz Bz.IV engine, the fuselage of the SF.3 deviated from the previous two models by having plywood covering instead of the usual fabric covering. In keeping with the CFT requirements, it was fitted with a machine gun for the observer and a radio transmitter. It was sent to the Seeflugzeug-Versuchs-Kommando or SVK (Seaplane Testing Centre) at Warnemünde for testing and evaluation, but its fate is unknown. One school of thought considers that it may have crashed during testing and no record of the event survived.

In the meantime, Sablatnig continued with developing the SF model and on 17 February 1917, delivered the Sablatnig SF.4 to the Navy. Armed with a single synchronised, fixed, forward-firing Spandau machine gun, only one of these aircraft was built, as it failed to make the grade when in competition with other seaplane manufacturers. The feedback from the tests laid the way open for the development of the SF.5. This was an improved version of the SF.2 and so successful was the aircraft that 101 were built and delivered to the Navy. This model carried no armament but was fitted with a radio transmitter.

What was rather strange was the fact that the Sablatnig factory in Berlin was in the Koepenickerstrasse, which was almost in the centre of the city. Even more unusual was the fact that the company, in addition to its own production, took over sub-contract work for Friedrichshafen. Sablatnig did, however, have a small dockyard at the Müggelsee for floatation tests. Efforts were made to acquire additional premises at Warnemünde, which were successful later in 1917.

The first of the landplanes made its appearance in 1917: the Sablatnig SF.6 (B.I). It was, in reality, an SF.2 with the floats replaced by an undercarriage, and was intended for training duties only.

The company reverted back to making seaplanes with the SF.7 and dispensed with the bracing wires, replacing them with 'I'-type interplane struts. Three of these aircraft were built and accepted by the Navy in September 1917.

A second land model was produced at the end of 1917, the SF.C.I. A conventional two-seater, the C.I. was of wood and fabric construction and physically differed very little from the other two-seater aircraft manufactured by various companies. It was armed with one manually operated Parabellum machine gun mounted in the observer's cockpit and was capable of carrying six 50 kg bombs. Only two were built, as the aircraft did not come up to the requirements of Idflieg.

A second C-model, the C.II, was built, incorporating the interplane 'I' struts that were a feature of the SF.7. It was powered by a 240-hp Maybach Mb.IV engine which gave it a top speed of 94 mph, but only the prototype was built.

In January 1918 came the Sablatnig SF.8. This was a dual-control seaplane designed and produced specifically as an instruction aircraft for flying schools. The SF.8 was sent to Warnemünde for intensive testing and passed, with the result that an additional forty were ordered. It is not known if all the aircraft were delivered, but at least twenty found their way onto the Navy's inventory.

Sablatnig continued to try and develop a landplane without a great deal of success. The appearance, in the spring of 1918, of two Experimental C-types, both variants of the C.II aircraft, gave some hope but only the single models were ever built. A C.III was developed and was fitted with a large single wing, similar to that of the Fokker D.VII; again, only the one was built.

The need for bombers prompted Josef Sablatnig to produce a single-engine, two-seater night bomber, the Sablatnig N.I. A small number were produced during the latter half of 1918, but the end of the war put an end to any more production of aircraft by Sablatnig.

It is a sad irony that during the Second World War, Josef Sablatnig was arrested and sent to Auschwitz concentration camp for assisting Jewish people to escape from Germany. He died in Auschwitz.

## SPECIFICATIONS

### Sablatnig SF.I

| | |
|---|---|
| Wing Span: | 62 ft 8 in (19.1 m) |
| Length: | 28 ft 6½ in (8.6 m) |
| Height: | 14 ft 3¼ in (4.35 m) |
| Weight Empty: | 2,233 lb (1,015 kg) |
| Weight Loaded: | 3,630 lb (1,650 kg) |

| | |
|---|---|
| Engine: | One 160-hp Mercedes D.III six-cylinder, in-line, water-cooled |
| Maximum Speed: | 78 mph (125 km/h) |
| Service Ceiling: | 21,000 feet (6,400 m) |
| Endurance: | 2-3 hours |
| Armament: | None |

## Sablatnig SF.2

| | |
|---|---|
| Wing Span: | 60 ft 9½ in (18.5 m) |
| Length: | 31 ft 3 in (9.2 m) |
| Height: | 13 ft 11¼ in (4.25 m) |
| Weight Empty: | 2,372 lb (1,078 kg) |
| Weight Loaded: | 3,733 lb (1,697 kg) |
| Engine: | One 160-hp Mercedes D.III six-cylinder, in-line, water-cooled |
| Maximum Speed: | 81 mph (130 km/h) |
| Service Ceiling: | 21,000 feet (6,400 m) |
| Endurance: | 2-3 hours |
| Armament: | None |

## Sablatnig SF.4

| | |
|---|---|
| Wing Span: | 39 ft 4½ in (12.0 m) |
| Length: | 27 ft 4 in (8.33 m) |
| Height: | 12 ft 3 in (3.73 m) |
| Weight Empty: | 1,756 lb (798 kg) |
| Weight Loaded: | 2,372 lb (1,078 kg) |
| Engine: | One 150-hp Benz Bz.III six-cylinder, in-line, water-cooled |
| Maximum Speed: | 98 mph (157 km/h) |
| Service Ceiling: | 21,000 feet (6,400 m) |
| Endurance: | 2 hours |
| Armament: | One forward-firing Spandau machine gun |

## Sablatnig C.I

| | |
|---|---|
| Wing Span: | 52 ft 6 in |
| Length: | 28 ft 6½ in |
| Height: | 10 ft 6 in |
| Weight Empty: | 2,310 lb |
| Weight Loaded: | 3,380 lb |
| Engine: | One 180-hp Argus As.III six-cylinder, in-line, water-cooled |
| Maximum Speed: | 75 mph |
| Service Ceiling: | 21,000 feet |
| Endurance: | 2-3 hours |
| Armament: | One manually operated Parabellum machine gun mounted in the observer's cockpit Six 50 kg bombs |

## Sablatnig C.II

| | |
|---|---|
| Wing Span: | 41 ft 0¼ in (12.5 m) |
| Length: | 27 ft 2½ in (8.3 m) |

| | |
|---|---|
| Height: | 10 ft 6 in (3.2 m) |
| Weight Empty: | 2,354 lb (1,070 kg) |
| Weight Loaded: | 3,520 lb (1,600 kg) |
| Engine: | One 240-hp Maybach Mb.IV six-cylinder, in-line, water-cooled |
| Maximum Speed: | 94 mph (150 km/h) |
| Service Ceiling: | 21,000 feet |
| Endurance: | 2-3 hours |
| Armament: | One manually operated Parabellum machine gun mounted in the observer's cockpit |
| | One forward-firing Spandau machine gun |

## Sablatnig SF.5

| | |
|---|---|
| Wing Span: | 56 ft 9½ in |
| Length: | 31 ft 6 in |
| Height: | 11 ft 8 in |
| Weight Empty: | 2,314 lb |
| Weight Loaded: | 3,531 lb |
| Engine: | One 150-hp Benz Bz.III six-cylinder, in-line, water-cooled |
| Maximum Speed: | 92 mph |
| Service Ceiling: | 21,000 feet |
| Endurance: | 2 hours |
| Armament: | None |

## Sablatnig SF.8

| | |
|---|---|
| Wing Span: | 52 ft 6 in (16.0 m) |
| Length: | 33 ft 5½ in (10.2 m) |
| Height: | 12 ft 5½ in (3.8 m) |
| Weight Empty: | 2,603 lb (1,183 kg) |
| Weight Loaded: | 3,465 lb (1,574 kg) |
| Engine: | One 150-hp Benz Bz.III six-cylinder, in-line, water-cooled |
| Maximum Speed: | 81 mph (130 km/h) |
| Service Ceiling: | 21,000 feet |
| Endurance: | 2 hours |
| Armament: | None |

## Sablatnig N.I

| | |
|---|---|
| Wing Span: | 52 ft 6 in |
| Length: | 28 ft 6½ in |
| Height: | 10 ft 6 in |
| Weight Empty: | 2,618 lb |
| Weight Loaded: | 4,092 lb |
| Engine: | One 220-hp Benz Bz.IV six-cylinder, in-line, water-cooled |
| Maximum Speed: | 78 mph |
| Service Ceiling: | 21,000 feet |
| Endurance: | 3 hours |
| Armament: | One manually operated Parabellum machine gun mounted in the observer's cockpit |
| | One synchronised, fixed forward-firing Spandau machine gun |
| Maximum Speed: | 78 mph (125 km/h) |

# Siemens-Schuckert Werke GmbH

Although Siemens-Schuckert's first incursion into the world of aviation was in 1907, the company actually started life back in 1847, when it manufactured telegraph equipment. It was known as Siemens-Halske OH before it merged with the Schuckert Werke and became the famous Siemens-Schuckert Company.

In 1907, the German General Staff approached the company with a view to building a 'military' non-rigid airship. The Type-M, as it was called, was completed but was not the success anticipated. This was followed by a much larger version that by all accounts was very successful, but for some unknown reason the project was dropped. Two years later the company was approached again, this time to build three aircraft, all to be powered by the 50-hp Argus four-cylinder water-cooled engine. After two years and three aircraft, which could only be described as mediocre at best, the company went back to its original business of electrical manufacture. During this time, however, the company created a section that investigated the development of aero engines, in particular the rotary model. This resulted in the appearance in 1914 of the Sh.I, a 90-hp, nine-cylinder rotary engine.

Then in 1914, with the outbreak of war, the German Government requested that all companies respond to the war effort. Siemens-Schuckert re-activated the aviation department under the control of Dr Walter Reichel, who was assisted by Dr Hugo Natalis and designer/pilots Franz and Bruno Steffen. The company's first effort was a single-engined monoplane that had been constructed for Prince Friedrich Sigismund of Prussia, based on a design by Swedish aircraft builder Villehad Forssman. Two of the Siemens-Schuckert Bulldogs, as they were known, were built in 1915 and submitted to the Idflieg for testing. One of the aircraft was fitted with a 100-hp Siemens-Halske Sh.I rotary engine, the other with a 100-hp Mercedes S I. Both the aircraft were rejected on the grounds of poor performance and even worse handling qualities.

Not put off by the rejection, Siemens-Schuckert produced the B model designed by Franz Steffen. Designed and constructed as an unarmed reconnaissance aircraft, the Siemens-Schuckert B was powered by a 100-hp Siemens-Halske Sh.I rotary engine which gave it a top speed of 95 mph. It had a wingspan of 40 ft 8 in and a fuselage length of 20 ft 4½ in. The wing spars were constructed of tubular steel, a new innovation for the time. The one and only model built was delivered to the Brieftauben Abteilung at Ostend (for testing purposes) at the request of the commanding officer. During one of the test flights the aircraft crashed and what was left of the usable parts were returned to the factory.

One of the types of aircraft that had been requested by the Government were bombers. Siemens-Schuckert responded by submitting two R-plane (*Riesenflugzeug*

– giant aircraft) designs. Two of the company's designers, Villehad Forssman and Bruno Steffen, based their designs on the Sikorsky-built four-engined bomber *Ilia Mourumetz*. Both men had been in Russia at the time the heavy bomber had been built, Forssman building airships and Steffen as a pilot serving on the Russian Front.

The first design by Forssman, who can best be described as a man of vision and vivid imagination, copied the Sikorsky configuration line for line. The Forssman R, as it was called, had four uncowled 110-hp Mercedes engines mounted on the lower wing, driving two-bladed propellers. The top speed of the aircraft is said to have been 115 mph, but there is a great deal of scepticism regarding this. The pilot's cabin was enclosed and fitted with ample transparent panels, giving him an excellent view all around. The observer/gunner was not so fortunate: his position in a pulpit fitted on the nose was completely exposed. The 78 ft 9 in wingspan initially had only single struts fitted, but it was soon realised that additional struts, including diagonal ones, were required.

There were a number of continuing problems; when one was solved, more suddenly appeared. The aircraft was underpowered, and the aircraft had only been subjected to a couple of ground runs when the first test pilot refused to fly the aircraft, stating it was unstable. A second pilot, Leutnant Walter Höhndorf, was requested to fly the aircraft. On his first run the aircraft hopped into the air twice then went over on its nose. The aircraft was rebuilt, and despite its glossy, streamlined look it was riddled with structural weaknesses. After the accident no pilot could be found to fly the aircraft and it was placed in a hangar.

In an effort to save the reputation of the company, the Steffen brothers were approached to test fly the aircraft, which they did on condition that they were allowed to make certain modifications. This was agreed. Bruno Steffen was to fly the aircraft and five members of the Idflieg Acceptance Commission were invited to go along. Not surprisingly all five refused, and it was left to Bruno Steffen to fly the aircraft alone. The Idflieg acceptance specifications called for the aircraft to reach a height of 2,000 metres in 30 minutes while carrying a load of 1,000 kg and enough fuel to sustain a 4-hour flight.

The brothers installed a device that allowed all four throttle levers to be operated in unison. After examining the design drawings, Franz Steffen warned his brother that the fuselage was weak behind the cockpit and to be careful on take-off and landings. The flight in October 1915 was relatively uneventful and the Idflieg accepted the aircraft, but only for training purposes. Shortly after acceptance the aircraft broke its back due to vibration while the engines were being run up.

The second of the designs submitted was the Siemens-Schuckert SSW R.I. This had been designed by the Steffen brothers and given the designation SSW R.I 1/15 (the 15 referred to the year of manufacture) and was built at the SSW-Dynamowerk, Berlin. It was powered by three 150-hp Benz Bz.III engines turning two, twin-bladed propellers. Two of the engines were placed in the nose of the aircraft with their crankshafts facing aft; the third engine was mounted behind the gearbox on a lower level and facing forward. Each engine was connected to a common gearbox by means of a combination of leather-cone and centrifugal-key clutches. When the required number of revolutions was reached the centrifugal-key clutch engaged automatically, while the leather-cone clutch was disengaged manually.

The SSW R.I/15 had a wingspan of 91 ft 10 in and a fuselage length of 57 ft 5 in. It had a top speed of 68 mph, an operational range of 320 miles and an endurance of four hours. The evaluation of the aircraft was carried out on the Eastern Front because the threat from the air was considered to be less than that it would face on the Western Front, where the low-performance, low-flying bomber would be extremely vulnerable.

The SSW R.II 2/15 was the next model to appear, just three weeks after the first flight of the R.I. This would later make its appearance over the Western Front. It was the first of six aircraft contracted by Idflieg at a cost of 170,000 marks, without engines. The first model was powered by three 240-hp Maybach HS engines that were supplied by the Government. There were problems right from the outset as the engines were no more than modified airship engines and totally unfit for operational use. Consequently the aircraft were plagued with problems throughout their manufacture and operational time. Eventually common sense prevailed and the engines were replaced, initially by 220-hp Benz Bz.IV types and later by the 260-hp Mercedes D.IVa.

It was decided that the relative success of this new bomber justified the creation of two new units or Riesenflugzeugabteilungens (Rfa 500 & Rfa 501). These units were created, initially as part of an existing unit, and only as and when the aircraft came off the production line, and as can be appreciated, this happened very slowly. Only two of these units were created as there were never enough of the aircraft built to justify any more.

A third model appeared, the SSW R.III, and this was almost immediately sent to Rea at Döberitz together with the SSW R.I and R.II and assigned for training duties. The appearance of the SSW R.IV allowed the replacement of the R.I and R.IIs at Rfa 501.

There followed a number of variations up to SSW R.VII 7/15 with different wingspans and engines. All these models gave sterling service to the German Army and carried out numerous raids.

The fighter aircraft side of the company switched back to the monoplane design and produced the Siemens-Schuckert E.I. Powered by a 100-hp Siemens-Halske Sh.I rotary engine, the E.I had a top speed of 93 mph. It was of conventional construction, the box-type fuselage being covered in plywood with dope-painted fabric wings. With a wingspan of 32 ft 10 in, a fuselage length of 23 ft 3½ in, the aircraft had an endurance of 1½ hours. Armed with a single synchronised, fixed, forward-firing Spandau machine gun, twenty E.Is were ordered by the Army and delivered at the beginning of October 1915.

A second model was built at the beginning of 1916, the E.II. Powered by an in-line, water-cooled 120-hp Argus As.II engine, it was constructed using some of the usable parts recovered from the crashed Siemens-Schuckert B. The only model built crashed during tests while being flown by Franz Steffen, brother of Bruno Steffen, one of the company's designers. This was followed by the E.III, which was just an E.I fitted with a 100-hp Oberursel rotary engine. Only six examples of this model were built.

A return to the biplane design resulted in the appearance of the Siemens-Schuckert D.D5. Only one model of this single-seater fighter was built. Powered by a 110-hp Siemens-Halske Sh.I rotary engine, the D.D5 bore more than a passing resemblance to the Type B. Passed to the Idflieg for evaluation, the D.D5 was rejected for its lack of handling and the poor visibility from the cockpit. Using the information gained from the evaluation, the Siemens-Schuckert Company set to work to produce another fighter. The Allies were enjoying success with their French Nieuport fighters and whenever one was captured, the aircraft was handed over to the German manufacturing companies to see if they could use any of the refinements built into the aircraft. The Siemens-Schuckert Company had recently received one and set to work copying it; the result was the Siemens-Schuckert D.I. The first test flight of this aircraft was by Bruno Steffen, whose brother Franz Steffen died in the crash of the Siemens-Schuckert B.

The aircraft was then passed to Idflieg for evaluation with the result that an order was placed for 150 of them. In November 1916 production started, but within weeks problems arose. It was nothing to do with the aircraft, but with the supply of the rotary engines, so it was decided to use the 110-hp Siemens-Halske Sh.I engine that had recently been developed by another branch of the company. This was a revolutionary engine, inasmuch as the crankcase rotated in one direction at 900 rpm and the crankshaft in the opposite direction at 900 rpm. This gave an engine speed of 1,800 rpm for a propeller speed of 900 rpm, which resulted in greater efficiency.

The engine was mounted within an open-fronted, horseshoe-shaped cowling with the lower half completely cutaway allowing exhaust fumes to freely escape. The fuselage was of a box-girder construction with four main longerons of spruce with plywood formers. It was covered with slab-sided plywood and doped fabric, with the exception of the foremost section that had metal panels in which large ventilation slits had been cut. Tail surfaces and aileron were made of steel tubing and covered in doped fabric.

The wings were staggered and the original French designed planform retained, although the four centre-section struts were vertical in both side and front views.

The problems with delivery of the engines improved slowly, but by mid-1917 other fighters had improved markedly, leaving the Siemens-Schuckert D.I way behind. So much so, in fact, that only ninety-five of the original order were completed before it was cancelled by the Army. The D.I ended up in training schools, although a number did see action on the Western Front and gave a good account of themselves. There was a D.Ia model that had a slightly larger wing area, and two D.Ibs with an improved Siemens-Halske Sh.I engine, none of which mounted to anything.

At the beginning of 1917, Siemens-Schuckert designers came up with a design for a triplane fighter that was powered by two 120-hp Siemens-Halske Sh.I high-compression engines. This unusual fighter had a nacelle situated between the wings, with 'push-pull' engines mounted fore and aft with the pilot sitting in the middle. The tail assembly, with twin rudders, was mounted on tubular outrigger booms. It was fitted with twin, synchronised, forward-firing machine guns. The Siemens-Schuckert D.DrI, as it was called, crashed on its maiden flight and no effort was made to rebuild it.

The natural successor to the D.I was the D.III. There were a number of D.II prototypes, but they only tested some of the ideas and theories that had appeared on the drawing board. Idflieg, impressed with the D.II prototypes and with the relative success of the D.I, made a pre-production order for twenty D.IIIs in December 1916. This was followed by a further order for thirty more in January 1917, but there was a proviso, and this was that there was to be continued development of a D.IV model and three prototypes were ordered.

During the construction of the D.III, two prototypes were built, the first being the Siemens-Schuckert D.III (Short). Each of the two had a tubby, rounded fuselage, but there were distinctive differences. The first model had a wingspan of 27 ft 10½ in and a fuselage length of 19 ft 8 in. The second, the D.III (long), had a wingspan of 29 ft 7 in and a fuselage length of 19 ft 8 in. Both the aircraft were fitted with the Siemens-Halske Sh.III engine. From these two prototypes came the added information that made the Siemens-Schuckert D.III one of the finest single-seat fighter aircraft in the German Army.

The D.III was powered by the eleven-cylinder 160-hp Siemens-Halske Sh.III engine, which was one of the most powerful engines available at the time and had a top speed of 112 mph. There were teething problems with the engine involving piston seizure. This manifested itself when the aircraft was supplied to Jagdstaffel 15 of Jagdgeschwader II. It was commanded by one of Germany's most experienced pilots, Hauptmann Rudolph Berthold, who, despite the problems he and his fellow pilots were having, continued to support the aircraft. There were also opponents of the aircraft, among them Oberleutnant Hermann Göring, whom, one suspects, was hand-in-glove with his friend Anthony Fokker in trying to get the Idflieg to purchase Fokker aircraft.

An improved engine was fitted into the D.III and one of the aircraft, flown by Siemens test pilot Rodschinka, was taken to an unprecedented 26,586 feet in 36 minutes. The Siemens-Schuckert D.III was now looked upon totally differently and, because of its superb climbing ability, was used by Kampfeinsitzer Staffeln 4a, 4b, 5, 6 and 8 as interceptors. It is recorded that on one sortie, Oberleutnant Fritz Beckhardt shot down two Breguet B 14s while they were on a reconnaissance mission at a height of 23,000 feet.

The Siemens-Schuckert D.IV was produced in March 1918 with a redesigned upper wing, the lower half of the engine cowling cut away and cooling louvres cut into the propeller spinner. The maximum speed was increased to 118 mph and the climb rate increased. A total of 280 D.IVs were ordered, but not all the aircraft would be delivered before the war was over. Production of the aircraft was controlled by the rate of delivery of the engine, and that was at times painfully slow.

The D.IV had a wingspan of 27 ft 4½ in, a fuselage length of 18 ft 8½ in and a height of 9 ft 2½ in. It was armed with two synchronised, fixed, forward-firing Spandau machine guns.

The first deliveries of the Siemens-Schuckert D.IV went to the Marine Jagdgeschwader, which was under the command of Oberleutnant zur See Osterkamp, and Jasta 14. Later Jasta 22 and Kest 2 were to receive a small number of the aircraft, but a number of other Geschwaders, including the famed Richthofen Geschwader, did not.

Then, in March 1918, from the Siemens-Schuckert factory in Berlin came the SSW R.VIII, the largest aircraft in the world at the time. The R.VIII had a wingspan of 157 ft 6 in, a fuselage length of 70 ft 10 in and a height of 24 ft 3 in. It was powered by six 300-hp Bass & Selve BuS.IVa engines, which turned two tractor and two pusher propellers and gave the 35,000 lb aircraft a top speed of 77 mph. With a maximum operating ceiling of 13,124 ft, the SSW R.VIII had a range of 559 miles.

The aircraft was given a new designation of R.23, in line with other R-planes. The cockpit, unlike the previous SSW models, was open, giving the two pilots an excellent all-round view. The aircraft commander/observer had a fully enclosed cabin situated behind the cockpit, which was fully equipped with map table and navigation equipment. It also had a dorsal fin in which a ladder was fixed to enable the upper gunner get to his post. The aircraft was a revolution for the time, but unfortunately, or fortunately depending on your position, the war ended before the aircraft was completed. This also ended the building of the R.24, which was running alongside the R.23 and was three-quarters completed.

One Siemens aircraft that spent a great deal of time as a prototype was the Siemens-Schuckert D.IIe. It had started life as a D.II and was built with dual-girder wing spars and unbraced wings. It was later fitted with 'I'-type interplane struts with no bracing. On tests it was found that the wings flexed alarmingly, and so it was returned to the factory for bracing cables to be added. After more tests it was returned to the factory for refurbishment to D.IV standards and sent to Geschwader II for evaluation tests. It was returned to the factory for modifications to be made and a new engine, the Siemens-Halske Sh.III, to be fitted. It was returned to Geschwader II in July 1918, where it stayed until the end of the war and is believed never to have seen action.

Three prototypes of the Siemens-Schuckert D.V appeared in August 1918, all with different types of wing bracing. The last of the three competed in the D-Types Competition at Aldershof.

A deviation from the biplane heralded the arrival of the Siemens-Schuckert D.VI. Designed to replace the D.IV, the D.V was a parasol fighter fitted with a jettisonable fuel tank beneath the fuselage. Powered by a Siemens-Halske Sh.IIIa engine which turned a four-bladed propeller, the D.V had a top speed of 137 mph and a climb rate of 1,200 feet per minute. It had a wingspan of 30 ft 9 in and a fuselage length of 21 ft 4 in. Only two of the aircraft were built, neither of which saw action, as they were not ready for testing until after the Armistice.

The Siemens-Schuckert Company was never a household name in aviation like Fokker, Dornier and Rumpler were, but they were, without doubt, one of the most innovative of all the aircraft manufacturers of the First World War. A perfect example of this was that between 1915 and 1918, not only did they build some of the finest aircraft, but they also developed a number of glider bombs that were the forerunner of today's guided missile programme. In 1918, the company developed a 300 kg and 1,000 kg torpedogleiter (glider bomb) and trials were carried out from the Zeppelin L.35. Thankfully, none of the bombs were launched in anger, but they did give the world an insight of what was to come.

After the war, the company continued to make engines, but under the Treaty of Versailles they were restricted to low-powered engines for sporting aviation. Some years later the Bristol Company granted them a licence to produce the Bristol Jupiter engine, which eventually led to the creation of the Bramo engine. In 1939, the Siemens-Schuckert Company became part of the Bavarian Motorwerke – Flugmotorenwerke Brandenburg GmbH and faded into obscurity.

## SPECIFICATIONS

### Siemens-Schuckert D.I

| | |
|---|---|
| Wing Span: | 24 ft 7½ in (7.5 m) |
| Length: | 19 ft 8¼ in (6.0 m) |
| Height: | 8 ft 11 in (2.7 m) |
| Weight Empty: | 946 lb (430 kg) |
| Weight Loaded: | 1,485 lb (675 kg) |
| Engine: | One 110-hp Siemens-Halske Sh.I rotary |
| Maximum Speed: | 96 mph (155 km/h) |
| Service Ceiling: | 26,240 feet (8,000 m) |
| Endurance: | 2 hours |
| Armament: | Twin fixed, forward-firing, Spandau machine guns |

### Siemens-Schuckert D.III

| | |
|---|---|
| Wing Span: | 27 ft 8 in (8.5 m) |
| Length: | 18 ft 8½ in (5.7 m) |
| Height: | 9 ft 2¼ in (2.8 m) |
| Weight Empty: | 1,175 lb (534 kg) |
| Weight Loaded: | 1,595 lb (725 kg) |
| Engine: | One 160-hp Siemens-Halske Sh.III rotary |
| Maximum Speed: | 112 mph (180 km/h) |

Service Ceiling:     26,240 feet (8,000 m)
Endurance:           2 hours
Armament:            Twin fixed, forward-firing, Spandau machine guns

## Siemens-Schuckert D.IV

Wing Span:           27 ft 4½ in (8.35 m)
Length:              18 ft 8½ in (5.7 m)
Height:              8 ft 11 in (2.72 m)
Weight Empty:        1,190 lb (540 kg)
Weight Loaded:       1,620 lb (735 kg)
Engine:              One 160-hp Siemens-Halske Sh.III rotary
Maximum Speed:       118 mph (190 km/h)
Service Ceiling:     26,240 feet (8,000 m)
Endurance:           2 hours
Armament:            Twin fixed, forward-firing, Spandau machine guns

## Siemens-Schuckert D.V

Wing Span:           29 ft 1 in (8.86 m)
Length:              18 ft 8½ in (5.6 m)
Height:              8 ft 11 in (2.7 m)
Weight Empty:        1,131 lb (514 kg)
Weight Loaded:       1,615 lb (734 kg)
Engine:              One 160-hp Siemens-Halske Sh.III rotary
Maximum Speed:       112 mph (207 km/h)
Service Ceiling:     26,240 feet (8,000 m)
Endurance:           2 hours
Armament:            Twin fixed, forward-firing, Spandau machine guns

## Siemens-Schuckert E.I

Wing Span:           32 ft 9½ in (10 m)
Length:              23 ft 3½ in (7 m)
Height:              8 ft 11 in (2.7 m)
Weight Empty:        1,041 lb (473 kg)
Weight Loaded:       1,481 lb (671 kg)
Engine:              One 100-hp Siemens-Halske Sh.I rotary
Maximum Speed:       100 mph (185 km/h)
Service Ceiling:     20,240 feet (6,169 m)
Endurance:           1½ hours
Armament:            One fixed, forward-firing, Spandau machine gun

## Siemens-Schuckert D.Dr.I (Triplane)

Wing Span:           39 ft 9¼ in (12.1 m)
Length:              19 ft 1 in (5.8 m)
Height:              8 ft 1 in (2.4 m)
Weight Empty:        1,496 lb (456kg)
Weight Loaded:       2,002 lb (610 kg)
Engine:              Two 120-hp Siemens-Halske Sh.I rotary
Maximum Speed:       100 mph 185 km/h)
Service Ceiling:     20,240 feet (6,169 m)

Endurance:               1½ hours
Armament:                Two fixed forward-firing Spandau machine guns

## Siemens-Schuckert R (Forssman)

Wing Span:               78 ft 9 in (24 m)
Length:                  54 ft 2 in (16.5 m)
Height:                  17 ft 1 in (5.2 m)
Weight Empty:            8,820 lb (400 kg)
Weight Loaded:           11,466 lb (5,200 kg)
Engines:                 Two 220-hp Mercedes D.IV
                         Two 110-hp Mercedes
Maximum Speed:           75 mph (120 km/h)
Service Ceiling:         12,468 feet (3,800 m)
Endurance:               4 hours with Mercedes engines
Range:                   Not known

## Siemens-Schuckert R.I

Wing Span:               91 ft 10 in (28 m)
Length:                  57 ft 5 in (17.5 m)
Height:                  17 ft 1 in (5.2 m)
Weight Empty:            8,820 lb (400 kg)
Weight Loaded:           11,466 lb (5,200 kg)
Engines:                 Three 150-hp Benz Bz.III
Maximum Speed:           68.4 mph (110 km/h)
Service Ceiling:         12,468 feet (3,800 m)
Endurance:               4 hours
Range:                   323 miles (520 km)

## Siemens-Schuckert R.II

Wing Span:               92 ft 7 in (28.22 m) with Maybach engines
                         124 ft 8 in (38 m) with Mercedes engines
Length:                  58 ft 1 in (17.7 m) with Maybach engines
                         60 ft 8½ in (18.5 m) with Mercedes engines
Height:                  15 ft 1 in (4.6 m)
Weight Empty:            11,797 lb (5,350 kg) with Maybach engines
                         13,561 lb (6,150 kg) with Mercedes engines
Weight Loaded:           15,767 lb (7,150 kg) with Maybach engines
                         18,654 lb (8,460 kg) with Mercedes engines
Engines:                 Three 240-hp Maybach HS
                         Three 260-hp Mercedes D.IVa
Maximum Speed:           80.8 mph (130 km/h) with Maybach engines
                         68.4 mph (110 km/h) with Mercedes engines
Service Ceiling:         12,468 feet (3,800 m)
Endurance:               5¼ hours with Maybach engines
                         4 hours with Mercedes engines
Range:                   559 miles (900 km)

## Siemens-Schuckert R.VIII

| | |
|---|---|
| Wing Span: | 157 ft 6 in (48 m) |
| Length: | 70 ft 10 in (21.6 m) |
| Height: | 24 ft 3 in (7.4 m) |
| Weight Empty: | 23,152 lb (10,500 kg) |
| Weight Loaded: | 35,060 lb (15,900 kg) |
| Engines: | Six 300-hp Bass & Selve BuS.IVa |
| Maximum Speed: | 77.7 mph (125 km/h) |
| Service Ceiling: | 13,124 feet (400 m) |
| Endurance: | 6 hours |
| Range: | 559 miles (900 km) |

# Flugzeug und Maschinenfabrik Thöne & Fiala

This company was the smallest of all the aircraft manufacturing companies to supply aircraft to the Luftfahrtruppen. The company was created by Johann Peter Thöne and Anton Fiala in 1913, the latter's background being in agricultural machinery design with the Gebrüder Blaha Company. The financial side of the Thöne & Fiala Company was controlled by Thöne, a very wealthy Viennese businessman, who left the designing and manufacturing side to his partner. This was one company that was not controlled by Camillo Castiglioni.

Anton Fiala had started designing aircraft as far back as 1908, when he persuaded the Blaha Company to build a biplane designed by a young engineer by the name of Raoul Hofmann. Encouraged by this, Fiala studied aeronautics and became involved in the design and construction of a number of different aircraft, including the Boemches airship. With the formation of the new company in 1913, Fiala approached Emil Uzelac of the Luftschifferabteilung (LA) in January 1914 with the intention of trying to obtain a contract to build an aircraft for the military. Relying on his background, Fiala put forward a number of ideas, but Uzelac was not convinced and suggested that Fiala visit some of the existing aircraft companies to see the standard required and to acquaint himself with the latest design and production techniques.

In March 1914, the Thöne & Fiala Company submitted a design after being told that there was a possibility of them getting a contract for a single aircraft. The design was rejected but such was the demand for aircraft manufacture that in September 1914 they were given a contract to build 'Spanish' replacement wings for the Lohner B.I biplane. This immediately gave them a foot in the door with the military and when, at the beginning of 1915, they were approached to build six Knoller B.I. biplanes, they felt that the door had been finally opened.

The reason that the company had been chosen by Knoller and the military was that in 1909, while studying aeronautics at the Technical University of Vienna, Anton Fiala had worked closely with Professor Richard Knoller. At the beginning of the war, Knoller became the engineering consultant to the LA and as such, any recommendations made by him carried considerable weight. Anton Fiala always maintained that the Knoller B.I. was in fact the Knoller-Fiala B.I., as many of the designs in the development of the aircraft were in fact his. Fifteen of the aircraft were eventually built, none of which saw action because of the numerous problems that were found. In fact, all of the aircraft were placed in storage and later destroyed.

For a time the company was relegated to repairing damaged aircraft and manufacturing fixtures for machine guns, but once again the necessity for additional aircraft forced Flars to put contracts out to other manufacturers. The demand for the Aviatik D.I. outstripped the production so contracts were issued to smaller companies to build the aircraft under licence. Thöne & Fiala received a contract to build fifteen of the first series of the aircraft, the first four being delivered in March 1918. By the end of October, they had built and delivered a total of thirty-four Aviatik D.I fighters. A contract was drawn up for the building of thirty Fokker D.VII fighters but the war ceased before it could be signed.

# Ungarische Lloyd Flugzeug und Motorenfabrik AG

The Lloyd Company was the brainchild of Heinrich Bier, the technical director of the Deutsche Flugzeug Werke (DFW), an Austrian officer in the reserve and also an accomplished pilot. He had been successfully demonstrating the latest DFW Mars monoplane to the Luftschiffer-Abteilung (LA), the department of the military that purchased aircraft, when, after they agreed to place an order for the aircraft, he persuaded them to get the War Ministry to grant permission for DFW to open a subsidiary factory in Hungary.

On 8 May 1914 the factory opened, with Heinrich Bier as General Manager. The factory, in fact, was part of the state prison, which had been made available to the company by the Hungarian Ministry of Justice. The workforce consisted of a number of inmates, supported by engineers and skilled workmen from the DFW factory in Leipzig.

The purpose of the factory was to build the DFW MD 14 biplane there and the first production order came on 29 July 1914. Given the designation C.I., the Ungarische Lloyd Flugzeug Company started production of one prototype to be followed by twelve production models, the first to be delivered on 15 August 1914.

Powered by a 145-hp Hiero engine, the fuselage was constructed using spruce longerons covered with plywood panels. The prototype had been covered in fabric, but after it had crashed, killing the test pilot, Viktor Wittman, plywood panels covered the fuselage. The wings had a swept-back appearance and were of unequal span, covered in fabric. Ailerons were fitted on the upper wing only.

Problems dogged production from the first and it wasn't until February 1915 that the first of the Lloyd C.I aircraft was accepted. The main stumbling block wasn't that there was insufficient labour; unskilled labour was in abundance within the prison system, but it was difficult getting them to develop the skills required. This was to be the case throughout the war and considering the large workforce, more than 600, the factory built only 279 aircraft during this period.

The Lloyd C.I was not a popular aircraft with pilots because it was difficult to handle, but it was the only aircraft available to the Austro-Hungarian Air Force that was capable of flying over the mountainous region of Montenegro. It was assigned to unarmed reconnaissance duties in the Balkans and the Tyrol and remained in service until 1916, when they were withdrawn and relegated to training duties.

In the meantime, production of the Lloyd C.II had started. The contract had been awarded in July 1915 for sixty-two of the aircraft, with an additional eight being ordered one year later. The construction of the aircraft itself was slow, but was made even slower by the unreliability of the licensed-built 145-hp Hiero

(Mar) engine built by the Marta company. The unreliability of aircraft engines was to be a source of constant complaint for both German and Austro-Hungarian aircraft manufacturers throughout the war. Construction of the C.II was almost identical to that of the Lloyd C.I.

The first C.IIs came off the production line in August 1915 and were sent to Fliks 16 and 17, which were stationed on the Italian Front. The Lloyd C.II proved to be an excellent reconnaissance aircraft, and as quickly as they came off the production line, they were put into service with almost every Flik on the front line. However, they were still plagued with problems with the Marta-built Hiero engines, despite Marta engineers being continually sent to the front line to repair them. Fliks stationed on the Russian Front were also supplied with the aircraft. Gradually the C.IIs were replaced as more reliable and faster aircraft appeared, and those that had survived were returned to training schools.

Because of the slow output from the Lloyd factory, mainly because of the delays in perfecting the veneer wing, the Lloyd C.III contract from Flars (Fliegerarsenal), the organisation responsible for the testing and production of all Army equipment, including aircraft, was given to the Wiener Karosserie und Flugzeugfabrik (WKF) Company. The problem with the veneer wing was that if the wing suffered a bullet or shrapnel hole, the veneer tended to peel back. No instructions to the front line ground crews had been issued on how to repair these holes, so subsequently repairs were extremely difficult to make. This invariably meant that the whole wing had to be replaced. In addition to this, condensation on the inner surface of the wing could cause the wing to warp and/or become delaminated.

The company built a total of forty-four of the aircraft and as the last one was delivered, Flars decided to order an additional sixteen aircraft: eight C.IIs and eight C.IIIs. This time, in order to keep the Lloyd factory operating, it gave the contract to them. In the meantime, the WKF Company were awarded contracts to build the Aviatik C.I and D.I.

The Lloyd C.III (WKF) and Lloyd C.III and C.IIs were assigned to Fliks operating on the Rumanian Front for both reconnaissance and advance training duties.

Then, in May 1916, Flars signed a contract with Lloyd for forty-eight C.IV biplanes, all to be powered by the 160-hp Daimler engine. The first of the aircraft were to be delivered in June 1916, but the problem in perfecting the veneer wing still had not been resolved and so, faced with further manufacturing delays, Flars reduced the order to twenty aircraft. In an effort to speed up production, they agreed that fabric-covered wings would be acceptable. However, it wasn't until December 1916 that the first of the C.IVs made its appearance. The first of the aircraft was found to be 463 lb (210 kg) overweight, which cost the company a heavy financial penalty fine. The order was split into two batches; the second batch were fitted with dual controls and assigned to training duties. The remaining C.IVs were assigned to Fliks operating on the Eastern and Italian Fronts.

The development of the Lloyd C.V had been approved by the LFT (Luftfahrtruppen) back in July 1916 and orders placed with Lloyd and WKF for forty of the aircraft. In December 1916, the airframes were inspected by Flars engineers and found to be defective. Instructions were issued with regard to correcting the problems and in March 1917 they were inspected again. Not one of the deficiencies had been corrected and the company's contract was now in default as they had been scheduled to deliver forty-six C.Vs in February.

With the threat of severe financial penalties hanging over them, the deficiencies were rapidly corrected, but it wasn't until July that the first five Lloyd C.Vs were accepted. The company was now at full stretch because they were also building the Aviatik C.I under licence and that was given priority over the C.V. The next twenty C.Vs were delivered without engines because the engines destined for them were given to the Aviatik C.Is.

The first of the C.Vs reached the front line Fliks in September 1917 and were greeted with a mixed response. The manoeuvrability and speed were good, but the replacing of the rudder bar inside the cockpit with pedals was causing some concern. The majority of pilots felt that the rudder pedals were not as sensitive as the rudder bar, causing the aircraft to be less responsive. A rudder bar replaced the rudder pedals within days. There were other complaints: nose-heaviness in a glide, tail heavy in a climb and poor longitudinal stability. The aircraft was clearly only to be used by experienced operational pilots.

Despite these complaints, production continued and the second series were fitted with a 220-hp Benz (Mar) engine. The airframe had to be modified to take the larger engine and this task fell to the engineers at WKF. Once again problems arose with the engine, causing further delays in the delivery of the aircraft. The priority given the Brandenburg C.I meant that what engines were available were allocated to them, resulting in further delays. When they did finally reach the front line Fliks, there were still the complaints regarding its handling qualities.

The Lloyd C.V was the last of the Lloyd-designed aircraft to be built by the company; until the end of the war they built aircraft under licence for various companies.

## SPECIFICATIONS

### Lloyd C.I

| | |
|---|---|
| Wing Span Upper: | 47 ft 3 in (14.4 m) |
| Wing Span Lower: | 44 ft 8 in (13.6 m) |
| Length: | 29 ft 3 in (8.9 m) |
| Height: | 10 ft 5 in (3.15 m) |
| Weight Empty: | 1,859 lb (843 kg) |
| Weight Loaded: | 2,931 lb (1,329 kg) |
| Max. Speed: | 80 mph (128 km/h) |

### Lloyd C.II

| | |
|---|---|
| Wing Span Upper: | 47 ft 11 in (14.8 m) |
| Wing Span Lower: | 45 ft 5 in (13.8 m) |
| Length: | 28 ft 11 in (8.8 m) |
| Height: | 10 ft 5 in (3.15 m) |
| Weight Empty: | 1,985 lb (900 kg) |
| Weight Loaded: | 2,931 lb (1,329 kg) |
| Max. Speed: | 80 mph (128 km/h) |
| Armament: | One machine gun in the observer's position mounted on a rail |

### Lloyd C.III

| | |
|---|---|
| Wing Span Upper: | 47 ft 11 in (14.8 m) |
| Wing Span Lower: | 45 ft 5 in (13.8 m) |
| Length: | 28 ft 11 in (8.8 m) |
| Height: | 10 ft 5 in (3.15 m) |
| Weight Empty: | 1,985 lb (900 kg) |
| Weight Loaded: | 2,888 lb (1,310 kg) |

Max. Speed: 80 mph (128 km/h)
Armament: One machine-gun in the observer's cockpit mounted on a rail

## Lloyd C.IV

Wing Span Upper: 43 ft 6 in (13.3 m)
Wing Span Lower: 41 ft 7 in (12.7 m)
Length: 26 ft 4 in (8 m)
Height: 9 ft 8 in (1.9 m)
Weight Empty: 1,859 lb (843 kg)
Weight Loaded: 2,860 lb (1,297 kg)
Max. Speed: 84 mph (135 km/h)
Armament: One machine gun in the observer's cockpit mounted on a rail

## Lloyd C.V

Wing Span Upper: 36 ft 9 in (11.2 m)
Wing Span Lower: 36 ft 1 in (11 m)
Length: 23 ft 7 in (7.2 m)
Height: 9 ft 8 in (1.9 m)
Weight Empty: 1,859 lb (843 kg)
Weight Loaded: 2,481 lb (1,125 kg)
Max. Speed: 102 mph (165 km/h)
Armament: One machine-gun in the observer's cockpit mounted on a rail

# Zeppelin-Werke Staaken GmbH

Although firms like Siemens-Schuckert and Luftverkehrsgesellschaft (LVG) had made tremendous inroads into the development of long-range bombers during the First World War, the most successful company by far was Zeppelin-Werke Staaken. It was the Staaken R-planes that bombed Britain during the hostilities and they were the only large bombers to have carried out attacks on the Western Front.

The birth of the Staaken R-planes can be traced back to the dream of one man: Hellmuth Hirth. In 1915, he had planned to build an aircraft that would fly across the Atlantic and appear at the World's Fair in San Francisco. The financial backing was assured by Gustav Klein, Director of the Robert Bosch Werke, but the arrival of the First World War put paid to his dream. But the concept had not been forgotten, and the airship manufacturer Graf Zeppelin took a long, hard look at the project and saw the potential for a terror weapon.

With the demise of the Naval Zeppelin *LZ*, the German Naval High Command started to take a long, hard look at Graf Zeppelin's design of the airship and at Graf Zeppelin himself. Graf Zeppelin, whose relationship with the German Admiral von Tirpitz had never been good and was at this point in time almost non-existent, turned his attention to the building of long-range bombers. Zeppelin approached the Robert Bosch Werke and persuaded them to allow Gustav Klein, thirty of their engineers and assorted other workmen to join him in building bombers.

Large sheds were rented from Gothaer Waggonfabrik AG (Gotha) on the Gotha airfield and work started on the giant bomber. A corporation was set up by the name of Versuchsbau GmbH Gotha-Ost (VGO), which was financed by Bosch and Zeppelin. Among the engineers that were invited to join the company were Claude Dornier and Ernst Heinkel, but only Dornier accepted. Both were later to become famous aircraft manufacturers in their own right. Almost from day one it was decided to use two different types of material in the construction of these giant bombers: wood and metal. Claude Dornier was given a relatively small hangar on Lake Constance, where he carried out experiments in building an all-metal aircraft with considerable success. This section of the company was known as Zeppelin-Werke Lindau GmbH, and the aircraft built there were given the prefix Dornier.

Claude Dornier, working diligently on the side of Lake Constance, started constructing a giant flying boat at the beginning of 1915, the Zeppelin-Lindau (Dornier) Rs.I. Powered by three 240-hp Maybach Mb.IV engines, this gigantic aircraft had a wingspan of 142 ft 8 in, a fuselage length of 95 ft 2 in, and a height of 23 ft 7½ in. The engines were mounted within the fuselage and turned three pusher propellers. On 12 October 1915, the Rs.I was at anchor on Lake Constance, the taxiing trials having been completed; the 22 December was set as the date of the first of the flight trials, but during the night gale-force winds rose up and the aircraft broke its moorings and ran aground. Within hours, the aircraft had been battered into pieces by large waves. Fortunately, a second machine, Dornier Rs.II, was already in production and was powered in exactly the same way. The only main difference was that the wingspan was considerably shorter at 108 ft 11 in and the fuselage length was 78 ft 4 in. On 30 June 1916 the Rs. II took to the air and within weeks the flight test programme was completed, the aircraft was dismantled and the parts used to construct the Zeppelin-Lindau (Dornier) Rs.IIb. This aircraft's engines were in a four-engined configuration and in a tandem arrangement; this was to become a characteristic of many of Claude Dornier's designs in later years.

The Rs.III appeared in October 1917 and, after trials, was scheduled to be delivered to the Navy at Norderney on the North Sea. There was concern about the delivery of the aircraft, as no one had ever flown a seaplane such a distance, and about how it would stand up to the heavy seas of the North Sea. On 19 February 1918, the aircraft took off and seven hours later touched down in the sea off Norderney. The flight was uneventful and the aircraft's response to the large waves of the North Sea was in the Navy's report:

> The aircraft passed the sea test with heavy seas - Beaufort 3 to 4; wind velocities between 33 and 36 feet per second and a payload of 4,400 lbs.

Work on the VGO.I-RML.1 (Versuchsbau-Gotha-Ost Reichs Marine Landflugzeug), as the aircraft was to be called, started in earnest in December 1914 and by the end of January 1915, work had to be halted as the engines were not ready. The 240-hp Maybach HS engines that had been chosen for the aircraft were a modified version of the HSLu airship engine. The aircraft was powered by three engines, one mounted in the nose driving a tractor propeller, the remaining two mounted in nacelles, supported between the wings by inverted struts, driving pusher propellers. The wings were fitted with unbalanced ailerons.

The rectangular fuselage was of the conventional slab-sided structure and constructed with a mixture of spruce longerons and welded steel tubing. With the exception of the plywood-covered top decking, the fuselage was covered in doped fabric. The fuselage narrowed down to a horizontal knife-edge at the biplane tail, which consisted of four small fins with unbalanced rudders along the top. The control cables from the cockpit to the tail rudders passed along the outside of the fuselage to large quadrants situated in the cockpit.

The aircraft had a flight crew of six: two pilots, a commander/observer and three mechanics, one for each engine. The cockpit was a large open one, with the observer in an enclosed section behind. Communications between the crew were relatively crude and were carried out by means of hand signals, blackboards and a series of bells. One wonders how, during a flight in an open cockpit or standing by one of the engines, anyone could have possibly heard any bells!

By the beginning of April 1915 the aircraft was completed, and on 11 April, piloted by Hellmuth Hirth, the VGO.I took to the air on its maiden flight. The success of its initial flight prompted the manufacturers to make plans for a long-distance cross-country flight from Gotha to the Maybach Werke, Friedrichshafen. The reason for the flight was firstly to see how the aircraft responded on long flights, and secondly to obtain improved and more reliable engines from Maybach.

It took almost six months for reliable engines to be installed in the aircraft, but then on the return flight, during a particularly bad snowstorm, disaster struck.

Flying over the Thüringen Forest two of the three engines cut out, leaving just the one. It soon became obvious that the aircraft could not stay airborne on the one engine and with tremendous skill the two pilots, Hans Vollmöller and Flugmaat Willy Mann, put the giant aircraft down in a small clearing. The aircraft was severely damaged but the crew were uninjured.

Engineers collected the remains from the site and returned them to the factory at Gotha. There the aircraft was rebuilt, only this time with a number of modifications made. The VGO.I had cowled engines installed with gun positions for what was now the mechanic/gunner in the front of the nacelle. On the top of the centre-section cabane a large, streamlined gravity tank was fitted. The rebuilt VGO.I flew again on 16 February 1916, and after tests was accepted by the Navy and assigned to Navy Kommando LR.1, which was commanded by Leutnant zur See Ferdinand Rasch. On the side of the aircraft were painted the letters RML.1 (Reich Navy Landplane 1). On the trip from Gotha to Alt-Auz, normally a three-day trip, problems arose from day one. The undercarriage collapsed and the engines overheated and had to be replaced, with the end result that it took three months to complete the flight.

Over the next few months the RML.1, as it was now referred to, was involved in a number of raids against Russian troop installations and air stations. Then, in late 1916, it was involved in another crash. On 10 March 1917 the rebuilt VGO.I (RML.1) took off on a test flight with Hans Vollmöller and Leutnant der Reserve Carl Kuring at the controls, together with Gustav Klein acting as observer. Shortly after take-off there was an explosion in the port engine nacelle and the engine stopped. Circling the airfield and preparing to make an emergency landing, the rudder pedals jammed. Vollmöller cut the engines and prepared to land, but the jammed rudders forced the aircraft into a right-hand turn and the aircraft smashed into the doors of the airship shed. All three crew were killed instantly.

While the VGO.I was being rebuilt after its first accident, work had been continuing on the VGO.II. The aircraft was identical in construction and specifications to the VGO.I, although there were a number of modifications made in the tail area. The vertical tail surfaces were reduced to two but the rudder areas were increased.

The aircraft was accepted by Idflieg on 28 November 1915 and given the designation R.9/15. Again the VGO was dogged with problems; this time the aircraft ran out of fuel on one flight after encountering very strong headwinds. The aircraft, flown by Leutnant Lühr and Leutnant Freiherr von Buttlar, had to make an emergency landing in which the undercarriage was ripped off. One experiment to place a rear gunner in the tail failed miserably, when, after the test flight, the gunner was removed from the aircraft more dead than alive. The oscillations experienced in the tail were so violent that the gunner became violently ill soon after take-off and stayed that way throughout the flight. Tests on a gun mounted within the fuselage were carried out, but came to nothing as there were serious problems with its accuracy.

The third in the series of Staaken R-planes, the VGO.III was well under construction in 1915. It had been decided to replace the three 240-hp Maybach HS engines with six 160-hp Mercedes D.III engines. Although lower in individual output, the total horsepower was jumped from 720-hp to 960-hp. Two engines were mounted side-by-side in the nose of the aircraft, driving a twin-blade tractor propeller; the remaining four engines were mounted in pairs in outboard nacelles and drove twin-bladed pusher propellers.

The aircraft was given the designation R.10/15 by Idflieg and assigned to RFa 500. Carrying a crew of seven, including a wireless operator, the aircraft completed seven bombing missions, including the bombing of the railway station at Riga. Then on 24 January 1917, the aircraft was lost, along with five of the crew, when it crashed on landing and burst into flames.

A deviation from building bombers was made in November 1916, when the Zeppelin-Lindau V.1 took to the air. This was an attempt at a single-seat fighter constructed mainly of metal. It had an egg-shaped nacelle constructed of steel struts that were covered in aluminium sheet and attached to open steel tail booms and struts. The tail and wings were covered in doped fabric. Wingspan was 34 ft 5½ in, with a fuselage length of 20 ft 7 in. The aircraft was fitted with a 160-hp Maybach Mb.III pusher engine.

The Allied push meant that an Allied air attack on the Staaken factory became more and more of a possibility. The German High Command decided that the factory should be moved to a place of relative safety, so the whole outfit was moved to Staaken, near Berlin. The first of the Staaken types then came off the production line, the Staaken R.IV.

The aircraft was powered by two 160-hp Mercedes D.III tractor engines that turned twin-bladed propellers of 13 ft 9 in diameter, and four 220-hp Benz Bz.IV pusher engines that turned two four-bladed propellers of 14 ft 1 in diameter. This giant aircraft had a wingspan of 138 ft 5½ in, a fuselage length of 76 ft 1 in, and a height of 22 ft 3½ in. Machine gun positions were built into the upper wings, directly above the engine nacelles. These, together with one ventral, two forward and two dorsal machine gun positions, made it one of the most heavily protected aircraft in the world. The aircraft was involved in a number of bombing missions on the Eastern Front and survived the war only to be broken up in 1919.

The Staaken R.V followed soon after the first test flight of the R.IV. The main difference between the two aircraft was that the outboard engines were reversed, with the result that all the engines were tractors, turning four-bladed propellers. Solving the technical problems that were thrown up by the new positioning of the engines, but eventually the aircraft was assigned to RFa 501 at Ghent and during its eight-month career flew sixteen combat missions. It crashed in October 1918.

The best known of all the German R-planes was the Staaken R.VI. This was the largest aircraft ever to go into production during the First World War and nineteen models were built, including a seaplane version. The first six were built by Zeppelin-Werke Staaken; the remainder were built under licence by Luftschiffbau Schütte-Lanz, Zeeson, Ostdeutsche Alabatroswerke GmbH, Schneidemühl and Automobil & Aviatik AG, Leipzig-Heiterblick. The design was based on the earlier Staaken types, the main difference being that the positioning of the engines was changed to four 260-hp Mercedes D.IVa push-pull engines in tandem, installed in two nacelles in the wings. It had four radiators, two at the front and two at the rear, the rear radiators being mounted slightly higher than those in the front.

Eighteen of the aircraft were built; eleven were destroyed during the war, the remainder fought throughout the last part of the war. A couple of the aircraft were even used commercially after the war.

The Staaken R.VII was similar to the R.IV inasmuch as unlike the R.VI, two of the engines powering a four-bladed tractor propeller were mounted in the nose; the remaining four engines powered two four-bladed pusher propellers. The undercarriage was relatively short and consisted of two sets of four wheels on each side with a two-wheeled nose section.

After tests the aircraft was accepted by Idflieg and assigned to RFa 500 on 14 August 1917. On its way to the front, the aircraft stopped at the airfield of Flieger Ersatabteilung in Halberstadt for emergency repairs. With the repairs completed, the aircraft took off on 19 August 1917 and headed for the front. As the aircraft rose in the air it became obvious that something was not right. The aircraft was at around 70 metres from the ground when the starboard wing dropped and the aircraft was forced into a tight turn. As the R.VII 14/15 reached a wooded hill at the end of the field, the starboard wing lurched downwards suddenly and hooked into one of the trees. The aircraft somersaulted into a rocky ravine on the other side of the hill. Only three of the nine crew-members survived and they were all badly burned.

Claude Dornier's attention was drawn to the development of a two-seat reconnaissance aircraft, the Zeppelin-Lindau C.I. The fuselage was of an all-metal construction covered in a sheet-metal skin; the wings, however, although constructed of aluminium, were covered in fabric. Powered by a 160-hp Mercedes D.III engine, which gave the aircraft a top speed of 93 mph, the C.I had a wingspan of 34 ft 5½ in, a fuselage length of 24 ft 4 in and a height of 9 ft. It was armed with a forward-firing, fixed, Spandau machine gun and a manually operated Parabellum machine gun. Tested by Idflieg, it failed to meet the requirements and was scrapped. The C.II was almost identical and only differed in the type of radiator used. Only a small number were built.

Another two-seater was constructed by the Zeppelin-Werke at the airship factory at Friedrichshafen. This model was designed by Paul Jarray, and was an entirely wooden machine, covered in doped fabric. The Zeppelin C.I and C.II were almost identical, with the exception of the tail surfaces on the C.II being removed and the tail frame being made of metal.

Powered by 240-hp Maybach Mb.IV engines which gave the aircraft a top speed of 125 mph, they had a wingspan of 39 ft 4½ in, a fuselage length of 26 ft and a height of 11 ft 9 in. Six C.Is and twenty C.IIs were built, none of which saw action. At the end of the war they were sold to the Swiss Air Force, who flew them until 1928.

Work was still continuing on the giant seaplanes, and the Rs.III, which arrived in October 1917, was a monoplane powered by four 245-hp Maybach Mb.IVa engines that gave the aircraft a top speed of 84 mph. It had a wingspan of 121 ft 8 in, a fuselage length of 74 ft 7½ in and a height of 26 ft 11 in. The tail booms that were so prominent in the Rs.II model were removed and were replaced by a fuselage made of steel longerons and alloy frames. The metal fuselage, with its biplane tail, was covered in fabric and mounted on top of the wing. The Rs.III had a short, wide hull that supported the two nacelles that contained the four tandem-mounted engines.

The first flight took place at Friedrichshafen on 21 October 1917 and was so successful that the aircraft was taken to Norderney, a flight of some seven hours. It underwent a series of tests but the Armistice occurred before it could be put into service. The last of the giant flying boats, the Zeppelin-Lindau Rs.IV, made its maiden flight in October 1918. The fuselage had a metal skin and a much-simplified cruciform tail section. It, like the previous model, was powered by four 245-hp Maybach Mb.IV engines which gave the aircraft a top speed of 90 mph.

The Rs.IV had one test flight and was then dismantled. Claude Dornier, who had been spearheading this programme, was able to use a great deal of the information he had gained from the test flights of these giant aircraft and incorporate them into the successful commercial flying boats he created after the war.

One of the most successful of all the Staaken giant bombers was the R.XIV. Three of the models were built: the R.XIV 43/17, 44/17 and 45/17. Four 12-cylinder, 350-hp Austro-Daimler engines initially powered the 43/17, but they proved to be too unreliable. These were replaced by four 300-hp Basse & Selve BuS.IVa, which also proved to be unreliable, so they were replaced by five 245-hp high-compression Maybach Mb.IVa engines. The reason for the sudden switch from four to five engines was that the increased weight of 2,000 kg required additional power. All three aircraft were ready by the early part of 1918.

Each of the aircraft was armed with six machine guns, two in the dorsal and ventral positions and one each in the engine nacelle positions. The cockpit was of the open type, while the bomb-aimer/observer/navigator's position was in an enclosed cabin situated in the nose.

At beginning of December 1917, the German Navy ordered two Staaken seaplanes. They bore a strong resemblance to the Staaken R.XIV inasmuch as the cockpit area was completely enclosed for both the pilots and the navigator/observer. There were noticeable differences; the fuselage was raised five feet above the lower wing, which in turn raised the tail as well. The reason for this was to protect both the fuselage and tail from spray and rough seas while landing and taking off. The two models, numbered Type 8301 and 8303, carried a crew of five and were armed as the R.XIV with the addition of two 20 mm Becker cannons in the rear position. Powered by four 260-hp Mercedes D.IVa engines, the 8301 and 8303 had a maximum speed of 80 mph, a wingspan of 138 ft 5½ in, a fuselage length of 68 ft 10½ in and a height of 22 ft 3½ in. Neither aircraft ever saw active service.

An improved version of the R.XIV, the R.XIVa, appeared in the middle of 1918 and was the last of the R-planes to be built by Staaken. Four of the aircraft were ordered by Idflieg and given the designation R.69 to R.72. Only the first three were completed and were too late to see any active service. All three aircraft were used by the German Army to fly cargoes up to the end of the war, and afterwards by the Inter-Allied Control Commission.

Also in February 1918, there appeared another version of the Staaken R.VI, the Staaken L Seaplane. The undercarriage was replaced with 39 ft 4½ in duraluminium floats and slightly larger ailerons. During the last of the test flights (carried out by Leutnant Haller) the engines failed while flying over land, and the aircraft crashed, killing all the crew. However, earlier results had convinced the Navy that the aircraft had a great deal going for it, so the Navy placed an initial order for two, followed later by a further four Staaken R-seaplanes based on the design and construction of the Staaken L.

An experimental two-seater seaplane fighter was built in May 1918, the Zeppelin-Lindau CS.I. The aircraft was of an almost all-metal construction with the exception of the wings and tail surfaces, which were covered in doped fabric, and was powered by a V-8 195-hp Benz Bz.IIIb engine which gave the aircraft a top speed of 93 mph. It had a wingspan of 43 ft 3 in and a fuselage length of 36 ft. It was armed with one fixed, forward-firing Spandau machine gun and a manually operated Parabellum machine gun. Only one was built.

The specifications of the Staaken giant bombers only differed in the variety of engines used and some minor modifications. Their contribution to the bomber aspect of the First World War was modest to say the least, and although they had made some impact it was not as great as the German Army had hoped. Nevertheless, they opened a new page in the annals of aviation history.

## SPECIFICATIONS

### Zeppelin C.I

| | |
|---|---|
| Wing Span: | 39 ft 4½ in (12 m) |
| Length: | 26 ft 0 in (7.9 m) |
| Height: | 11 ft 9 in (3.5 m) |
| Weight Empty: | 2,173 lb (985.6 kg) |
| Weight Loaded: | 3,201 lb (1,452 kg) |
| Engine: | One 240-hp Maybach Mb.IV six-cylinder, in-line, water-cooled |
| Maximum Speed: | 125 mph (231 km/h) |
| Service Ceiling: | 21,240 feet (6,473 m) |
| Endurance: | 1½ hours |
| Armament: | Two fixed forward-firing Spandau machine guns One manually operated Parabellum machine gun mounted in the rear observer's cockpit |

### Zeppelin-Staaken R.IV

| | |
|---|---|
| Wing Span: | 138 ft 5½ in (42.2 m) |
| Length: | 76 ft 1½ in (23.2 m) |
| Height: | 22 ft 3½ in (6.8 m) |
| Weight Empty: | 19,298 lb (8,753 kg) |
| Weight Loaded: | 28,677 lb (13,007 kg) |
| Engines: | Four 220-hp Benz Bz.IV six-cylinder, in-line, water-cooled |
| Maximum Speed: | 78 mph (144 km/h) |
| Service Ceiling: | 29,240 feet (8,812 m) |
| Endurance: | 6-7 hours |
| Armament: | Six manually operated Parabellum machine guns mounted in the nose ventral and dorsal positions |

### Zeppelin-Staaken R.VI

| | |
|---|---|
| Wing Span: | 138 ft 5½ in (42.2 m) |
| Length: | 72 ft 6¼ in (22 m) |
| Height: | 20 ft 8 in (6.2 m) |
| Weight Empty: | 17,426 lb (7,904 kg) |
| Weight Loaded: | 26,066 lb (11,823 kg) |
| Engines: | Four 245-hp Maybach Mb.IV or four 260-hp Mercedes D.IVa six-cylinder, in-line, water-cooled |
| Maximum Speed: | 84 mph (155 km/h) |
| Service Ceiling: | 14,240 feet (4,340 m) |
| Endurance: | 7-10 hours |
| Armament: | Four manually operated Parabellum machine guns mounted in the nose, ventral and dorsal positions |

### VGO.I - RML.I (Versuchsbau Gotha-Ost – Reichs Marine Landflugzeug)

| | |
|---|---|
| Wing Span: | 138 ft (42 m) |
| Length: | 78 ft 8 in (24 m) |
| Height: | 21 ft 7½ in (6.6 m) |

| | |
|---|---|
| Weight Empty: | 14,377 lb (6,520 kg) |
| Weight Loaded: | 29,992 lb (9,520 kg) |
| Engines: | Three 240-hp Maybach HS six-cylinder, in-line, water-cooled |
| Maximum Speed: | 68.4 mph (110 km/h) |
| Service Ceiling: | 9,843 feet (3,000 m) |
| Endurance: | 6-7 hours |
| Armament: | Six manually operated Parabellum machine-guns mounted in the nose ventral and dorsal positions |

## VGO.II

| | |
|---|---|
| Wing Span: | 138 ft 5½ in (42.2 m) |
| Length: | 78 ft (23.78 m) |
| Height: | 22 ft 11½ in (7 m) |
| Weight Empty: | 14,635 lb (6,637 kg) |
| Weight Loaded: | 22,498 lb (10,203 kg) |
| Engines: | Three 240-hp Maybach HS six-cylinder, in-line, water-cooled |
| Maximum Speed: | 68.4 mph (110 km/h) |
| Service Ceiling: | 9,843 feet (3,000 m) |
| Endurance: | 6-7 hours |
| Armament: | Six manually operated Parabellum machine-guns mounted in the nose ventral and dorsal positions |

## VGO.III

| | |
|---|---|
| Wing Span: | 138 ft 5½ in (42.2 m) |
| Length: | 80 ft 4½ in (24.5 m) |
| Height: | 22 ft 3½ in (6.8 m) |
| Weight Empty: | 18,963 lb (8,600 kg) |
| Weight Loaded: | 25,578 lb (11,600 kg) |
| Engines: | Six 160-hp Mercedes D.III |
| Maximum Speed: | 75 mph (120 km/h) |
| Service Ceiling: | 9,843 feet (3,000 m) |
| Endurance: | 6 hours |
| Armament: | Six manually operated Parabellum machine guns: one in the ventral, two in the dorsal and two in the nacelle positions |

## Zeppelin-Staaken R.V

| | |
|---|---|
| Wing Span: | 138 ft 5½ in (42.2 m) |
| Length: | 75 ft 5½ in (23 m) |
| Height: | 22 ft 3½ in (6.8 m) |
| Weight Empty: | 20,837 lb (9,450 kg) |
| Weight Loaded: | 28,687 lb (13,010 kg) |
| Engines: | Five 245-hp Maybach Mb.IVa |
| Maximum Speed: | 83.9 mph (135 km/h) |
| Service Ceiling: | 14,764 feet (4,500 m) |
| Endurance: | 6 hours |
| Armament: | Six manually operated Parabellum machine-guns: one in the ventral, two in the dorsal and two in the nacelle |

positions

## Zeppelin-Staaken R.VI

| | |
|---|---|
| Wing Span: | 138 ft 5½ in (42.2 m) |
| Length: | 72 ft 6 in (22.1 m) |
| Height: | 20 ft 8 in (6.3 m) |
| Weight Empty: | 16,934 lb (7,680 kg) |
| Weight Loaded: | 25,269 lb (11,460 kg) |
| Engines: | Four 260-hp Mercedes D.IV |
| Maximum Speed: | 80.8 mph (130 km/h) |
| Service Ceiling: | 12,467 feet (3,800 m) |
| Endurance: | 7-8 hours |
| Armament: | Six manually operated Parabellum machine-guns: one in the ventral, two in the dorsal and two in the nacelle positions |

## Zeppelin-Staaken R.VII

| | |
|---|---|
| Wing Span: | 138 ft 5½ in (42.2 m) |
| Length: | 72 ft 6 in (22.1 m) |
| Height: | 22 ft 3½ in (6.8 m) |
| Weight Empty: | 19,675 lb (8,923 kg) |
| Weight Loaded: | 28,561 lb (12,953 kg) |
| Engines: | Four 220-hp Benz Bz.IV Two 160-hp Mercedes D.III |
| Maximum Speed: | 80.8 mph (130 km/h) |
| Service Ceiling: | 12,631 feet (3,850 m) |
| Endurance: | 7-8 hours |
| Armament: | Six manually operated Parabellum machine-guns one in the ventral, two in the dorsal and two in the nacelle positions |

## Zeppelin-Staaken R.XVI

| | |
|---|---|
| Wing Span: | 138 ft 5½ in (42.2 m) |
| Length: | 73 ft 10 in (22.5 m) |
| Height: | 21 ft 4 in (6.5 m) |
| Weight Empty: | 22,932 lb (10,400 kg) |
| Weight Loaded: | 32,303 lb (14,650 kg) |
| Engines: | Two 530-hp Benz Bz.VI (Pusher) Two 220-hp Benz Bz.IV (Tractor) |
| Maximum Speed: | 80.8 mph (130 km/h) |
| Service Ceiling: | 12,172 feet (3,710 m) |
| Endurance: | 7-8 hours |
| Armament: | Six manually operated Parabellum machine guns: one in the ventral, two in the dorsal and two in the nacelle positions |

## Zeppelin-Staaken L

| | |
|---|---|
| Wing Span: | 138 ft 5½ in (42.2 m) |
| Length: | 72 ft 10 in (22.2 m) |
| Height: | 24 ft 2½ in (7.38 m) |
| Weight Empty: | 18,522 lb (8,400 kg) |

Weight Loaded:      26,019 lb (11,800 kg)
Engines:            Four 260-hp Mercedes D.IVa
Maximum Speed:      77.7 mph (125 km/h)
Service Ceiling:    8,202 feet (2,500 m)
Endurance:          10 hours
Armament:           Six manually operated Parabellum machine-guns:
                    one in the ventral, two in the dorsal and two in
                    the nacelle positions

## Zeppelin-Staaken 8303 Seaplane

Wing Span:          138 ft 5½ in (42.2 m)
Length:             68 ft 10½ in (21 m)
Height:             22 ft 3½ in (6.8 m)
Weight Empty:       19,845 lb (9,000 kg)
Weight Loaded:      27,563 lb (12,500 kg)
Engines:            Four 260-hp Mercedes D.IVa
Maximum Speed:      80 mph (130 km/h)
Service Ceiling:    8,202 feet (2,500 m)
Endurance:          10 hours

## Dornier Rs.I (Zeppelin-built)

Wing Span Upper:    142 ft 9 in (43.5 m)
Wing Span Lower:    123 ft 10 in (37.7 m)
Length:             95 ft 1½ in (29 m)
Height:             23 ft 7½ in (7.2 m)
Weight Empty:       16,357 lb (7,500 kg)
Weight Loaded:      23,153 lb (10,500 kg)
Engines:            Three 240-hp Maybach HS (Mb.IV)
Maximum Speed:      Never flown
Service Ceiling:    Never flown
Endurance:          Never flown
Armament:           None

## Dornier Rs.IIa/b

Wing Span Upper:    108 ft 11 in (33.2 m)
Wing Span Lower:    52 ft 6 in (16 m)
Length:             78 ft 4¼ in (23.88 m)
Height:             24 ft 11½ in (7.6 m)
Weight Empty:       16,045 lb (7,278 kg)
Weight Loaded:      20,190 lb (9,158 kg)
Engines:            Four 245-hp Maybach Mb.IVa
Maximum Speed:      79.5 mph (128 km/h)
Service Ceiling:    8,202 ft (2,500 m)
Endurance:          10 hours
Armament:           None

## Dornier Rs.III

Wing Span:          121 ft 4½ in (37 m)
Length:             74 ft 8 in (22.75 m)

| | |
|---|---|
| Height: | 26 ft 11 in (8.2 m) |
| Weight Empty: | 17,339 lb (7,865 kg) |
| Weight Loaded: | 23,523 lb (10,670 kg) |
| Engines: | Four 245-hp Maybach Mb.IVa |
| Maximum Speed: | 83.9 mph (135 km/h) |
| Service Ceiling: | 8,202 ft (2,500 m) |
| Endurance: | 10 hours |
| Armament: | Twin machine guns on top of fuselage and one machine gun in the nose |

# Epilogue

The successes and failures of the German and Austro-Hungarian aircraft industries, before and during the First World War, were in the main controlled by budgets allocated for aviation. The German military hierarchy thought from day one that the war would be a short one and would be won by the land forces. The Prussian aviation arm of the military, although considered as the Army's 'poor relative', was by 1914 well-prepared for war. The British had about 160 of what were considered 'front-line' aircraft, while the French had around 300 front-line aircraft and the Russians 400, most of which were French-built and only half were considered serviceable. In comparison, the Prussians had 450 aircraft, of which over 300 were deemed serviceable front-line aircraft.

It was the naval aviation arm of the German Navy that seemed to attract the most interest when, in 1910, Admiral von Tirpitz, as Secretary of State of the Imperial Naval Office, allocated 100,000 marks to investigate the suitability of aircraft for the Navy. The following year he raised the sum to 200,000 marks after receiving favourable reports about the use of aircraft as a reconnaissance tool.

In the case of the Bavarian Army, they turned to private aircraft manufacturers after their own dismal failure of trying to produce aircraft and having to depend on the Prussian Army to assist them. They chose the Euler Company, and as one senior Bavarian officer put it, 'Although they are not Bavarian at least they are not Prussian'. This epitomised the deep-seated animosity that festered between the two states. The problem was that the Bavarian Army and the Austro-Hungarian Army only had one fifteenth of the budget of the Prussian Army to spend on aviation. It was this and the underlying simmering hostilities between the Prussian and Bavarian states throughout the war that contributed to Germany's defeat.

# Also available from Amberley Publishing

## *The Setting of the Rising Sun*
### *Japanese Military Aviation 1877-1945*

TERRY C. TREADWELL

Telling the story of Japanese military aviation from the mid-Victorian era, a time when Japan was only just beginning to open up to the rest of the world, Terry Treadwell illustrates the story with a fascinating selection of images of the personalities and aircraft involved in the development of aircraft by the Japanese.

£17.99 Paperback

192 pages, 124 black and white illustrations

978-1-4456-0226-4

# Also available from Amberley Publishing

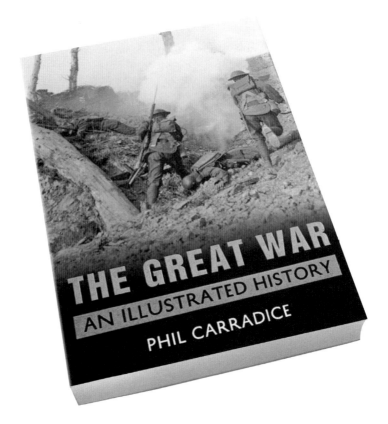

## *The Great War*
### *An Illustrated History*

PHIL CARRADICE

*The Great War – An Illustrated History* looks at the causes of the war and the actual events themselves. Naturally, much of it covers the war on the Western Front but there are also sections about other theatres of war – the Middle East, Gallipoli, the war in Africa, etc. The war at sea and in the air are also covered.

£14.99 Paperback

160 pages, 227 black and white illustrations
978-1-84868-881-0

Available from all good bookshops or to order direct
Please call **01285 760 030**
**www.amberleybooks.com**

# Also available from Amberley Publishing

## *Home Guard Manual*

Edited by Campbell McCutcheon

Two weeks before Dunkirk, Anthony Eden, Minister of War, announced to the nation on BBC radio his concept of a Local Defence Volunteer force. It was a grim time! The Germans were routing the French and British in Belgium and France, Norway was already lost, and within two weeks the cream of Britain's fighting forces would be weaponless and kit-less, seeking rescue from the beaches of Dunkirk. Find out about the real 'Dad's Army' from the manual used to train them.

£7.99 Paperback

240 pages, 50 black and white illustrations
978-1-4456-0047-5

Available from all good bookshops or to order direct
Please call **01285 760 030**
**www.amberleybooks.com**

# Also available from Amberley Publishing

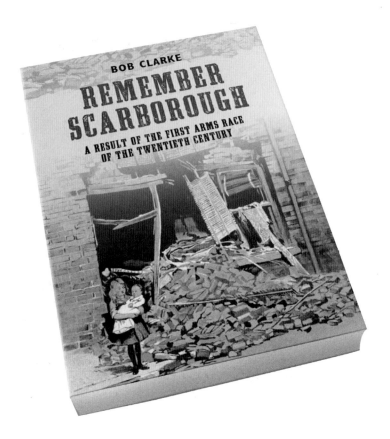

## *Remember Scarborough*
### *A Result of the First Arms Race of the 20th Century*

BOB CLARKE

On the morning of 16 December 1914, elements of the Imperial German Navy's High Sea Fleet shelled three east coast towns. Scarborough, Whitby and Hartlepool all suffered damage. Whilst Hartlepool saw the most loss of life, it was the attack on Scarborough that gripped the nation's imagination.